Cooking alla Giudia

ARTISAN BOOKS | NEW YORK

A Celebration of the Jewish Food of Italy

Cooking alla Giudia

BENEDETTA JASMINE GUETTA

To my mother,
who taught me everything

To Shlomi,
who gave me the courage to dream up this book

To Maya,
who will carry these recipes into the future

Contents

Introduction

This book is a tribute to the wonderfully rich but still mostly unknown culinary heritage of the Jews of Italy. While Jews have lived in Italy for thousands of years, the depth of their contribution to Italian cuisine today has been largely untold.

When describing one of the most popular cuisines in the world, it's tempting to paint Italian food with a broad brush: everyone agrees on the culinary merits of lasagna, pizza, cannoli, and tiramisu, no questions asked. However, the patchwork of subtleties that comprise Italy's mosaic of traditional dishes is often unfairly overlooked, even by native Italians. In order to properly understand Italian food, it's essential to consider the crossroads between Italian and Jewish culture. Jews, after all, have lived in the region since the days of ancient Rome, and through the ages, they have changed the way Italians eat—certainly for the better! For instance, if you ask someone in Italy about the origin of orecchiette pasta—the signature ingredient of the southern region of Apulia—most would state with absolute certainty that it comes from Southern Italy. Well, it turns out it most probably came from Provence, in France, brought by the Jews who settled in Apulia as early as the twelfth century.

Farther north, in the region of Veneto, one of the classic specialties of Venice is sarde in saor (sweet-and-sour sardines). Proud locals would surely swear that sarde in saor is a Venetian dish, but from the ingredients of the dish—especially the combination of raisins and vinegar—we know that the recipe must have been brought to Veneto by the Sephardic Jewish merchants who traveled to Italy from Spain.

The Jewish influence on Italian food goes well beyond dishes and recipes; it goes all the way back to the ingredients themselves. A classic example is the story of the adoption of eggplant by Italians. Today we know melanzane as a key ingredient in many Italian dishes—think of eggplant parmigiana—but this wasn't always the case. In the late Middle Ages, Jews in Spain learned from the Arabs how to cook eggplant, an ingredient that was practically unknown to the inhabitants of Italy. When the Jews were expelled from Spain, many of them relocated to Italy and brought with them their traditions and customs, including these bizarrely shaped vegetables. *Berenjenas*, as they were called in

Spanish, were regarded by Italians with great suspicion. Eggplants were disdained for ages as food suitable only for the Jews and for the poor—many people even thought they were poisonous—until the end of the seventeenth century, when Italian Christians slowly began to appreciate Jewish specialties like melanzane in concia (fried eggplant with vinegar) and thus adopted them in their cooking.

Just as Jews have shaped Italian cuisine, so has Italy—with its own ingredients and flavors, but also with its economic and political landscape—shaped the way its Jewish citizens cook and eat. Just look at zuppa di pesce (fish soup), a specialty of Italian Jewish cuisine that is greatly appreciated in Rome. In 1555, Pope Paul IV ruled that the thousands of Jews living in Rome had to move to a ghetto, a confined area located in one of the most undesirable quarters of the city, near the old fish market, and subject to constant flooding from the Tiber River. The conditions in the ghetto were terrible, with most of the Jews living in extreme poverty. However, the Jewish women there, demonstrating that necessity truly is the mother of invention, made the most of their dire circumstances. They would go to the fish market after it closed, collect all the heads and tails and other leftovers that the fishmongers had disposed of, and boil them in water to make a soup. This is the humble origin of zuppa di pesce, a staple in the Jewish Quarter in Rome that is now considered a local delicacy.

These are just some of the fascinating facts about Jewish Italian cuisine that can be uncovered by looking through the dusty recipe books of Italian Jews; they provide evidence of how migration, poverty, and even oppression can, over time, give rise to some extraordinarily delicious food. Knowing the stories behind the dishes makes them taste even better.

A Brief History of Jews in Italy and Their Cuisine

Jewish food all over the world, be it Sephardic, Mizrahi, or Ashkenazi, has developed in accordance with the historical and geographical circumstances of the Jews in the Diaspora. In this respect, Jewish Italian food is no exception: the birth and evolution of the Jewish Italian culinary tradition have been closely linked over the centuries to the history of the Jewish communities in Italy, and to the history of Italy as a whole.

Jews arrived on the Italian peninsula back in the Republican age of Rome. During the Jewish-Roman wars, beginning in 66 CE and spanning seventy years, thousands of Jews were taken from Jerusalem to Rome as slaves, an event depicted in images on the famous Arch of Titus, near the Roman Forum. The Jews were treated with tolerance by most of the Roman emperors, so their numbers swelled to more than fifty thousand in the first century, when they occupied urban centers and port towns, often earning their freedom and becoming merchants. However, when the emperor Constantine decriminalized Christianity in 313 CE and subsequently converted, he paved the way for Central Italy to become what it is today: the seat of the papacy.

The Roman Empire's collapse in the late fifth century resulted in the creation of a number of separate states, each with its own political landscape, a situation that characterized Italy until the late 1800s, when the country was finally unified. Jews were dealt with differently by the Christians in each state, and those differences determined the way they lived and, naturally, cooked. Italian Jews were also often expelled from one state and relocated in another one, but this forced mobility allowed for the expansion, rather than decline, of their culture.

Central and Southern Italy (in particular the region of Sicily and the city of Rome) were home to the earliest and largest Jewish communities in the country until the expulsion of the Jews in the late fifteenth century. Because Sicily was a major hub for commerce with Mediterranean and Middle Eastern countries, Sicilian Jews had long traded with the foreign occupiers who, over time, contended for Italy, including Arabs, Normans, Angevins, and Aragonese. From the Arabs, the Jews of Southern Italy learned to cook with ingredients previously unknown in the country, such as artichokes, eggplants, fennel, and cardoons, as well as many spices that later came to be identified as Jewish ingredients by the local population. When the Spanish monarchy banned the Jews from its kingdom in 1492, thousands of Jews who lived in Sicily fled north, expanding their cultural influence all over the peninsula. While the original Jewish settlements in Southern Italy disappeared, their culinary traditions survived, though in somewhat diluted form, and spread to other regions.

At around the same time the Jews emigrated from Southern Italy toward the central and northern regions, Jewish immigrants from Germany and France also relocated there, especially in Lombardy and Piedmont, joining the ranks of the Jews who had originally left Spain and Portugal.

In the early sixteenth century, though, a new pattern emerged: Jews began to be increasingly segregated in ghettos, closed enclaves that were instituted in most Italian cities to separate them from Christians.

In 1516, Venice was the first city to restrict Jews to a ghetto, and in fact, the term *ghetto* (from *geto*, meaning "foundry") was coined there. At the time, Venice was home to the wealthy and cosmopolitan Tedeschi Jews (German Jews who were mostly loan bankers), as well as to the Ponentini (from Spain and Portugal) and the Levantini merchants (from Egypt, Syria, and Turkey), whose joint influence on the local cuisine had made it sophisticated and varied. Trading with Africa and the Mediterranean, the Levantini taught Venetians to cook with pine nuts, raisins, and saffron and to preserve foods with vinegar, a technique that was later called *saor* in the Venetian dialect. The Ponentini brought with them marzipan (see page 270) and other almond treats, salted cod dishes (see pages 163 and 170), and a preference for citrus. The Tedeschi contributed some of their traditional dishes, such as gefilte fish and kneidlach, as well as recipes using duck and goose (see page 49) and, in particular, the use of goose fat in lieu of the pork and butter found in much Italian cooking, all of which enriched the local cuisine.

A taste for cooking similar to that of the Tedeschi Jews could also be found in Trieste, a port town on the far eastern border of Italy, not far from Venice. There the culinary habits of the Jewish communities had been influenced by the Habsburg monarchy that controlled the city. The local Jewish food included stuffed pancakes similar to Hungarian palacsinta; rich tarts and yeast-leavened cakes of Austrian origin, such as putizza di noci (page 335); and other Northern and Eastern European specialties, like the bean soup called *jota*, which the Jews prepared without the traditional pork.

In Rome, Jews were restricted to a ghetto in 1555, under a decree issued by Pope Paul IV. At the time, there were about two thousand Jews living in Rome. *Cum nimis absurdum* was a papal bull requiring Roman Jews to be segregated and to identify themselves with distinctive, mandatory types of clothing. It also limited their property rights and the learning of skilled trades, forcing Jews into unskilled work such as pawnbroking, moneylending, and the secondhand and rag-and-bone trades.

Rome's ghetto was among the poorest and most dense of any in Italy, and the food the Jews prepared there reflected their dire conditions. They lived on small, cheap fish from the local fish market; humble vegetables from the countryside; and cuts of meat nobody else wanted to buy, like offal (see, for example, minestra di ceci e pennerelli, page 95). As Jews were legally excluded from most professional activities, some got into the "street food" business, one of the few jobs they were allowed, specializing in preparing inexpensive scraps of vegetables fried in oil (see pezzetti fritti, page 63), as well as small bites of battered stockfish (see filetti di baccalà fritti, page 170), dishes for which the Roman Jews are still known to this day.

OPPOSITE, CLOCKWISE FROM TOP LEFT:
A view of the Roman Forum with the Arch of Titus; a bas-relief of the menorah looted by Romans from the Second Temple in Jerusalem on the Arch of Titus; the interior of the Great Synagogue of Rome; an artifact from the Jewish Museum of Rome.

The next pope, Pius IV, extended ghettoization to towns outside of Rome, and his successor, Pius V, further encouraged neighboring states to adopt such practices.

There were also lively Jewish communities in the northern regions of Lombardy and Piedmont, as well as closer to the center of the country, in Tuscany, Emilia-Romagna, and Marche, among other places. Most of these communities experienced the hardship of life in a ghetto, but that didn't deter the local Jews from developing their own culinary traditions.

The Jews of Piedmont, who lived in beautiful towns such as Casale Monferrato, Vercelli, Asti, and Cuneo, took much of their culinary style from neighboring France, in particular from the areas of Comtat Venaissin and Provence, whose Jewish populations had crossed the border to Piedmont beginning in the fifteenth century.

In Lombardy, towns like Mantua experienced a "Jewish Golden Age" during the sixteenth century. The Jews of Mantua left a lasting mark on the local Italian cuisine by importing pumpkin, which is still a specialty there, featured in local dishes such as pumpkin-stuffed pasta (see page 129).

In Tuscany, the Jews of towns such as Florence, Pisa, Siena, and Pitigliano created a number of what are known to this day as local Jewish specialties, such as cuscussù (page 181), triglie alla mosaica (page 167), and sfratti (page 301). One notable exception to the ghettoization of this region was Livorno, a lively port city with a thriving Jewish population. Thanks to a decree issued by Grand Duke Ferdinando de' Medici in 1593, the Jews there enjoyed religious freedom as well as tax exemptions. These favorable conditions drew many Sephardic Jews, particularly Portuguese conversos, who were cultured, affluent merchants, to the city. Along with them came extraordinary ingredients from the New World such as tomatoes, corn, green beans, and chocolate. Livorno's culinary influence extended well beyond the city's borders; in fact, between the sixteenth and nineteenth centuries, Livornese Jews settled in various North African and Levantine cities (Tunis, Tripoli, Aleppo, and Alexandria) to develop commercial businesses, and their recipes live on also in the traditional cuisine of those cities (see, for example, bocca di dama, page 257).

When Napoléon marched through Italy in the final years of the eighteenth century, he was generally greeted by Italian Jews as a liberator. In Venice, the site of the oldest Italian ghetto, the gates were opened in 1797, though the quarter itself has remained largely unchanged, with five of its synagogues still standing today. Rome's ghetto was opened in 1798 with the establishment of Napoléon's Roman Republic, but it was remodeled one year later with the restoration of the Papal States. It persisted—with a small window of freedom between 1808 and 1815—until 1870, making it the last remaining ghetto in Europe for many years, until the reintroduction of ghettos in Eastern Europe in the 1940s. Similarly, in Tuscany, liberation was brief, with Jews being allowed to leave the ghetto in 1799 but then forced back into it in 1814, when the Napoleonic Wars ended and power was restored to the Grand Dukes. The capital city of Tuscany, Florence, did not open its ghetto until 1848.

The unification of Italy began with a series of revolts in 1848: in 1861, the individual states of Italy were merged into a single kingdom under Victor Emmanuel II. For about seventy-five years, the Italian Jewish population enjoyed equal rights: Jews were recognized as citizens and could hold office, attend university, and integrate into the society they'd helped build for more than a thousand years. With that assimilation, however, came a loss of traditions and a loosening of those social connections that the many years of segregation had forcibly maintained.

The Holocaust further threatened the fragile Italian Jewish heritage. A first blow came in 1938, when the Fascist regime promulgated racial laws, which stripped Jewish citizens of their assets and restricted their civil rights. Then, in 1943, the Congress of Verona declared Jews in Italy to be noncitizens, and mass arrests and deportations began. Almost eighty-six hundred Italian Jews were funneled through three major transit camps in Italian territory to Auschwitz and other concentration camps, where most of them were killed. Hundreds more died in violent massacres in Italian towns and cities or in the transit camps themselves. Over the two-year period from 1943 to 1945, 20 percent of Italian Jews were murdered. Relative to other countries in central Europe, Italy lost a smaller percentage of its Jews, but the impact was still staggering.

After the Second World War, Italy as a nation experienced an economic boom that lasted through the 1950s and 1960s. During this time, the Italian Jewish population grew, due to an unlikely source: Mizrahi Jews. Italy became home to large waves of Jews fleeing the Arab world, especially Libya, an Italian colony that had grown very hostile to Jews following the birth of the State of Israel in 1948 and, later, its independence from Italy in 1951. After years of insecurity, in a single month in 1967, Italy helped more than six thousand Libyan Jews immigrate to Rome, where they remain a large and dynamic part of the community today.

In recent years, most of the Jews of Italy have settled in urban centers such as Milan and Rome, so the smaller historic communities of the Italian peninsula have shrunk or disappeared. However, the old recipes of the towns that were once home to Jewish populations are still

passed on, generation after generation, and the ones I have collected in this book serve as a testimony to the Jewish history of those places.

What Makes Food Jewish Italian?

In determining which recipes belonged in this book, I considered Jewish Italian food from two complementary perspectives. First, there are the recipes whose invention is attributed to the Jews of Italy by credible historical sources, or that are unique to the Italian Jewish community as far as available documentation can prove. Second, I consider a recipe Jewish if it's what Jews eat in their own homes, either day in and day out or for the holidays. Interestingly, many common Italian dishes fall into this category, occasionally with some small adjustments to make them fit for the Jewish table.

An adherence to the rules of kashrut, or Jewish dietary law, which often translates to a preference for certain ingredients over others, is decisive in determining the "Jewish Italian" identity of certain foods. The term *kashrut* refers to the set of rules that teach Jews which foods are permitted (kosher) according to Jewish law, and how to prepare them. These rules, which limit human freedom in choosing between pure and impure animals, have the precise importance of reminding Jews that only God is the master of the universe and that, for this reason, we must have pity not only for human beings but also for animals.

Kosher animals are defined as ruminant quadrupeds with split hooves, such as cows, sheep, and goats. Meeting just one of these two conditions is not enough for the animal to be considered kosher, as is the case with pigs and camels, which are, in fact, forbidden foods. Fowl such as chicken, geese, and ducks are kosher and are used in abundance in traditional Jewish Italian cooking. Fish with scales and fins are also considered kosher, but mollusks and crustaceans are forbidden. That is why, for example, Italian Jews have created their own versions of certain seafood dishes that are popular in Italy, such as caciucco (page 172), altering the ingredients to their needs.

Another important rule is to avoid ingesting the blood of animals, since blood is the symbol of life. Therefore, for meat to be kosher, the animal must be killed using a special system (shechitah) designed to prevent suffering and to eliminate as much blood as possible from the meat. Then, to be considered ready for consumption, the meat must be immersed in water, sprinkled with salt, and, finally, rinsed again.

Another strict ban Jews who keep kosher must abide by is never to eat meat and milk (or other dairy products) together. The specific ruling

ruling is found in both Exodus and Deuteronomy: "You shall not cook a goat in its mother's milk." For this reason, several hours must elapse between the time meat-based dishes are eaten and the time dairy-based foods are consumed. Hence, Jews categorize meals as one of three types: milk (halavi), meat (basari), and without meat or milk (pareve). You will find a dedicated index (beginning on page 343) to help you sort the recipes according to these categories.

To maintain compliance with these dietary laws, for many Jewish Italian dishes, certain traditional Italian ingredients are swapped with others: for example, goose fat for pork fat, and oil for butter. Italian specialties such as prosciutto and salami that are typically made with pork can be prepared with goose. Traditional baked goods such as cakes and cookies that are usually made with butter can be made with oil instead. And legendary but not kosher dishes such as lasagna—which feature meat and milk together—can be adapted thanks to a special béchamel (see page 121) that is made with broth instead of milk.

My Mission

Time has a way of eroding the past. One of the things that makes us human is to attempt to prevent this erosion, to keep the past alive. While some people erect monuments and dedicate plaques, and others capture likenesses in portraits and on film, I believe that sharing recipes is a very effective way to preserve our memories. Food is a part of human history, and it constitutes, in a way, our most fundamental and common form of culture.

I was born into an Italian Jewish family, and I have always been fascinated with the two culinary identities that have been part of my household. However, in the last decade, which I have spent writing about food, I have come to realize that the unique cuisine of the Jews of Italy, which has flourished and evolved for more than two thousand years, has not been as dutifully recorded as it should be to be preserved from looming oblivion. The size of the Italian Jewish community has dropped over the last century, and as of today, there are approximately only twenty-seven thousand Jews left in the entirety of Italy (less than 0.45 percent of the population). To give a sense of proportion, that is roughly the same number of Jews who reside in, for example, Minneapolis or Milwaukee, neither of which is a particularly Jewish city.

While gathering information for this book, I visited congregations big and small all over Italy, spoke with home cooks young and old, and came to a worrisome conclusion: a lot of dishes that were once considered standard Jewish Italian fare have already largely been forgotten, still treasured by, at most, a couple of elderly ladies who can cook them but have no one to pass the recipes down to. At this rate, in a few generations, the wealth of culinary heritage that constitutes the Jewish Italian legacy could be entirely lost.

That potential loss was the inspiration for this book. I believe that food keeps us alive not only literally but also figuratively. Because many recipes, stories, and memories that were once passed on via word of mouth are now in danger of disappearing, I made it my mission to save them. My humble goal was to make this book the most comprehensive and accurate collection of Jewish Italian recipes ever published.

Along with the recipes, you will find descriptions of the main cities and regions of Italy from a Jewish perspective, with some historical insights and travel tips for approaching the local Jewish culture, as well as recommendations for those curious foodies who stumble into town. You will also find information on the major Jewish holidays. The life of a Jew has a very specific rhythm, marked by the holidays in the Jewish calendar, and Italian Jews have special holiday foods that enrich celebrations with symbolic meaning as well as nourishment.

I have made every effort to faithfully describe the food that is cooked and enjoyed in the Jewish communities in the various regions of Italy, and to provide guidance to those who want to learn to cook the way Italian Jews have done for centuries, along with historical references to put the recipes in context. Cultural value aside, this book also aims to introduce you to the food I love to eat and cook—comforting, easy to prepare, and made in the style of an Italian *mamma*. It is food that calls for sharing with family and friends around the table, in the true spirit of Italian Jewish culture.

Ingredients

Although passionate cooks always care about the ingredients that go into their dishes, Italians can be particularly obsessive, especially when it comes to the local products they are proud of, such as olive oil and Parmesan cheese. Before approaching the recipes in this book, please take a few minutes to read these notes on ingredients, and consider looking for a well-stocked local Italian market or deli, such as Eataly in New York and Los Angeles, to source authentic Italian products for your pantry—or seek them out online.

BREAD · A few recipes in this book call for slices of stale bread. Unless otherwise stated, the bread I use is white sourdough, and one slice is approximately 5 by 3 by ½ inch (13 by 8 by 1 cm) and weighs approximately 3½ ounces (100 g). In most cases, you can substitute ¼ cup (25 g) dry bread crumbs for 1 slice of stale bread.

BROTH · For homemade broth, turn to page 78. I make broth in large quantities and freeze it. Note that whenever I call for broth in a recipe, any broth (vegetable, chicken, or beef) will do unless otherwise specified. I know you can't always have homemade broth on hand, so go ahead and use stock cubes, preferably organic ones, or good store-bought stock instead.

CHEESE · While not many of these recipes call for cheese, always keep some good-quality Parmesan and Pecorino on hand. You don't need to buy it fresh very often: cut it into smaller wedges or grate it, place it in an airtight container or a heavy-duty freezer bag, and store it in the freezer for up to 12 months.

DRIED AND CANDIED FRUIT · Some of these recipes call for dried or candied fruit. Good-quality candied fruit, in particular, is not easy to find in US supermarkets, but it can be purchased online.

EGGS · Large eggs were used for testing these recipes. Use good-quality free-range eggs if you can.

FISH · Italy is a peninsula surrounded by water, so many of our traditional dishes feature fish. The local fish found in Italian markets are not always available in North America, but I've tried to provide alternatives whenever possible. Seek out a local fishmonger to procure good-quality fish.

MATZO AND MATZO FLOUR · Many recipes in this book call for Passover ingredients such as matzo and matzo flour. These can be found year-round in kosher shops and many supermarkets, and they have a long shelf life, so even if you buy them for Passover, they will last you a while. In Italy, there are two types of matzo: the common one found all over the world and a thicker version, which is roughly three times as thick as regular matzo. Unfortunately, it is not easy to find thick matzo in the United States. The recipes in this book will work with either type, but if you ever come across the thicker type, try it. As for matzo flour, there are also two types, matzo meal, which is coarser, and matzo cake meal, which is finer. Unless otherwise specified in the recipe, either will work.

OIL · The Jews of Italy cook mostly with oil and use little to no butter. Choosing the right type of oil for cooking these recipes is simple: use extra-virgin olive oil for everything other than frying or baking. For frying and baking, use sunflower (my first choice) or peanut, or at least an oil from a single source (such as grapeseed), not a mixed one. If you like the flavor of olive oil and you come across a brand that has a very mild taste, you can use it for baking, but I often find the taste of olive oil to be too strong, so I avoid it in those cases. If you are on a budget, I urge you to save money on everything else you buy but not on the oil, because the quality of the oil you use makes a huge difference. My favorite Italian extra-virgin olive oil brands found in American supermarkets are Bertolli and Colavita, but some Californian olive oils are also great.

SALT · I always use kosher salt for cooking. Salting food is very much a matter of taste, and I tend to eat quite salty. I have provided some guidance for amounts in each recipe, but you should taste and adjust the amount to your liking.

SPECIAL CUTS OF MEAT AND OFFAL · This book includes a few recipes that call for offal and such, because a major part of traditional Jewish Italian cuisine relied on offal for inexpensive nutrition, and I want to honor that. Make friends with your butcher, if you haven't already: you'll be surprised how easily accessible and affordable good meat can be when you source lesser-known cuts of good quality.

TOMATOES · In the United States, fresh tomatoes, unfortunately, are usually nothing like Italian ones. For recipes that call for fresh tomatoes, look for heirloom varieties—these are as close as they get to Italian standards. For recipes that call for tomato puree, I almost always recommend passata, which is simply tomatoes that have been pureed and passed through a sieve. Tomato puree can be found in most supermarkets; sometimes popular Italian brands such as Mutti or Pomì are available, and I recommend them. Should your local Italian market carry "rustic" passata, snatch it up: it's coarsely pureed passata, the best there is for cooking. Canned tomato sauces, which generally have added flavorings and/or salt, are not the same as passata, so steer away from canned sauce. If you can't find passata, you can substitute canned crushed tomatoes, but you'll have to puree them with a blender and increase the cooking time to allow for the fact that crushed tomatoes contain more liquid than passata.

VINEGAR · Vinegar is used extensively in this book, as many historical Jewish Italian recipes have a sweet-and-sour-flavor that depends on vinegar. For these recipes, you'll mostly need white wine vinegar, but a few of them call for red wine vinegar or balsamic. If you are buying balsamic vinegar, do invest in a small bottle of real Italian balsamico; most American brands are of lesser quality and often contain added sugar and food coloring.

Tools and Utensils

These are the items you should have in your kitchen to fully enjoy cooking from this book.

IMMERSION BLENDER · While not strictly essential, an immersion blender will make your sauces, soups, and dressings perfectly creamy.

KITCHEN SCALE · A kitchen scale is a prerequisite for accurate baking. These recipes give both volume measures and metric measures, but I highly recommend you follow the metric measurements if you can. Cups and spoons are just not precise enough; with a scale, there is no possibility of error. Invest in a small digital scale: these cost very little, take up almost no space, and will improve your baking results beyond belief.

KNIVES · Good cooking starts with good knives. Get a Santoku or a chef's knife, a paring knife, and a serrated bread knife, and you are good to go. And please keep them sharp!

POTS AND PANS · Use nonstick pots and pans if possible; they can be coated in ceramic, granite, or Teflon, depending on what you can afford. And treat yourself to a proper Dutch oven: it's a fairly expensive item, but it will noticeably improve everything you stew and roast. The other pots and pans I find most useful include the following.

- Small skillet: 8 inches (20 cm) wide and 1½ to 2 inches (4 to 5 cm) deep

- Medium skillet: 10½ inches (27 cm) wide and 1½ to 2 inches (4 to 5 cm) deep

- Large skillet: 11 inches (28 cm) wide and 2 to 3 inches (5 to 8 cm) deep

- Sauté pan: 10 inches (25 cm) wide and 3½ inches (9 cm) deep

- Small saucepan: About 7½ inches (19 cm) wide and 3½ inches (9 cm) deep; it should comfortably hold 1¼ quarts (1.2 L)

- Medium saucepan: About 8½ inches (22 cm) wide and 3½ inches (9 cm) deep; it should comfortably hold 1¾ quarts (1.7 L)

- Large saucepan: About 9½ inches (24 cm) wide and 4½ inches (11 cm) deep; it should comfortably hold 3 quarts (2.8 L)

- Stockpot: About 10 inches (25 cm) wide and 5½ (14 cm) inches deep; it should comfortably hold 4½ quarts (4.3 L)

SPICE GRINDER · Of course you can buy most spices and nuts already ground, but freshly ground spices taste a lot better.

STAND MIXER · If money and space aren't a concern, buy a stand mixer. For a more affordable solution, get a handheld mixer. You'll need a mixer to make the desserts, especially the ones that require whipping egg whites.

THERMOMETERS · Get one thermometer for deep-frying, another for candymaking or measuring sugar temperature (or look for a combination deep-fry/candy thermometer), and a third one for meats. Thermometers are especially useful if you are a beginner cook; they will prevent you from making discouraging mistakes.

Antipasti

STARTERS

ARANCIO ACCONDITO
Orange and Olive Salad

SERVES 4

—

**4 oranges
(see headnote)**

**½ cup (90 g) pitted
black olives**

**3 tablespoons extra-
virgin olive oil**

**2 tablespoons white
wine vinegar
(optional)**

**Kosher salt and
freshly ground
black pepper**

Arancio accondito translates as "dressed orange." This humble salad, made simply with good oranges and black olives, was once a classic winter dish, especially among poorer Jews. People would eat the salad sandwiched inside a piece of bread, which sounds like an odd practice, but it's actually quite clever: the bread soaks up all the juices of the salad, maximizing the flavor while providing a heartier meal.

The salad is incredibly tasty—it's the perfect mix of sweet, salty, and tangy—and it comes together in minutes. It can be spiced up with a variety of other ingredients; try the basic recipe first, then try it the Roman or Sicilian way (see the Variations). Use the best-quality oranges you can find, preferably blood oranges, though common navel or Cara Cara oranges will work too.

———

Carefully peel the oranges: with a sharp knife, cut off the ends of each orange, stand it on a flat surface so it won't tip over, and cut off all the peel and white pith, working your way around the orange.

Once the oranges are peeled, with only orange flesh in sight, thinly slice them and arrange the slices on a plate. Sprinkle the black olives over the oranges.

Dress the salad with the olive oil, adding the vinegar for an extra kick of sour, if you like, then season with salt and pepper to taste and serve.

VARIATIONS

• In Rome, some cooks used to add small cubes of boiled beef left over from making broth to make the salad more nourishing.

• In Southern Italy, especially in Sicily, a similar dish is prepared with the addition of thinly sliced fennel, a sprinkling of oregano, a handful of olives, and a pinch of crushed red pepper flakes.

TORTA DI ERBETTE
Spinach, Artichoke, and Green Pea Pie

SERVES 6

—

FOR THE CRUST

1⅔ cups (200 g)
    all-purpose flour

8 tablespoons
    (1 stick/113 g)
    cold butter or
    margarine, cubed

Pinch of kosher salt

About ½ cup
    (120 ml) water

FOR THE FILLING

6 fresh artichokes
    or 2½ cups (250 g)
    frozen artichoke
    wedges

2 tablespoons extra-
    virgin olive oil

1 onion, thinly sliced

1 pound (450 g)
    fresh spinach or
    one 10-ounce
    (285 g) box frozen
    spinach

1½ cups (200 g)
    fresh or frozen
    peas

1 teaspoon kosher
    salt

Freshly ground
    black pepper

2 large (100 g) eggs,
    lightly beaten

Savory pies are great make-ahead dinner options. This one is a simple starter that keeps very well for a couple of days and can be served at any temperature: it's perfect for Shabbat, which is when it's usually prepared in Rome, but you could make it for a warm-weather picnic as well.

If you are in a rush, you can skip the homemade crust and use frozen puff pastry instead. If you do, there is no need to blind-bake the pie shell.

———

Sift the flour into a large bowl. Add the cubed butter or margarine and rub into the flour with your fingertips until the mixture resembles fine bread crumbs.

Stir in the salt, then gradually add the water, mixing and kneading with your hands to make a firm dough (you may need a little more or less water).

Knead the dough briefly, shape it into a disk, and wrap it in plastic wrap. Chill it in the refrigerator while you make the filling.

To prepare the filling, start with the artichokes, which take the longest to cook. If you are using fresh artichokes, with kitchen shears or sharp scissors, remove the thorny tips from the leaves. Peel off the first layer of the outer leaves and discard, as they are tough and chewy. Shave the stems of the artichokes with a potato peeler.

Cut the artichokes in half, scrape out and discard the fuzzy choke at the center, and quarter the artichokes.

Add the artichoke quarters to a large saucepan of boiling water and cook over medium heat for 30 minutes, or until soft; drain.

Pour the olive oil into a large sauté pan set over medium-low heat, add the onion, and cook until soft and translucent, a couple of minutes. Add the spinach, peas, and, if using fresh vegetables, ½ cup (120 ml) water. Reduce the heat to medium-low, partially cover the pan, and cook for 10 minutes, or until the spinach is wilted and the peas are tender.

Add the fresh or frozen artichokes to the pan, sprinkle with the salt and pepper to taste, and stir the vegetables to combine. Increase the heat to medium-high and cook for about 1 minute, so the last bits of cooking liquid evaporate.

Transfer the cooked vegetables to a bowl and let cool to room temperature, then stir in the beaten eggs.

Preheat the oven to 400°F (200°C).

Cut out two 10-inch (25 cm) rounds of parchment paper. Take the chilled dough from the refrigerator, place it on one of the rounds of parchment, and roll it out with a rolling pin to the size of the paper. Place the dough, still on the parchment paper, in a 9-inch (23 cm) pie dish. Crimp the edges for a decorative finish or use the tines of a fork to create a pattern in the edges of the dough.

Place the second round of parchment paper in the crust and fill the pan with pie weights or dried beans. Bake for 10 to 15 minutes, until the crust is set and just barely starting to brown. Carefully remove the parchment and weights.

Pour the vegetable mixture into the prebaked crust, smoothing it with a spatula, and bake for 20 to 25 minutes, or until the filling has set and a knife inserted in the center of the pie comes out clean. If the edges of the crust start to brown excessively before the filling is done, cover the edges with foil for the last few minutes of baking.

Let the pie cool for 15 to 20 minutes before serving. Leftovers keep well in the fridge for a couple of days and can be reheated in the oven or served at room temperature.

VARIATION

• If you don't have to worry about making a dairy-free meal, a generous sprinkle of grated Parmesan or Pecorino cheese and a few tablespoons of ricotta make a great addition to the pie filling.

Bagna Cauda, Two Ways

Bagna cauda is a warm sauce made with garlic and anchovies, typical of the region of Piedmont, that is prepared seasonally at around the time of the grape harvest. It's served in a fondue pot or a bowl, with raw and cooked vegetables for communal dipping. While the origins of the dish are uncertain, bagna cauda has been a part of Piedmontese cuisine since the sixteenth century; there are reasons to believe that it was the Jews who first introduced anchovies to the peasants in Piedmont.

There are two versions of the recipe, one in which the garlic and anchovies are slow-cooked together in olive oil, and another in which the garlic is boiled in milk. I've included both versions here, but you might want to try the one with milk first, as the garlic flavor is less pungent and intense, making it suitable for less-adventurous palates.

The simplest and most traditional way to serve bagna cauda is with just peppers (raw or grilled and cut into strips) or blanched sticks of cardoon, if you can get your hands on that short-seasoned thistle, but potatoes, onions, cabbage, cauliflower, and celery, among other vegetables, are great for dipping too (see Note). Don't forget hard-boiled eggs, for a bit of protein, and, most important, bread, which will allow you to scoop up the last few precious drops of bagna cauda left in the bowl.

Olive Oil Bagna Cauda

SERVES 2 TO 4

—

10 to 12 garlic cloves, depending on your taste for garlic

Two 2-ounce (55 g) tins anchovy fillets in olive oil

½ cup (120 ml) dry red wine (optional)

1 cup (240 ml) extra-virgin olive oil

4 tablespoons (½ stick/57 g) cold butter or margarine, cut into chunks

Kosher salt

A mix of vegetables, plus hard-boiled eggs and bread, for serving (see Note)

Peel the garlic cloves and thinly slice them with a sharp knife.

Remove three-quarters (3 ounces/82.5 g) of the anchovy fillets from their tins and drain them on paper towels. Reserve the remaining anchovies for another recipe, such as Orecchiette with Broccoli Rabe (page 111) or Fried Vegetables and Squash Blossoms (page 63).

Some people like to soak the anchovy fillets for a few minutes in red wine, but this step is optional. Drain them well if you do so.

Place the garlic and anchovies in a small saucepan with the olive oil and cook over very low heat for 30 minutes, or until the garlic is soft and the anchovies are falling apart.

Just before removing the pan from the heat, stir in the butter and add salt to taste.

If you want a smoother sauce, give the bagna cauda a whiz in a food processor or with an immersion blender.

Serve hot or at room temperature, with the vegetables for dipping, along with hard-boiled eggs and bread. Or store in the fridge for a day or two; reheat before serving, if desired, or just bring to room temperature. Stir well before serving.

- continued -

Milk-Based Bagna Cauda

SERVES 2 TO 4

—

10 garlic cloves

Two 2-ounce (55 g) tins anchovy fillets in olive oil

¼ cup (60 ml) milk

¼ cup (60 ml) extra-virgin olive oil

Kosher salt (optional)

A mix of vegetables, plus hard-boiled eggs and bread, for serving (see Note)

Peel the garlic cloves and thinly slice them with a sharp knife.

Remove three-quarters (3 ounces/82.5 g) of the anchovy fillets from their tins and drain them on paper towels. Reserve the remaining anchovies for another recipe, such as Orecchiette with Broccoli Rabe (page 111) or Fried Vegetables and Squash Blossoms (page 63).

In a small saucepan, bring the milk to a gentle simmer over very low heat. Add the garlic and cook for 15 minutes, or until it is soft.

Meanwhile, place the anchovies in a medium saucepan with half of the olive oil and cook over very low heat for 15 minutes, or until the anchovies fall apart.

Whiz the garlic milk and anchovies in the food processor, then transfer the mixture to the saucepan.

Add the remaining olive oil and simmer over very low heat for 20 to 30 minutes; the oil should never bubble, and the sauce should develop a very creamy texture. Taste; add salt, if desired.

Serve warm or at room temperature, with the vegetables for dipping, along with hard-boiled eggs and bread.

Leftovers can be stored in the fridge in an airtight container for a day or two; reheat before serving, if desired, or just bring to room temperature. Leftover bagna cauda goes very well with polenta and with roasted meats.

NOTE

Prepare a mix of accompaniments to serve with the bagna cauda. Arrange them on your nicest platter; here are some suggestions.

- Strips of raw or roasted mixed bell peppers
- Cardoons, trimmed, sliced, and blanched
- Onions, cut into wedges and roasted
- Beets, cut into wedges, roasted, and peeled
- Cabbage, cut into wedges and roasted
- Cauliflower, cut into wedges and roasted
- Celery ribs, trimmed and sliced
- Potatoes, quartered and boiled
- Parsnips, peeled, sliced into sticks, and roasted
- Hard-boiled eggs, cut into quarters
- Sourdough bread, cut into thick slices and toasted

Savory Cheese Pie, or "Pie of the Jews"

MAKES TWO 9-INCH (23 CM) PIES; SERVES 10

—

3¾ cups plus 1 tablespoon (480 g) all-purpose flour, plus more for dusting

½ teaspoon kosher salt

12 tablespoons (1½ sticks/170 g) cold unsalted butter, plus 1 tablespoon for greasing the pan and 1 tablespoon for the top of the pie

¾ cup (170 g) vegetable shortening or 12 tablespoons (1½ sticks/170 g) margarine, at room temperature (see Notes)

1¼ cups (300 ml) water

½ teaspoon fresh lemon juice

1½ cups (130 g) thinly shaved Parmesan cheese

Tibuia is a savory pie made with buttery, flaky layers of puff pastry and shaved Parmesan cheese. This pie is typical of the city of Finale, in Emilia-Romagna, where it's eaten as a starter or a snack, but it's also quite similar to the Middle Eastern puff pastry hand pies called *bourekas*, due to its Jewish history.

Serve small slices of this pie during happy hour with a nice glass of wine, or as a simple starter.

————

In a medium bowl, mix the flour and salt together. Take 3 tablespoons of the cold butter and 3 tablespoons of the shortening or margarine and rub it into the flour/salt mixture with your fingertips until it resembles sand. (If you prefer, you can use your stand mixer for this task.) Set the remaining butter and shortening (or margarine) aside to come to room temperature.

In a small cup, mix the water and lemon juice, then stir into the flour-fat mixture to make a soft, smooth dough.

Dust a rolling pin and the counter with flour. Divide the dough into 2 portions and roll each portion out into an 8-by-6-inch (20 by 15 cm) rectangle.

By this point, the butter and shortening should have come to room temperature, but if they have not, microwave them briefly to achieve a spreadable consistency.

Position one dough rectangle so a short side is toward you. Spread 1½ tablespoons of the soft butter and 1½ tablespoons of the soft shortening evenly over the top two-thirds of the first dough rectangle, leaving a ½-inch (1 cm) border of dough at the top and sides. Fold the bottom third up over the middle third and then the top third down over that, as you would fold a letter. You should end up with an 8-by-2-inch (20 by 5 cm) rectangle. Wrap the dough in plastic wrap and refrigerate for about 15 minutes. Repeat with the second portion of dough.

After the dough has chilled, take one portion out of the fridge and roll it out a second time, then repeat the process above, spreading the dough with both fats and folding as you did before. Repeat with the second portion of dough. Wrap the dough and chill again for 15 minutes.

Repeat the process of adding the fats and folding the dough a third time. Then roll and fold the dough one last time, without adding any fat. Wrap the dough and chill for at least 45 minutes.

– continued –

Preheat the oven to 400°F (200°C). Grease two 9-inch (23 cm) pie pans or round cake pans with the 1 tablespoon butter.

One at a time, unwrap both rectangles of dough and roll each one out to a thickness of ⅓ inch (8 mm), or slightly thinner if you can. Place a pie pan (or cake pan) on top of one sheet of dough and use a knife to cut out 3 disks the diameter of the bottom of the pan. As this is a laminated dough, you want to avoid rerolling the dough multiple times: think ahead, measure well, and start cutting only when you think you have the size under control. (Most 9-inch/23 cm pie pans are only about 5 inches/13 cm across at the bottom, so if you measure the disks using the bottom of the dish for size, you are sure to have no excess dough on the sides.) Repeat with the second portion of dough to make a total of 6 disks.

Place a disk of dough in the bottom of one pie pan, brush it with some water, and sprinkle one-quarter of the Parmesan on top of the dough. Repeat with a second disk of dough and another one-quarter of the Parmesan. Cover the pie with a third disk of dough and decorate the surface by gently scoring it with a knife to form very small squares. Brush the surface of the pie with half of the remaining tablespoon of butter. Repeat with the second pie pan and the remaining ingredients.

Bake the pies for 25 to 30 minutes, or until golden on top. Remove from the oven and let cool slightly.

Cut the pies into small slices to serve. Leftovers will keep well in the fridge, wrapped in foil, for a few days, and can be reheated in the oven.

NOTES

- If you don't want to use shortening or margarine, feel free to use all butter in the recipe; the result will be equally flaky and delicious.

- To prepare this dish in advance, you can make the dough ahead and freeze it, tightly wrapped, for a few weeks. The evening before you want to make the pies, thaw the dough overnight in the fridge, then assemble and bake the pies the following day.

A STORY OF LOVE AND VENGEANCE • The "pie of the Jews," it has been said, was brought to Italy from Turkey by the Belgradi family, and the recipe was kept a secret within the Jewish community for generations. In 1861, a Jewish man by the name of Mandolino Rimini decided to marry a Catholic girl and convert to Catholicism. As the community loudly disapproved of his choices, he decided to punish his fellow Jews and share the famous pie recipe with the Christians. To further offend his former community, he added lard to the dish, so it was no longer kosher. His version of the recipe became a local specialty, and it still goes by the name torta degli ebrei today, although it is, ironically, still not kosher, just as the rebellious convert wanted it.

Beef Hand Pies

MAKES 8 TO 10
HAND PIES
—

FOR THE FILLING

2 tablespoons extra-
virgin olive oil

1 small onion, finely
chopped

1 pound (450 g)
ground beef
(see Note)

½ teaspoon kosher
salt

Freshly ground
black pepper

FOR THE DOUGH

1⅔ cups (200 g)
all-purpose flour

½ cup (120 ml) water

1 tablespoon extra-
virgin olive oil

½ teaspoon kosher
salt

Sunflower or peanut
oil for deep-frying

This vintage Roman recipe for hand pies brings back fond memories of generations of mothers and grandmothers who were not afraid to fry. Tortiglioni are made with a very simple dough called *pasta matta* ("crazy dough") and filled with meat and onions. They are similar to empanadas, and some people refer to these hand pies as impanate instead of tortiglioni, which gives away their Sephardic origins.

———

To prepare the filling, pour the olive oil into a large nonstick skillet set over medium heat, add the onion, and cook until soft and translucent, about 10 minutes. Increase the heat to medium-high, add the beef, season with the salt and pepper to taste, and stir with a spoon for a minute, breaking up any lumps, then cover and cook for 5 minutes. Remove the lid and cook, uncovered, for 5 more minutes, or until the beef is browned. Transfer to a bowl and set aside to cool.

To prepare the dough, in a large bowl, mix the flour, water, olive oil, and salt together. Then knead with your hands for a couple of minutes, to make a smooth dough. Cover the bowl with plastic wrap and let the dough rest for 30 minutes at room temperature.

Tortiglioni can be shaped like half-moons or like large rectangular ravioli.

Divide the dough into 8 to 10 portions. Roll out each piece into a disk about ¼ inch (6 mm) thick, if you want to make half-moon–shaped tortiglioni, or a square approximately 5 inches (13 cm) across for rectangular tortiglioni. To forms the pies, put about 1½ tablespoons of the meat mixture in the center of each piece and fold the dough over the filling. Press the edges together with your fingers to seal tightly. Should the edges not stick together, wet a finger with a little water, rub it along the inside edges of the dough, and try again.

Pour 1½ to 2 inches (4 to 5 cm) of sunflower or peanut oil into a large saucepan and heat over medium heat until a deep-fry thermometer reads 350°F (180°C). You can test the oil by dropping a small piece of food, such as a slice of apple, into it: if it sizzles nicely but doesn't bubble up too wildly, the oil is ready. (An apple is said to help minimize the smell of the frying oil, so I generally go for that, but any bit of food will do.) When the oil is ready, fry the hand pies, in batches, to avoid crowding the pan, for 1 to 2 minutes per side, until lightly golden.

Drain the fried pies on a paper towel–lined plate and serve warm.

Tortiglioni are best enjoyed freshly fried. However, leftovers can be reheated in a 350°F (180°C) oven if necessary.

NOTE

If you have leftover boiled meat from making broth or from another dish, this recipe is a good place to repurpose it. Just grind the meat coarsely in a food processor and mix it into the cooked onions.

VARIATION

For a fish variation, combine any cooked white fish with mashed boiled eggs, parsley, and some coarsely chopped canned anchovy fillets to make the filling.

Chicken Hand Pies

MAKES 15 TO 18
HAND PIES
—

FOR THE DOUGH

½ cup (120 ml) light extra-virgin olive oil or sunflower oil

½ cup (120 ml) warm water

¼ teaspoon kosher salt

2¾ cups plus 1 tablespoon (350 g) all-purpose flour

FOR THE FILLING

2 tablespoons extra-virgin olive oil, plus more for greasing

1 onion, chopped

¾ pound (340 g) skinless, boneless chicken (thighs work best), cut into small pieces

¼ teaspoon ground allspice

Kosher salt and freshly ground black pepper

3 slices stale sourdough bread

1 cup (240 ml) chicken or vegetable broth, homemade (page 78) or store-bought

1 large (50 g) egg, lightly beaten

Buricche are small hand pies that have been prepared in the city of Ferrara, in the Emilia-Romagna region, since the Middle Ages. They're similar to Turkish borekas, evidenced by the name of the dish. Buricche can be either savory—with fillings of beef, chicken, chicken liver, cooked fish, pumpkin, or eggplant—or sweet, with an almond paste filling (for that version, the dough is also sweetened a little). In Venice, where the name of the pies is spelled *burriche*, the traditional filling is turkey, onion, and pine nuts. In the old days, the dough would have been made with rendered chicken or goose fat, but today olive oil is more common.

———

To make the dough, in a large bowl, mix the oil, warm water, and salt. Gradually add the flour, mixing and kneading with your hands until a soft, elastic, but no longer sticky dough has formed. Cover the dough with plastic wrap and set aside at room temperature while you prepare the filling.

To make the filling, pour the olive oil into a large nonstick skillet set over medium heat, add the onion, and cook gently, stirring often, until soft and translucent, about 10 minutes. Add the chicken, season it with the allspice and salt and pepper to taste, and cook for 10 minutes, or until the chicken is cooked through and is golden brown in spots. Remove from the heat and let cool.

Preheat the oven to 350°F (180°C). Lightly oil a large baking sheet.

In a medium bowl, soak the bread in the broth until softened, then remove it and squeeze it well to remove all the liquid.

In the bowl of a food processor, combine the softened bread (you might not need all of it, so start with half and go from there), chicken, and egg and process to a thick paste. You are looking for a texture similar to that of meatballs.

Place the dough on a floured counter and divide it into 15 to 18 portions. Roll the portions out into disks about ¼ inch (6 mm) thick. Put 1½ tablespoons of the chicken mixture in the center of each disk and fold over the dough to form a half-moon. Press the edges together with your fingers to seal tightly and crimp them with a fork. If the edges do not stick together, wet a finger with water, rub it along the inside edges of the dough, and try again.

Place the buricche on the prepared baking sheet and bake for 25 to 30 minutes, until golden. Serve warm.

Buricche are best fresh, but you can reheat leftovers in the oven.

MALIGNANE SCINICATE
Marinated Eggplant

SERVES 4 TO 6

—

3 or 4 medium
eggplants

Kosher salt

5 tablespoons (40 g)
all-purpose flour

Sunflower or peanut
oil for deep-frying

1 garlic clove

½ teaspoon saffron
threads

Leaves from a few
sprigs of fresh
oregano

Freshly ground
black pepper

1 tablespoon fresh
lemon juice

1 tablespoon
unsweetened
grape juice
(optional)

1½ tablespoons red
wine vinegar

Italians didn't eat eggplant for decades after the vegetable had been introduced into the country (see page 9), as they suspected it of being poisonous (the name *malignane* is related to the word *malign*, which means "evil") and considered them a food fit only for the poor and the Jews, who had long enjoyed the ingredient. This is one of the oldest Jewish Italian recipes and features fried eggplant that is briefly marinated in vinegar, herbs, and precious saffron threads.

———

Cut the eggplants into 1-inch (3 cm) cubes. Put the eggplant cubes in a large colander, toss with a little salt, and place a heavy plate on top of the eggplant. Set the colander in the sink or over a bowl and let the eggplant release any bitter liquids for at least 30 minutes (weighting the eggplant with a plate will help release more liquid faster).

Briefly rinse away the salt under cold running water, drain the eggplant cubes, and pat thoroughly dry with paper towels. Place the eggplant cubes in a bowl, add the flour, and toss to coat.

Pour 1½ to 2 inches (4 to 5 cm) of oil into a large saucepan and heat over medium heat until a deep-fry thermometer reads 350°F (180°C). You can test the oil by dropping a small piece of food, such as a slice of apple, into it: if it sizzles nicely but doesn't bubble up too wildly, the oil is ready. (An apple is said to help minimize the smell of the frying oil, so I generally go for that, but a bit of any food will do.)

Working in batches to avoid crowding the pan, fry the eggplant cubes until golden, 3 to 4 minutes. Using a slotted spoon, transfer the eggplant to a paper towel–lined plate to drain and cool.

Mash the garlic clove in a garlic press or with the side of a knife. In a small bowl, mix the garlic with the saffron, oregano leaves, salt and pepper to taste, the lemon juice, grape juice, if using, and vinegar.

Transfer the eggplant to a large skillet. Pour the marinade over the top and briefly reheat the eggplant over medium heat, stirring well to combine the ingredients. Serve hot or at room temperature.

Leftovers keep well in the fridge, in a bowl covered with plastic wrap or in an airtight container, for a couple of days.

Fried Eggplant with Melon

SERVES 4

—

2¼ pounds (1 kg) eggplants (see headnote)

2½ cups (600 ml) extra-virgin olive oil

½ teaspoon kosher salt

1 tablespoon chopped parsley

2 garlic cloves, crushed

1 cantaloupe, peeled, halved, seeded, and sliced into wedges

Fried eggplant might seem like a straightforward side dish, but this version comes with an interesting companion: melon. In Italy, cantaloupe is commonly paired with prosciutto for a refreshing starter, but as many Jews don't eat pork, they created this dish to enjoy in the same way. These melanzane al funghetto are a Venetian specialty, not to be confused with a dish that goes by the same name in Southern Italy but features tomatoes and basil.

For best results, look for eggplants that are somewhat elongated and thin, not large and round. Japanese eggplants will work well in this recipe. Note that the sliced eggplant has to dry overnight to ensure the crispest result.

————

Trim the eggplants and slice them lengthwise into quarters. If you have large eggplants, scrape out some of the seedy pulp, to end up with 4 slimmer slices. Cut the slices diagonally into rhomboidal wedges, like you would to make some very chunky potato fries.

Lay out the eggplant wedges on a baking sheet, cover them with a kitchen towel, and let them sit at room temperature overnight.

The next day, in a large saucepan, heat the olive oil over medium heat for a minute, then add all the eggplant wedges. It will look like there are too many in the pan at first, but they will eventually shrink and soften. Sprinkle the eggplants with the salt, then add the parsley and garlic. Cover and cook, stirring once or twice so that the eggplants that are at the top make it to the bottom at some point, for approximately 5 minutes. Check the eggplants after the first couple of minutes. If they look very dry, add a splash of water. When the eggplant wedges have softened and offer little to no resistance when pierced with a fork but still retain their shape, turn the heat to high and cook, uncovered, for 5 minutes, stirring constantly. Drain the eggplant in a colander (and discard the oil).

Let the eggplants cool to room temperature, then place them in the fridge to chill.

Serve the eggplant cold, with the sliced melon.

Leftover eggplant keeps well in the fridge, in a bowl covered with plastic wrap or in an airtight container, for a couple of days.

Fried Zucchini in a Garlic-Herb Marinade

**SERVES 4 TO 6
AS A STARTER
OR SIDE DISH**

—

2¼ pounds (1 kg)
zucchini

Sunflower or peanut
oil for deep-frying

3 garlic cloves, finely
minced

A handful of parsley
or basil leaves,
or both, finely
chopped (see
Variations)

¼ teaspoon kosher
salt

Freshly ground
black pepper

½ cup (120 ml) white
wine vinegar

3 tablespoons extra-
virgin olive oil

Starting in the spring and then all the way to the end of summer, fried zucchini is a staple recipe on every Roman Jewish family's Shabbat menu. Any type of zucchini will work, but in Rome, concia is made with the special Italian zucchini called *zucchine romanesche*; they are small and light green with thin, pale stripes and have beautiful flowers. If you can't find them, try Persian zucchini or Mexican squash.

This marinated fried zucchini dish is generally made ahead, to ensure that the flavors blend well, and is served as a starter or a side, but it also makes the best snack on top of crusty pizza bianca (page 328), or sandwiched between two slices of crunchy bread such as ossi (page 327).

————

Slice the zucchini lengthwise into ¼-inch-thick (6 mm) strips. People debate the best way to slice the zucchini for this dish; some like to cut the slices at an angle to obtain wide ovals instead of strips. Any shape will do as long as your slices are even in thickness.

If you are not pressed for time, let the zucchini slices dry on a baking sheet lined with paper towels for a couple of hours, so they lose some of their moisture. If you are in a hurry, go straight to frying.

Pour about 2 inches (5 cm) of sunflower or peanut oil into a large saucepan and heat over medium heat until a deep-fry thermometer reads 350°F (180°C). (You could use a deep skillet for frying if you prefer, but I find that a saucepan helps contain the oil if it bubbles up too much.) You can test the oil by dropping a small piece of zucchini into it: if it sizzles nicely but doesn't bubble up too wildly, the oil is ready.

Working in batches to avoid crowding, gently place some zucchini slices into the pan, making sure that they all lie flat and do not overlap. Fry, turning once, for about 5 minutes, until deeply golden, almost brown. Transfer the slices to a tray lined with paper towels to drain and continue frying the zucchini in batches.

Place one-third of the fried zucchini in one layer in a deep rectangular dish. Sprinkle with some of the minced garlic, herbs, and salt and season with pepper to taste. Repeat with two more layers, finishing with one last sprinkle of minced garlic, herbs, salt, and pepper.

Cover the zucchini with the vinegar, top with the olive oil, and refrigerate for at least 5 hours, and up to 24 hours. Bring to room temperature to serve.

Leftovers keep well in the fridge, covered with plastic wrap or in an airtight container, for a couple of days.

VARIATIONS

- You can swap eggplant for the zucchini to make concia di melanzane.

- Some concia recipes feature parsley, some basil, some both parsley and basil, and some mint. Find your favorite combination!

Goose Prosciutto and Salami

In the late Middle Ages and throughout the Renaissance, many Jews who were fleeing persecution resettled in Northern Italy, particularly in the cities of Venice, Ferrara, Mantua, and Pavia. The local climate was suitable for breeding geese, and since the Jews could not eat pork, they commissioned their butchers to make charcuterie similar to that of the Christians using goose meat. Goose was kosher, nutritious, and very affordable.

Today, finding kosher charcuterie made with goose is nearly impossible in Italy. There are, however, a few people who still make it at home. Among the last remaining experts is Anna Campos, a master of Jewish Venetian cuisine, who shared these goose prosciutto and salami recipes with me.

Smaller in size than its nonkosher counterpart but equally tasty, kosher prosciutto is prepared, dried, and seasoned for a relatively short time. Traditionally, it would be crafted around Hanukkah and kept in a cellar for three to four months, to be ready right on time for Passover.

Venetian goose salami are called *luganegotti*. They are different from goose salami prepared in other parts of the country because they are air-dried, whereas others, such as those produced in the city of Mortara, are boiled and then cured.

Be aware that making your own goose charcuterie from scratch is a time-consuming and challenging project, but once you become familiar with the task, you'll find yourself tempted to do it again. For this recipe, you can use both legs and one breast to make the two prosciutti and one salami, or you can use all the meat for prosciutto. NUMBERED STEPS PICTURED ON PAGE 51

MAKES 2 PROSCIUTTI AND (OPTIONAL) 1 SALAMI (SEE HEADNOTE)

—

¾ cup (175 g) kosher salt

2 tablespoons freshly ground black pepper

2 tablespoons ground allspice

1 whole goose (or 2 skin-on, bone-in legs and 2 skin-on boneless breasts; see Notes, page 52)

- ingredients continued -

In a small bowl, mix together the salt, pepper, and allspice.

If you have a whole goose and you are going to butcher it yourself, start here.

Place the cleaned goose breast side up on a cutting board [1] (see Notes, page 52). Use a very sharp knife to remove the legs of the goose: find the soft, fatty spot in each thigh where the leg connects to the body and start cutting around the leg from there, then move on to cutting into the tendon, so that the leg will pull away easily.

At this point, decide if you want your prosciutto on the bone or not. If not, separate the leg meat from the bones and set the bones aside. In either case, leave the skin attached to the legs; you can make prosciutto using just the meat, but the skin adds flavor.

Next, cut down along the breastbone to separate the breast meat from the body. Carefully remove each breast, leaving the skin on. Then trim away the excess bits of skin and fat so you have 2 neatly shaped breasts.

- continued -

At this point, any meat left on the bones is for the salami. With the help of another person, pull on the bones from opposite sides to crack the carcass apart, then carve off all the meat and set aside in a bowl. The bones can be saved to flavor broths and soups, and the skin of the neck, if you have it, can be saved for the salami.

You should now have on the counter [2]:

- 2 legs, both of which will become prosciutto

- 2 breasts, both of which can become prosciutto (or use one for salami and one for prosciutto)

- Some odd bits and pieces of meat and skin, for the salami, if you are making it

If you have bought pieces of goose, start here.

Leave the bones in the legs for prosciutto on the bone, or remove it (see above).

To make the prosciutto, place the legs and breast(s) in a glass bowl and rub generously all over with one-third of the spice mix [3, 4]. Cover loosely with plastic wrap and refrigerate. The total resting time in the fridge is 7 days. For the first 6 days, remove any liquid that might have formed each day, and rub the meat on the third and fifth days with half of the remaining spice mix (if you are making a salami, reserve some of the spice mix for it).

On the sixth day, take out the legs and use a sterile needle and food-safe thread to sew the meat around the bone (or on itself, if you decided to avoid the bone) to perfect the shape of your prosciutto. The breasts don't require any sewing.

- continued -

THE PORK OF THE JEWS · Goose was historically nicknamed "the pork of the Jews" because thrifty Jewish cooks used the entire bird, just as pigs were fully exploited by the poorer Christians. Traditionally, after prosciutti and salami were made, the leftover bits of goose fat and skin would be fried together to make gribole, a specialty that was probably brought to Northern Italy in the late thirteenth century by the Ashkenazi Jews who escaped from Central and Eastern Europe: it doesn't take a philologist to figure that gribole must have been the local version of what in America is called *gribenes*.

As for the leftover bones and the meat still attached to them, Venetians cook the thigh bones with barley and broth to make a flavorful soup, and they grill the bones from the rib cage, which are called *pissaore*—there isn't much meat left to eat there, but they are very tasty!

Put the meat back in the fridge, cover it loosely with plastic wrap, and press it down with a weight (a heavy jar will do) for 24 hours.

Pat the meat dry with a paper towel. Traditionally, the meat is left to cure outside in the winter, loosely wrapped in a cloth, or in a wine cellar in the summer, but for safety reasons, keep it refrigerated instead. The ideal temperature is 37 to 44°F (3 to 7°C). The prosciutto is safe to eat as soon as a month into the drying, but it's best if left to cure for 3 to 4 months.

To make the optional salami: If you bought pieces of goose, you will have the 2 skin-on breasts for this. If you butchered a whole goose, you will have the leftover meat and skin from the carcass plus the reserved breast. Finely chop the meat with a knife or grind in a food processor.

If using the reserved neck skin, sew it together to form a long wide rectangle and rub the skin with the reserved spice mix.

Place all the filling inside the skin and roll it up tightly, sewing as you go, to obtain an oblong salami shape. Poke some very small holes in the skin with a sterile needle to let the air escape and squeeze it well to remove as much air as possible.

You can make one long salami or create multiple smaller ones by tying the salami with string at regular intervals as many times as you like.

If using store-bought synthetic casings, soften them in warm water before using, then turn inside out and rub the inside with the reserved spice mix and turn right side out to fill the casing.

Exactly like prosciutto, traditionally the salami is left to cure and dry in the open air outside in the winter, or in a wine cellar in the summer, but you should be cautious and let it cure in the fridge instead. The salami is ready to eat after 2 to 3 weeks.

NOTES

- Your local butcher may be able to source a goose for you, or you may have to order it online. You might also be able to source only goose pieces, which will work too. Generally, any goose should come plucked, cleaned, and emptied of all its entrails.

- When you're inspecting the whole goose, before you start cutting it, you're supposed to say, "No ghe se più le oche de 'na olta" ("Geese are not as good as they used to be"). Anna, who taught me the recipe, says that complaining about the goose is of vital importance to the process, and I do what I'm told!

Shabbat

Shabbat, the holiday that begins before sunset every Friday evening with the lighting of the candle and lasts until the appearance of three stars in the sky on Saturday night, is the most important Jewish celebration. On Shabbat, Jews give thanks to God for the creation, as prescribed by the fourth commandment.

Jews in Italy honor Shabbat in the same way as other Jews around the world. We recite the blessing called the *kiddush*. During the kiddush, we bless a glass of wine and two loaves of challah (page 323), the slightly sweet egg bread. Wine is the symbol of joy, and the bread references the double portion of manna that God gave the Jews in the desert.

Shabbat is a day of rest, so all work, travel, and commerce are suspended. Cooking food on Shabbat (even simply using an open flame) is prohibited, so the traditional Shabbat dishes are prepared in advance to be served cold or gently warmed up for many hours on a countertop hot plate, which is (fortunately) allowed.

Depending on the region of Italy, different dishes grace the Shabbat table. In Northern Italy, families often eat hearty dishes such as lasagna (page 121); golden saffron rice (see page 233) accompanied by slow-cooked stews, such as traditional brasato with wine and carrots (page 191) or with squash (page 189); or a simple roast of veal (page 200) with potatoes and other vegetables. Some families also serve various versions of cholent (page 96) and hamin (page 192), although these dishes are more common among Jews of Ashkenazi descent than among strictly Italian Jews.

In Central and Southern Italy, favorite Shabbat dishes include tender beef stracotto (*stracotto* literally means "overcooked") in a rich tomato sauce (page 186), regional lamb specialties such as abbacchio e patate (page 205), and couscous with meatballs and vegetables (page 181), as well as vegetarian starters and sides including concia di zucchine (marinated fried zucchini; page 46), pomodori a mezzo (oven-roasted tomatoes; page 212), and pomodori al riso (tomatoes stuffed with rice; page 231).

In most households, you will find either a freshly baked cake (page 249) or some cookies, which are served for dessert on Friday night as well as for breakfast and an afternoon snack on Saturday. In Italy, we can't buy challah ready-made (our small communities don't create enough demand for Jewish food to be produced and sold at scale), so we either bake that too (page 323) or we bless a simple but delicious crunchy bread such as ossi (page 327) instead.

A unique Shabbat dish that the Jews of Italy prepare is called Pharaoh's Wheel (page 118), a baked pasta made with meat, pine nuts, and raisins. It is prepared for only one Shabbat a year, the Shabbat Beshalach, and it serves as an elaborate metaphorical reminder of the liberation of the Jews from Egyptian slavery.

Favorite Shabbat dishes include (clockwise from top left) Dairy-Free Lasagna (page 121), Sandra's Shabbat Cake (page 249), Slow-Cooked Pot Roast (page 186), Yellow Rice for Shabbat (page 233), Fried Zucchini in a Garlic-Herb Marinade (page 46), Challah (page 323), Libyan-Style Spicy Tomato Fish Steaks (page 72)

CECI SPASSATEMPI
Crispy Fried Chickpeas

SERVES 4 TO 6
AS A SNACK

—

1 cup (200 g)
dried chickpeas
(see Note)

Extra-virgin olive oil
for deep-frying

½ teaspoon kosher
salt

Freshly ground
black pepper

Ceci spassatempi are a very simple salty treat. They are made with blanched dried chickpeas, which are fried to perfection in olive oil until golden and crispy. The Jews of Rome prepare them to celebrate the holiday of Sukkot and eat them by the handful as a crunchy snack. Ceci spassatempi are very addictive: you'll find yourself sneaking them off the plate where they are draining. I recommend cooking just a small quantity; because they soften as they sit, these are best eaten fresh out of the hot oil.

————

Place the dried chickpeas in a large bowl, cover generously with cold water, and leave them on the counter overnight to soak.

The next day, blanch the chickpeas: Set out a colander and fill a bowl that can hold your colander with ice. Drop the chickpeas into a large saucepan of boiling water, blanch for 2 minutes, and drain them in the colander, then set the colander in the bowl filled with ice to prevent the chickpeas from cooking further.

Drain the chickpeas. Rub off as much of the outer skins with your fingers as you can and discard them.

Dry the chickpeas well with a clean kitchen towel: this is very important, because any residual moisture will cause the chickpeas to steam instead of crisp, and drying will also make the frying much messier.

Pour 1 inch (3 cm) of olive oil into a medium skillet and heat over medium-high heat until a deep-fry thermometer reads 350°F (180°C). You can test the oil by dropping a chickpea into it: if it sizzles nicely but doesn't bubble up too wildly, the oil is ready.

Working in 2 batches, carefully add the chickpeas to the skillet and fry, stirring once or twice, until golden and crispy, about 5 minutes. (If you have a grease splatter screen, this is a great time to use it.) Using a slotted spoon, transfer the chickpeas to a paper towel–lined plate to drain.

- continued -

Place the fried chickpeas in a medium bowl, sprinkle with the salt and pepper to taste, toss to coat, and serve right away.

The chickpeas are meant to be eaten as a snack as soon as they are fried, but if you have any leftovers, you can use them as a substitute for croutons in salads or soups.

NOTE

Canned chickpeas can be used for this recipe, but the result will not be as good. Fried blanched dried chickpeas soften without becoming mushy, but canned chickpeas often lose their bite. If you don't have time to soak and blanch dried chickpeas, though, go ahead and use canned: 1 cup (185 g) dried chickpeas equals approximately 3 cups (490 g) cooked or canned.

VARIATION

For roasted chickpeas, preheat the oven to 450°F (230°C); place a baking sheet in the oven while it preheats. Toss the blanched chickpeas with 1 tablespoon olive oil and ¼ teaspoon kosher salt, then spread them out in a single layer on the hot baking sheet. Roast, shaking the pan halfway through, until the chickpeas are crispy, 20 to 25 minutes.

CHICKPEAS TO PASS THE TIME • During the Jewish holiday of Sukkot, Jews generally head to the local synagogue to have a meal in the communal sukkah set up there. A few generations ago in Rome, some of the ladies in the congregation would bring trays of kosher food to share with other people under the sukkah, and on those trays you would find the delicious crispy fried chickpeas called *spassatempi* (literally, "chickpeas to pass the time"). Younger generations haven't experienced this tradition, but older people have keen memories of eating crispy chickpeas under the sukkah, and they now prepare their own small batches at home.

CARCIOFI ALLA GIUDIA
Deep-Fried Artichokes

SERVES 4 AS A STARTER

—

1 lemon, halved

4 medium or 8 baby artichokes

Extra-virgin olive oil for deep-frying

Kosher salt and freshly ground black pepper

Lemon wedges for serving (optional)

Carciofi alla giudia are world-famous and one of the few Jewish Italian dishes known outside Italy. They are as much a part of Rome as the Colosseum, and, yes, we are very proud that they are a Jewish specialty. In Italy, the dish is made with Romanesco artichokes, which are harvested between February and April in the coastal region northwest of Rome. These Italian artichokes are, in my experience, much softer than artichokes generally grown in the States. However, you can easily prepare outstanding carciofi alla giudia with medium-sized globe artichokes or baby artichokes as long as you opt for the purple variety of globe artichokes, which are generally softer than the green ones.

Please note that these artichokes are fried in extra-virgin olive oil, rather than the sunflower or peanut oil used in other recipes in this book. Outside Italy, good-quality olive oil is expensive and so generally is used in small amounts for salad dressings and the like, but carciofi alla giudia are well worth the splurge. It's the double-frying in the olive oil that will make your carciofi perfectly crispy.

———

Fill a 1-quart (1 L) bowl with water and squeeze the juice of the lemon into it.

Remove the tough outer leaves of one artichoke to expose the more tender leaves within and then, using kitchen shears or a paring knife, cut off the top half of each leaf. Trim the base and peel the stem, then scoop out the hairy choke in the center of the artichoke with a sharp spoon (if possible) and discard. Once all the cutting and trimming is done, the artichoke should look like a rosebud. Place the artichoke in the lemon water. Repeat with the remaining artichokes.

When all the artichokes are trimmed, drain and pat dry. One at a time, put the artichokes on a clean work surface and press down on them gently to force the leaves to open; alternatively, use your fingers to spread out the leaves.

In a medium saucepan, heat the olive oil over medium heat until it reaches 300°F (150°C) on a deep-fry thermometer. You can check the oil temperature by dipping the handle of a wooden spoon in it—when the oil is ready, it will gently sizzle and bubble up around it. Drop a couple of artichokes at a time into the hot oil and press them down with a fork or with tongs. Cook for 5 to 10 minutes, depending on size. Transfer the half-cooked artichokes to a plate lined with paper towels to drain and repeat with the remaining artichokes. Using a fork or your fingers, try to separate the leaves of the artichokes so they open up like a flower.

Raise the heat and bring the oil to 350°F (180°C) to fully fry and crisp up the artichokes.

Fry the artichokes one at a time: Add the artichoke stem side up to the hot oil and cook for 3 to 4 minutes, then flip it with kitchen tongs and fry until the leaves brown, pressing the artichoke gently down into the oil so that it opens up like a flower. Transfer to a plate lined with paper towels to drain.

Once the artichokes have cooled slightly, sprinkle them with salt and pepper. Serve immediately, with a few slices of lemon on the side, if desired.

"ALLA GIUDIA" BUT NOT KOSHER? • In 2018, the Chief Rabbinate of Israel declared that carciofi alla giudia are not kosher, because they might conceal nonkosher insects. Roman Jews disagree, arguing that the artichoke leaves are so thick and dense that insects cannot penetrate the artichoke. In my opinion, carciofi alla giudia are kosher.

PEZZETTI FRITTI E FIORI DI ZUCCA
Fried Vegetables and Squash Blossoms

SERVES 4

12 squash blossoms, washed, stamens and stems removed

6 canned anchovy fillets, halved

6 mini mozzarella balls, cut in half, or 1 big mozzarella ball, cut into twelve ¾-inch (2 cm) cubes

2 cups minus 1 tablespoon (240 g) all-purpose flour

Kosher salt

2⅔ cups (630 ml) sparkling water or beer

Sunflower or peanut oil for deep-frying

2¾ cups (250 g) cauliflower or broccoli florets

2⅔ cups (250 g) Romanesco broccoli florets

2 artichokes, cleaned, trimmed, and cut into wedges

1 cup (120 g) bite-size slices pumpkin

Many street food vendors in Rome sell small paper packets of freshly fried bits and pieces—*pezzetti*—of vegetables, a great snack invented by the Jews to make the most of food scraps. Today most restaurants in the Ghetto serve pezzetti fritti, alongside delicious stuffed fried squash blossoms. Pezzetti—especially fried pumpkin—are often found on the Jewish dinner table on Rosh Hashanah, while Catholic Romans, ironically, often eat pezzetti as a starter to their Christmas meal.

To prepare the squash blossoms, gently open each blossom's petals, without breaking them, and insert half of an anchovy and half of a mini mozzarella ball or a mozzarella cube inside. Set aside.

To make the batter, in a medium bowl, combine the flour and a pinch of salt, then whisk in the sparkling water or beer until the batter is smooth.

In a medium saucepan, heat about 2 inches (5 cm) of oil over medium heat until a deep-fry thermometer reads 350°F (180°C). You can test the oil by dropping a small piece of food, such as a slice of apple, into it: if it sizzles nicely, the oil is ready. (An apple is said to help minimize the smell of the frying oil, so I generally go for that, but any bit of food will do.)

Working in batches to avoid crowding the pan, one by one, dredge the blossoms in the batter, shaking off the excess and trying to keep the petals closed at the top. Gently lay the blossoms in the oil and cook, flipping once with a slotted spoon, until golden brown, 2 to 3 minutes. Transfer the blossoms to paper towels to drain and sprinkle with salt.

Again working in batches, batter and fry the cauliflower, Romanesco, artichoke, and pumpkin pieces. Drain on paper towels and sprinkle with salt.

Serve immediately.

Fried pezzetti and fiori di zucca are very delicate and best enjoyed freshly made. Leftovers don't really keep well, but they can be reheated in the oven if necessary.

VARIATION

Pezzetti can also be made with ricotta cheese, thoroughly drained and shaped into disks, to celebrate the holiday of Shavuot. Don't try frying ricotta until you have grown pretty confident about frying like this, because ricotta can be messy, especially if it's not drained enough.

Fried Rice Balls

SERVES 4

—

3 tablespoons extra-virgin olive oil

½ onion, finely chopped or ground in a food processor

2 cups (400 g) Carnaroli or Arborio rice

½ cup (120 ml) dry white wine

4 cups (1 L) chicken or vegetable broth, homemade (page 78) or store-bought

1 recipe Tomato Sauce with Chicken Giblets (page 136) or Tomato Sauce (see page 100)

2 large (100 g) eggs

2⅓ cups (230 g) bread crumbs or matzo crumbs

Sunflower or peanut oil for deep-frying

Kosher salt

Whenever you make risotto (page 135), leftovers seem to be inevitable: a cup of rice appears so little when it's uncooked but grows so much in the pot! The solution to the problem of leftovers is rice balls, known in Italian as supplì. Frying them makes the leftovers all the more delicious.

This recipe makes fried rice balls starting with freshly cooked risotto. But when you have leftover risotto on hand, you can also use this recipe; you need about ⅓ cup of leftover cooked risotto per person.

———

Pour the olive oil into a large nonstick skillet set over medium heat, add the onion, and cook for 5 minutes, or until translucent. Add the rice to the skillet and cook, stirring with a wooden spoon, for a couple of minutes, so that the grains gently toast in the oil.

Pour in the wine and let it evaporate for a minute or two. Add a ladleful of the chicken broth, reduce the heat to medium-low, and cook, stirring, as the rice gradually absorbs the broth. Once it does, add another ladleful of broth and cook, stirring, until it is absorbed. Continue cooking the rice, adding more broth a ladleful at a time as it is absorbed, until the grains are tender but not mushy, 20 to 30 minutes. Turn off the heat.

Stir the tomato sauce into the risotto and mix well. (If using leftover risotto, stir the sauce into the rice.) Let the rice cool to room temperature before proceeding, or let cool and refrigerate, covered, overnight.

To make the supplì, moisten your hands to keep the rice from sticking to them and roll the rice mixture into 2½-inch (6 cm) balls; set them aside on a plate.

In a small bowl, lightly beat the eggs with a fork. Put the bread or matzo crumbs in another small bowl.

Dip each rice ball in the eggs, then coat it well with bread crumbs and transfer to a plate. Repeat this procedure for a double coating and return the balls to the plate.

Pour 2 inches (5 cm) of sunflower or peanut oil into a large saucepan and heat over medium heat until a deep-fry thermometer reads 350°F (180°C). You can test the oil by dropping a small piece of food, such as a slice of apple, into it: if it sizzles nicely but doesn't bubble up too wildly, the oil is ready. (An apple is said to help minimize the smell of the frying oil, so I generally go for that, but any bit of food will do.)

Working in batches to avoid crowding the pan, fry the rice balls, rolling them around with a slotted spoon while they cook, until deep golden on all sides, about 5 minutes.

Drain the rice balls on paper towels, season with salt, and serve straightaway.

NOTES

- The rice balls can be shaped and coated up to 2 days ahead. Refrigerate them in an airtight container until ready to fry.

- If you don't keep kosher or are using plain tomato sauce here, consider inserting a small morsel of mozzarella in the middle of each rice ball; you could also add Parmesan cheese when making the risotto, for additional flavor.

- Leftover stracotto sauce (page 186), coda alla vaccinara (page 196), or ragù left over from lasagna making (page 121) also works very well for making rice balls.

Marinated Fried Sardines

SERVES 4 TO 6

—

2¼ pounds (1 kg) fresh sardines (see Note)

About 3 tablespoons all-purpose flour, for dusting

Sunflower or peanut oil for deep-frying

Kosher salt

¼ cup (40 g) raisins

½ cup (120 ml) dry white wine

¼ cup (40 g) pine nuts

3 tablespoons extra-virgin olive oil

4 white onions, thinly sliced

1 cup (240 ml) white wine vinegar

1 teaspoon sugar

Freshly ground black pepper

Sarde in saor is one of the most traditional Venetian cicchetti, or nibbles: fillets of fresh sardines are fried and then marinated in vinegar with soft onions, and just enough raisins and pine nuts are sprinkled on top.

While the origins of the dish are uncertain, it is very likely that it was brought to Italy from Spain by Sephardic Jews, as we know that this traditional way of serving (and preserving) fish was common in Spain. There are not many old sources that describe the dish, but one of the earliest ones, which dates back to 1908, includes candied citron in the recipe, a hint that points directly to the Jewish community and its taste for citrus.

On the Jewish table, the dish is a classic for Shabbat and the holidays, as it is best prepared at least 24 hours in advance and then served at room temperature. It's also a preferred starter for the Rosh Hashanah menu, because sweet-and-sour fish has historically been a symbol of prosperity and luck.

If your knife skills are not top-notch, consider asking the fishmonger to clean and debone the sardines for you.

———————

Clean the sardines and remove the heads and backbones, leaving the sardines opened out like a book. Rinse them in cold water, pat dry with paper towels, place in a colander, and let drain for 15 minutes. If you are short on time, you can leave the sardines whole; just be careful with the bones when you eat the sardines.

Place the flour in a shallow dish. Add the sardines and toss to coat evenly.

Pour 1½ inches (4 cm) of sunflower or peanut oil into a large skillet and heat over medium heat until a deep-fry thermometer reads 350°F (180°C). You can test the oil by dropping a small piece of food, such as a slice of apple, into it: if it sizzles nicely but doesn't bubble up too wildly, the oil is ready. (An apple is said to help minimize the smell of the frying oil, so I generally go for that, but any bit of food will do.)

Carefully drop a batch of sardines into the oil, without crowding the pan, and fry for 2 minutes on each side, or until golden. Use a slotted spoon or a spider to carefully lift the fried sardines out of the pan, so that they don't fall apart. Set on paper towels to drain, and sprinkle with salt. Carry on in batches until you've cooked all the sardines.

– continued –

Place the raisins in a small bowl, cover with the wine, and let soak and soften for 15 minutes; drain.

Meanwhile, in a small skillet, toast the pine nuts over medium heat until lightly colored, about a minute. Transfer to a plate.

Pour the olive oil into a large skillet set over low heat, add the onions, and cook, stirring often, for about 10 minutes, until they're translucent.

Add the vinegar, sugar, and pepper to taste to the onions, then stir in the raisins and pine nuts and cook until the liquid has reduced by about half. Remove from the heat.

In a deep dish, layer the sardines with the onion, raisins, and pine nuts. Finish by pouring any remaining cooking liquid over the top. Let cool to room temperature, then cover with plastic wrap and allow to marinate for about 24 hours in the fridge.

Serve the sardines at room temperature.

Leftovers keep well in the fridge, covered with plastic wrap, for a couple of days.

NOTE

The sardines used for this dish in Venice are very big and meaty. If you can't get big sardines, small ones will be perfectly fine too, although they will be harder to debone and will fry quite quickly.

COPPIETTE DI CARNE SECCA
Roman Beef Jerky

SERVES 20 TO 25

—

One 2¼-pound
(1 kg) beef rump
cap or beef
clod roast or a
2¼-pound (1 kg)
piece of brisket,
fat on

1 teaspoon kosher
salt

Freshly ground
black pepper

In the days when kosher charcuterie wasn't available, Roman Jews used to home-cure the fresh buffalo meat they sourced from the countryside. It was the wind that blew through the windows and across the balconies of the Ghetto on sunny days that served as a rather unusual "cooking method" for cured meats. Coppiette are the best example of this ancient tradition. These thin slices of fatty meat are dried until they resemble a slightly softer version of what Americans know as beef jerky. The traditional way to make coppiette—still in use today in most Roman households—involves hanging the meat outside to air-dry, covered in gauze to protect it from animals and bugs. However, this recipe explains how to make it using your oven or a dehydrator. In Italy, a specific cut of beef called *coda di pezza* or *fascia di pezza* is always used for coppiette; for this recipe, I've suggest more readily available cuts, but the result will be quite similar.

Coppiette is an addictive snack for every day, but it makes for a special treat to serve alongside pizza bianca (page 328).

———

Pop the meat into the freezer for 15 to 20 minutes to make it easier to slice. Then take it out and slice it about ⅛ inch (3 mm) thick. For chewier jerky, slice the meat with the grain. For more tender jerky, slice against the grain. (A friendly butcher will slice the meat for you, so try asking. The only important thing is that each slice of meat has a layer of fat on one edge.) Season the slices of beef with the salt and pepper to taste.

To dry the jerky in the oven, preheat the oven to 120°F (50°C). Line a baking sheet with aluminum foil and place it at the lowest level of your oven (or even on the oven floor) to catch any drips.

Remove two racks from the oven and lay the strips of meat in a single layer on the racks, then place the racks in the top and middle of your oven. Bake the meat with the oven door propped slightly open until the jerky is dry yet still pliable, about 1 hour, flipping the position of the racks about halfway through.

To dry the jerky in a dehydrator, lay the strips out in a single layer on the trays of your dehydrator. Follow the dehydrator's instructions to dry the beef until it is firm yet still a little bit pliable.

Remove the jerky from the oven or dehydrator, let it cool to room temperature, and transfer it to an airtight container. It will keep in the fridge for up to 1 month.

Tuna Pâté

SERVES 4 TO 6

—

1 large potato, boiled
and peeled

2 hard-boiled-egg
yolks

Three 6-ounce
(170 g) cans
yellowfin tuna
packed in olive oil,
drained

Juice of 2 lemons

4 tablespoons
(½ stick/57 g)
butter or
margarine, at room
temperature

A spoonful of
capers, plus
more for garnish
(optional)

¼ teaspoon kosher
salt

Lemon slices
(optional)

Tuna pâté is one of my favorite foods in the world, and I ask my
mother to prepare it for my birthday year after year: it may be a very
1980s kind of recipe, but it never falls out of fashion in my household.
You can make the pâté in advance, keep it in the fridge, and serve it
cold; this works especially well for Shabbat and the holidays, when
you're not able to cook. Make sure to serve it with crunchy sourdough
bread, toast slices, or crackers.

This pâté also works well as a sandwich filling for a quick lunch.

———

In a food processor, grind together the boiled potato and egg yolks until
smooth. Transfer to a small bowl and set aside.

In the food processor (no need to clean it), process the tuna, lemon
juice, butter, and capers, if using, together. Transfer to a medium bowl,
add the potato mixture and salt, and mix together.

Using your hands, shape the tuna mixture into a log approximately
9 inches (23 cm) long and 3 inches (8 cm) thick. Wrap it tightly in a
clean kitchen towel and refrigerate to chill for at least 2 hours, or as long
as overnight.

Remove the pâté from the kitchen towel and pat gently with your
fingers to remove the marks from the towel, in order to get a smooth
surface. Transfer the pâté to a serving plate and slice it about ½ inch
(1 cm) thick.

Serve the pâté cold, with lemon slices and capers for garnish, if
desired.

Store leftovers in the fridge wrapped in plastic wrap or in an airtight
container for a day or two, but no longer.

Libyan-Style Spicy Tomato Fish Steaks

SERVES 4

½ cup (120 ml) extra-virgin olive oil

1 large onion, finely chopped

5 tablespoons (75 g) tomato paste (see Notes)

½ to 1 teaspoon pure chili powder

2 garlic cloves, crushed

1½ cups (355 ml) water

½ teaspoon kosher salt

4 thick yellowfin, ahi, or albacore tuna steaks, about 4 ounces (115 g) each (see Notes)

½ teaspoon ground caraway (see Notes)

Juice of ½ lemon

Rome is home to two Jewish communities: Roman-born and -raised people, who define themselves as "di piazza" ("from the square"), and Libyan Jews, first-generation (and now second- and third-generation) immigrants who fled their native country in the 1960s and found a safe haven in Italy. The most famous Libyan Jewish specialty, hraimi, fish in a spicy tomato sauce, has become a regular dish in the homes of most Roman Jews, Libyan or not, as a mainstay of Shabbat dinner. Serve hraimi as a starter, with some crunchy ossi buns (page 327) fresh out of the oven alongside: I guarantee there will be no leftovers.

———

Pour the olive oil into a large nonstick sauté pan or skillet set over low heat, add the onion, and cook until it is translucent, about 10 minutes.

Add the tomato paste, chili powder, and crushed garlic to the pan, then pour in the water, add the salt, and bring to a simmer over medium heat. Put the fish in the skillet and cook for 15 minutes, or until the sauce thickens.

Add the ground caraway to the sauce and cook for a few more minutes, then add the lemon juice and take the pan off the heat. Let the hraimi cool to room temperature.

Serve, providing plenty of bread to "clean up" all the sauce once the fish is eaten.

In the unlikely event that you have leftovers, hraimi keeps well in the fridge, covered or in an airtight container, for 2 days.

NOTES

• You can substitute ½ cup (115 g) tomato puree (passata) for the tomato paste.

• Grouper and cod fillets work well here instead of tuna. One of my favorite shortcuts is using canned tuna, but only if high-quality canned tuna in big chunks is available. In that case, prepare the sauce and add the tuna at the end, when the sauce is ready.

• If you don't have ground caraway, cumin is an excellent substitute.

Milan and Lombardy

Lombardy, in the northern part of Italy, close to Switzerland, is a region that includes two main places of Jewish interest: the capital city of Milan and the town of Mantua, about 93 miles (150 km) to the east, as well as a handful of other towns with Jewish history—Cremona, Como, Vicenza, and Pavia.

Jews established themselves in this area as early as the fourth century, but there is only limited evidence of Jewish life here before the end of the twelfth century. Toward the end of the thirteenth century, some Jews of German origin moved to Lombardy, mainly to the town of Cremona. In the fourteenth century and the first half of the fifteenth century, a few small communities were established in the region, but the Jews were under constant threat from the local population, despite the favorable treatment accorded them by a few sympathetic political figures, including the Visconti and Sforza Dukes of Milan and the Duchy of Gonzaga in Mantua.

In 1565, Jews were expelled from the Duchy of Milan under Philip II of Spain (Milan and the surrounding area having been passed to Spanish rule in 1535), and they resettled in Cremona, Mantua, and other nearby cities.

For a brief time during the Renaissance, the Jews of Lombardy enjoyed some freedom, but the Great Plague of 1665 put an end to Jewish prosperity, as anti-Semitism drove out nearly half the population.

After Lombardy passed to Austria in 1713, a few Jews again settled in the region, and after the incorporation of Lombardy into the Kingdom of Italy (1859–61), many former members of now-disintegrating small Italian communities also moved to the area.

During the Second World War, Milan's Jewish community reached an estimated population of twelve thousand, many of them refugees. In 1938, the community was badly affected by the racial laws, with five thousand Jews fleeing and nearly a thousand deported. But in the 1950s, refugees from Arab countries settled in Milan, replenishing the community and increasing the population to about seven thousand, where it currently remains.

Today Milan is the main hub of Jewish life in Lombardy. The city is home to more than twenty synagogues (where people can pray according to the rites of their country of origin because, as they say, "two Jews, three opinions"), multiple kosher restaurants, a Jewish school for all grades, a Shoah memorial, and the Center for Contemporary Jewish Documentation, which contains a precious archive and a great library.

Visitors should check out the central synagogue, Hechal David u-Mordechai, which was opened in 1892, reconstructed after bombings in 1943, and renovated in a very contemporary style in the 1990s. Within the synagogue building, there are actually two temples: one upstairs, for Italian Jews, and one downstairs, for Jews of Sephardic origin.

When it comes to food, the kosher restaurants of Milan offer a cuisine that is not particularly grounded in local tradition, as gentiles and Jews

LEFT: *The facade of the Central Synagogue in Milan*
ABOVE: *A view of the Navigli area*

alike there seem to prefer Middle Eastern Jewish flavors when they dine out, probably because they can enjoy Milanese food at home. You can try a milk meal with pasta and pizza at Carmel, or go to Ba Ghetto, which offers, quite confusingly, Jewish Roman specialties such as carne secca (page 69), concia (page 46), pasta amatriciana (page 108), carbonara (page 114), and abbacchio (page 205). To indulge in sweets and pastries, as well as delicious savory roschette (page 330), a stop at Tuv Taam is in order.

Those who don't adhere to the Jewish dietary rules should enjoy a meal in a proper old Milanese restaurant, such as Osteria del Treno, Trattoria Milanese, Trattoria Madonnina,

or Trattoria Aurora, where they can have a taste of delicious risotto (page 135), brasato (pages 189 and 191), arrosto (page 200), bagna cauda (page 35), and other classic dishes.

Just a short day trip of approximately 80 miles (129 km) from Milan, Mantua (Mantova) is also well worth a visit. There are only a handful of Jews left in Mantua today, so you'll have to pack a picnic if you care to keep kosher. In town, you can observe the beautiful reconstruction of the Norsa-Torrazzo synagogue, with its original eighteenth-century furniture; some remains of the ghetto, particularly the nicely decorated palace of the rabbi, which dates back to the seventeenth century; and the ancient cemetery.

Another day trip of Jewish interest is a visit to Soncino, which is only 40 miles (64 km) from Milan. The city is home to the beautiful Museum of Printing. In the building that now houses the museum, a Jew named Israel Nathan established the only Jewish printing house of his time and printed the first complete Hebrew Bible in the second half of the fifteenth century.

Zuppe e minestre

SOUPS

DAYENU
Passover Egg Soup

SERVES 6

—

2 quarts (2 L) broth, preferably beef, homemade (recipe follows) or store-bought

3 matzos, split in half

4 large (76 g) egg yolks

Dayenu, which translates as "it would have been enough," is a line from a song Jews sing on Passover. The song is about all the gifts God gave our people, such as taking us out of slavery in Egypt and offering us the Torah. The idea behind the song is that had God given us only one of the gifts, it would have still been enough for us to be grateful.

The soup called *dayenu* is very nourishing and "enough" to be a meal in itself because it contains not only a rich, meaty broth but also eggs and matzo, which create a creamy texture. Although it is a Passover staple for Jews all over Italy, it is believed to have originated in Piedmont.

———

In a medium pot, bring the broth to a boil. Drop the matzo into the pot and cook until soft but not mushy, approximately 15 minutes.

Right before serving, beat the egg yolks in a small bowl with a whisk for a minute. Add the egg yolks to the broth, stirring them quickly with the whisk so that they mix smoothly into the broth rather than curdling. Serve immediately.

VARIATIONS

• For a twist, add a pinch of cinnamon to the broth. For an even more nutritious meal, add 10½ ounces (300 g) spinach, boiled and chopped, to the soup just before serving.

• This soup is also great with chicken broth instead of beef broth.

BRODO VEGETALE, DI POLLO, E DI MANZO
Vegetable, Chicken, or Beef Broth

MAKES 1½ QUARTS (1.4 L)

—

VEGETABLE BROTH

3 carrots

1 parsnip

2 celery ribs

2 zucchini

2 tomatoes

Broth is an essential ingredient in many recipes, as well as a nourishing soup on its own. When broth is called for in a recipe in this book, it is always possible to substitute good store-bought stock, but nothing beats homemade broth: it makes any dish richer and more flavorful.

The trick to always having broth on hand is to prepare it in large quantities and freeze it in portions sized for later use: you can freeze individual cubes in an ice cube tray and then transfer to freezer bags for when you just need a bit of broth; or freeze in 16-ounce (450 ml) jars, for a two-person meal, or 2-quart (2 L) jars for large cooking

1 onion

3 quarts (2.8 L) water

1 tablespoon kosher salt, plus more to taste

Freshly ground black pepper

CHICKEN (OR HEN OR TURKEY) BROTH

Ingredients for Vegetable Broth (see above)

2¼ pounds (1 kg) skin-on chicken, hen, or turkey pieces

1 garlic clove

3 bay leaves

A few sprigs of parsley

BEEF BROTH

Ingredients for Vegetable Broth (see above)

2¼ pounds (1 kg) beef (chuck or flank work best)

¾ pound (350 g) beef bones

2 cloves

projects. I even freeze broth in 8-ounce (240 ml) jars to give away to family and friends when they have a cold: homemade broth can be a cure-all!

———

To make vegetable broth, peel the carrots and parsnip, and peel away the outer part of the celery ribs. Cut the carrots, parsnip, celery, and zucchini into chunks. Quarter the tomatoes and onion.

Place all the vegetables in a stockpot, cover with the water, and add the salt and pepper to taste. Bring the water to a boil over medium heat, then lower the heat to medium-low and simmer until the vegetables are very soft and the liquid has reduced and concentrated, about 2 hours. Adjust the salt and pepper to taste and remove from the heat.

With a slotted spoon, lift the vegetables from the pot and set them aside to serve later, if desired.

To make either the chicken or beef broth, follow the recipe for vegetable broth, adding the additional ingredients to the pot with the vegetables before covering them with water and adding the salt and pepper.

Bring the water to a boil over medium heat, then lower the heat to medium-low and simmer until the vegetables are very soft and the liquid has reduced and concentrated, about 2 hours (or up to 4 hours if you have the time). With a slotted spoon, skim any foam from the broth as it cooks. When the broth is ready, adjust the salt and pepper to taste.

With a slotted spoon, lift the vegetables and meat from the pot and transfer to a platter to serve later. Discard the herbs and/or spices and remove the meat from the bones (discard the bones). The meat can be served with the broth or saved for other recipes, such as Beef Hand Pies (page 40), Meat-Filled Pasta in Broth (page 90), or the Roman variation of Orange and Olive Salad (page 30).

Passover staples include (clockwise from bottom left) Passover Egg Soup (page 78), Passover lasagna (see page 122), Passover Lamb with Artichokes and Fava Beans (page 206), Stuffed Turkey Meatloaf (page 155), Honey Matzo Fritters (page 274), Passover Seder plate with Charoset (page 240)

Rice Soup with Turnips

SERVES 4

—

3 turnips

1½ quarts (1.4 L) beef or chicken broth, homemade (page 78) or store-bought

1½ cups (300 g) Carnaroli or Arborio rice

Rice soup with turnips is a very simple dish that used to be served all over Italy in the days when most people did not have much money. It's considered a classic dish in Piedmont, in the north, but also farther south in Rome: two separate regions brought together by the humble but flavorful turnip, which, when paired with rice, makes for a very inexpensive yet nutritious soup. This recipe is traditionally prepared for the holiday of Sukkot.

———

Wash and peel the turnips and slice very thin. Put the slices in a bowl of cold water and let them soak for an hour to wash away the bitterness.

Pour the broth into a large pot and bring to a simmer over medium heat.

Drain the turnips in a colander, rinse under running water, and add them to the broth, then add the rice. Reduce the heat to low and cook the soup for 15 minutes, or until the turnips are soft and the rice is tender. Serve.

INDIVIA REHAMINÀ

Curly Endive and Bread Soup

SERVES 4

—

4 cups (1 L) broth, preferably beef, homemade (page 78) or store-bought

1 head curly endive (see Note)

4 slices stale sourdough bread

Kosher salt and freshly ground black pepper

Curly endive, *indivia* in Italian, was one of the basic ingredients in Roman dishes of the old days. Most people grew this prolific plant in their backyard or found it very inexpensively at the market and used it to add some substance to their dishes.

This is a humble but flavorful soup, and it is a great way to use up bread that you've had a little too long. Just make sure to use a good rich broth, preferably homemade—your soup will be as good as your broth.

———

Pour the broth into a large saucepan and bring to a boil over medium heat.

Meanwhile, wash the endive carefully and chop it coarsely.

Add the chopped endive to the broth and cover with the slices of bread. Reduce the heat to low and cook, covered, for about 1 hour, until the bread falls apart and blends nicely into the soup. Season with salt and pepper to taste and serve.

NOTE

If you can't find curly endive, you can substitute escarole, or even lettuce, if you have some on hand that is slightly past its prime.

MINESTRA DI LENTICCHIE DI ESAÙ
Esau's Lentil Soup

SERVES 6

1½ cups (300 g) dried lentils

1⅛ pounds (500 g) lean ground beef

Kosher salt and freshly ground black pepper

¼ cup (60 ml) extra-virgin olive oil

2 carrots, diced

1 celery rib, chopped

1 onion, minced

1 garlic clove, crushed in a press or minced

1 cup (225 g) tomato puree (passata)

5 cups (1.2 L) water

1 bay leaf

Chopped parsley for garnish (optional)

The biblical story of Esau, who sold his birthright for a plate of lentils, is well known, but nobody knows today how that dish was really cooked and what made it so good that it was worth more than the rights reserved for a firstborn son in biblical times. Jews in older Tuscan communities tried to imagine how the legendary lentil dish might have been prepared and came up with a recipe for the dish. They forgot, though, that at the time of Esau, tomatoes had not yet been discovered—a significant mistake, but one that shows the great passion Italians have for tomatoes!

Put the lentils in a colander and rinse under running water. Transfer the lentils to a large bowl and cover with water. Cover the bowl and let the lentils soak overnight.

The next day, in a large bowl, mix the ground meat with a scant teaspoon of salt and a generous pinch of pepper. Use your hands to form the meat into small meatballs the size of a walnut. Set the meatballs on a plate as you form them.

Pour the olive oil into a sauté pan or a large saucepan set over medium-low heat, add the carrots, celery, onion, and garlic, and sauté until soft, about 10 minutes.

Add the meatballs to the pan, increase the heat to high, and cook, turning the meatballs occasionally, for about 10 minutes, until evenly browned.

Pour the tomato puree into the pan and simmer for 5 minutes, then add the water and 1 teaspoon salt and bring to a simmer.

Add the drained lentils and bay leaf, reduce the heat to low, cover the pan, and cook for 30 minutes.

Check to see if the lentils are soft. If necessary, you can add more water and continue cooking the lentils for a bit longer, but be careful to not let them overcook, or they will be overdone and mushy.

Serve hot, with a little chopped parsley on top, if you wish.

Leftover soup keeps well in the fridge, in a bowl covered with plastic wrap or in an airtight container, for a couple of days. It can be reheated in a saucepan or in the microwave.

Pasta, Broccoli, and Potato Soup

SERVES 4

3 tablespoons extra-virgin olive oil

1 garlic clove, smashed

1 small yellow onion, thinly sliced

1¾ cups (400 g) tomato puree (passata) or finely diced canned tomatoes

½ teaspoon kosher salt, or more to taste

1 head Romanesco broccoli, leaves trimmed, core removed, chopped into florets

1 potato, peeled and cut into 1-inch (3 cm) cubes

4½ cups (1.1 L) water

3 ounces (85 g) spaghetti, broken into pieces, or ¾ cup (about 60 g) small pasta of your choice

Freshly ground black pepper

Grated Pecorino or Parmesan cheese for serving (optional)

Minestra cucinata, which translates literally as "soup that has been cooked," is a rustic soup that is one of the oldest dishes in Jewish Roman cuisine. Back in the day, the basic version of minestra cucinata was a thick, garlicky tomato soup with broken pieces of spaghetti or other pasta (it was sometimes also called *minestra spezzata*, or "broken soup"). Nowadays, a richer version of the dish, featuring Romanesco broccoli and potatoes, also goes by the name minestra cucinata. You can omit the Romanesco and potatoes, if you like; the soup is excellent either way.

––––––––––

In a large saucepan, heat the olive oil over medium-low heat. When the oil begins to shimmer, stir in the garlic and onion and cook for about 5 minutes, until golden.

Add the tomato puree and salt and stir to combine. Add the Romanesco and potato cubes and stir well. Add the water and bring to a simmer over medium heat, then lower the heat to medium-low and let the soup cook for approximately 40 minutes, until the vegetables are quite tender.

Add the broken spaghetti or other pasta and cook for 10 to 15 minutes, depending on the type of pasta (check the box for the suggested timing). If the soup thickens too much before the pasta is ready, add a ladleful of water and continue simmering until the pasta is al dente and the vegetables are soft. Adjust the salt if needed and add freshly ground pepper to taste.

Serve the soup hot or warm, with some grated Pecorino or Parmesan cheese on top, if desired (it's optional, if you want to keep the meal pareve).

VARIATION

You can make the Romanesco and potato version of the soup even richer by adding small cubes of beef chuck or a similar relatively fatty cut at the beginning of the recipe. Add the meat along with the onion and garlic and brown it thoroughly in the oil before proceeding.

BOCCETTE IN BRODO
Meatballs in Broth

SERVES 4

—

1⅛ pounds (500 g) lean ground beef

½ teaspoon kosher salt

1 recipe Beef Broth (page 78), with its vegetables

Boccette translates as "marbles" or "small balls," and that's precisely the shape of the meatballs in this very nutritious soup. Boccette in brodo makes the best winter comfort food on weekdays and weekends alike, and it's guaranteed to please your entire family. It's also a great choice for a make-ahead meal, as it keeps well in the fridge and can be frozen as well.

————

In a large bowl, mix the ground beef and the salt together, then use your hands to shape the mixture into small balls, roughly the size of a walnut. Place the meatballs on a plate as you go.

In a large pot, bring the broth to a gentle boil. Add the meatballs, reduce the heat to medium-low, and simmer for 30 minutes, or until the meatballs are cooked through. Add the reserved vegetables from making the broth and heat briefly over medium heat.

Serve straightaway, or reheat when needed.

NOTES

- If you want to make this ahead and save the broth and meatballs for another time, it's best to freeze them separately. Let the broth cool to room temperature and freeze it in a freezer container. Place the cooked meatballs on a baking sheet, let them cool to room temperature, and flash-freeze until hard, about 1 hour, then transfer to a labeled gallon-size (4 L) freezer bag, removing as much air as possible.

- Thaw the broth and meatballs overnight in the fridge, and reheat together to serve.

VARIATION

A very similar old Jewish Roman dish that features boccette is called *zuppa di erbe*. To make it, cook the boccette in a rich minestrone—a chunky vegetable soup—instead of clear broth.

Meat-Filled Pasta in Broth

SERVES 6 TO 8

—

FOR THE CARCIONCINI

1⅛ pounds (500 g) ground beef (see Note)

Scant ½ teaspoon kosher salt

Freshly ground black pepper

A quadruple recipe Fresh Egg Pasta (page 103)

All-purpose flour and cornmeal for dusting

2 quarts (2 L) beef broth, homemade (page 78) or store-bought

Pinch of ground cinnamon

Carcioncini, small meat-filled pasta shapes similar to agnolotti, are a classic Rosh Hashanah dish in Rome. Served in a nourishing hearty broth, they make the perfect first course for any winter dinner. The same pasta is also served on the eve of Yom Kippur, as it provides liquids and nutrients to help you through the fast, and again at the end of the fast, for an easier recovery. The quality of carcioncini is measured by their size: the smaller they are, the better the cook!

———

To prepare the carcioncini, in a medium bowl, mix the ground beef with the salt and pepper to taste. Set aside.

Cut the pasta dough into 4 equal pieces. Wrap 3 of the pieces in plastic wrap, so they don't dry out, and set aside while you work with the remaining piece of dough.

On a floured surface, roll the first piece of dough into a 9-by-13-inch (23 by 33 cm) sheet.

Using a teaspoon and your fingers, scoop up equally sized tiny balls of the filling and arrange them on the bottom half of the pasta sheet, leaving a 1½-inch (4 cm) border of dough at the bottom edge and at the ends of the dough and spacing the balls of filling approximately 1 inch (3 cm) apart.

Fold the top half of the pasta sheet over the filling and press out the air around each portion of filling. With a sharp knife or a crimped pastry wheel, cut the sheet into individual carcioncini. (Each carcioncino should be approximately 1 by 1½ inches/3 by 4 cm.) Place the carcioncini on a baking sheet dusted with a thin layer of cornmeal, which will help prevent sticking. Working quickly, repeat with the remaining dough and filling. You should have approximately 160 carcioncini. The carcioncini can be frozen and then cooked directly from frozen, or cooked straightaway.

In a medium pot, bring the broth to a boil and add the cinnamon. Add the carcioncini, working in batches if necessary. The carcioncini are ready when they float to the top. Remove the pasta with a slotted spoon and transfer it to bowls, then add a ladleful of broth to each one.

NOTE

The recipe can also be made with leftover boiled beef, finely ground in a food processor.

PASTA E FAGIOLI CON LUGANEGA DI MANZO
Pasta and Bean Soup with Sausage

SERVES 4 TO 6

—

**FOR THE SAUSAGE
OR MEATBALLS**

7 ounces (200 g)
   ground beef

3 ounces (85 g)
   beef fat

1 garlic clove,
   crushed in a press
   or minced

½ teaspoon kosher
   salt

½ teaspoon ground
   allspice

¼ teaspoon freshly
   ground black
   pepper

FOR THE SOUP

2 small onions

1 carrot, peeled

1 celery rib

5 tablespoons
   (75 ml) extra-virgin
   olive oil, plus more
   for serving

1 sage leaf

1¼ cups (250 g)
   cranberry or other
   red or dark beans

½ teaspoon kosher
   salt

Freshly ground
   black pepper

7 cups (1.7 L) boiling
   water

1¾ cups (150 g)
   small pasta,
   such as ditalini

Among the nutritious, hearty dishes that Venetians enjoy during the winter, pasta e fagioli surely ranks high as one of the most beloved local comfort foods. The Jews of Venice often prepare pasta and beans for Shabbat and enrich it with a homemade beef sausage, called *luganega*, or with meatballs made with the same sausage meat, to make it more festive. This is a very forgiving recipe, a great make-ahead dish that also works well for feeding larger groups.

If you want to make the luganega sausage, you will need artificial sausage casings.

———

In a food processor, grind the beef and fat together to a coarse paste.

Transfer the ground beef to a bowl, add the garlic, salt, allspice, and pepper, and mix well with your hands.

To make one sausage, soak an artificial sausage casing briefly in water; drain well. Using a piping bag, stuff the casing with the meat filling. Secure each end of the casing tightly with a knot and poke a couple of minuscule holes in it with a sterile needle to release the excess air.

To make meatballs, divide the meat into about 25 small portions and shape into well-rounded balls. Place on a tray as you shape the meatballs and set aside.

To make the soup, in the clean bowl of the food processor, grind together the onions, carrot, and celery. Or finely chop the vegetables with a chef's knife.

Pour the olive oil into a large saucepan set over medium heat, add the vegetables and sage leaf, and cook for 10 minutes, or until all the vegetables are soft and the onions are translucent.

Add the beans to the saucepan and season with the salt and pepper to taste. Cover with 5 cups (1.2 L) of the boiling water, reduce the heat to low, cover, and cook for 2 hours, or until the beans are tender.

Remove 1 cup (250 g) of the beans from the saucepan, transfer to a blender, and process until smooth. Set aside.

Add another 1 cup (240 ml) boiling water to the saucepan and bring the beans to a simmer again over medium heat. Add the sausage or meatballs to the saucepan and simmer for 10 more minutes, or until the meat is cooked through.

- continued -

Add the remaining 1 cup (240 ml) boiling water to the pan, increase the heat to high, and add the pasta. Cook until the pasta is al dente, approximately 10 more minutes (if in doubt, check the cooking time on the box).

Taste the pasta to check for doneness; when it's ready, add the reserved pureed beans to the pan and stir well. At this point, the soup should be very thick. If you like, you can adjust the consistency either by adding a bit of water to thin the soup or letting it simmer a bit longer to make it creamier. Remove from the heat and, if you used the sausage, cut into slices.

Serve immediately, with a tablespoon of olive oil drizzled over the top.

Leftovers keep well in the fridge, in a bowl covered with plastic wrap or in an airtight container, for a couple of days. They can be reheated in the microwave or in a saucepan over low heat, with a bit of hot water if needed.

VARIATION

If you have goose bones and leftovers from making prosciutto and salami (page 49), add them to the soup as it cooks to make it richer and even more flavorful.

Chickpea Soup with Tendons and Gristle

SERVES 4

—

1 pound (450 g) dried chickpeas

10 ounces (285 g) tendons and gristle, preferably from beef shin (see headnote)

1 celery rib, diced

1 carrot, diced

½ white onion, diced

2 tablespoons extra-virgin olive oil

One 4-inch (10 cm) marrowbone, split in half vertically (optional)

½ teaspoon kosher salt, or more to taste

Freshly ground black pepper

½ cup (115 g) tomato puree (passata)

Crunchy bread for serving

Pennerelli is the name in Roman dialect for nervetti, pieces of tendons and gristle that butchers cut off meat before it is sold. Nervetti are generally inexpensive, but cooking them requires a lot of patience, so traditionally hardly anyone bothered to prepare them other than the savvy Jews of the Ghetto.

Tendons and gristle are somewhat hard to come by, but you can ask your butcher to set some aside for you. If your market can't provide tendons and gristle, try Asian grocery stores, as tendons are more common in Japanese and Vietnamese cuisines.

———

Put the chickpeas in a colander and rinse under running water. Transfer to a large bowl and cover with water. Cover the bowl with plastic wrap and let the chickpeas soak overnight.

The next day, bring a large pot of water to a boil. Add the tendons and gristle and blanch for 2 to 3 minutes. Drain in a colander and rinse away any scum; rinse out the pot.

Using a sharp knife, slice the tendons diagonally, against the grain, into pieces about 1 inch (3 cm) long.

Place the celery, carrot, and onion in a Dutch oven or other deep heavy pot. Pour the olive oil over the vegetables and cook over medium heat for 10 minutes, or until the onion is soft and translucent.

Add the tendons and gristle, marrowbone, salt, and pepper to taste to the pot, then pour in enough water to cover by 2 inches (5 cm). Bring the water to a gentle simmer, reduce the heat to low, and simmer, tightly covered, for 2 hours.

During the first 2 hours of cooking, the tendons will look hard and gummy. Don't panic, as the situation will change as the collagen breaks down and the tendons soften.

Drain the soaked chickpeas, add the chickpeas and tomato puree to the pot, and simmer over low heat for about 2 more hours, or until the chickpeas are soft and the tendons and gristle are tender. If the tendons don't appear ready yet, just keep simmering until they give in. Check a piece of tendon to make sure it is tender. (If you cook the tendons over high heat instead, they will stay gummy indefinitely; there is no way back.) Check the pot occasionally and add water if the soup is too thick.

When you're ready to serve, extract the marrow from the bone and mix it into the soup. Taste and adjust the salt if necessary.

Serve hot, with slices of crunchy bread alongside.

CHOLENT DI CASA MIA
My Family's Cholent

SERVES 6

⅓ cup (80 ml) extra-virgin olive oil

1½ large onions, chopped

3 potatoes, peeled and halved

2 pounds (900 g) beef for stew, such as brisket, flanken, or chuck, cut into chunks

One 4-inch (10 cm) marrowbone, split in half vertically (optional)

1¼ cups (220 g) mixed dried adzuki and cannellini beans (see Note)

½ cup (110 g) pearl barley

2 teaspoons sweet paprika

1 teaspoon ground cumin

1 teaspoon kosher salt

1 tablespoon tomato paste

3½ quarts (3.3 L) beef, chicken, or vegetable broth, homemade (page 78) or store-bought, or water

3 large (150 g) eggs, shells thoroughly rinsed

In the United States and in many other Jewish communities around the world, *cholent* and *hamin* are two names for the same dish, a traditional stew with meat, beans, and barley that is generally served on Shabbat. In Italy, though, the dish is slightly different, as Italian hamin contains ingredients, such as chard, that are not usually part of a cholent in the Ashkenazi version. This recipe makes an Ashkenazi-style cholent; for an Italian hamin, see page 192. This cholent is almost embarrassingly simple to make, but as long as you let it simmer for enough time, you'll be rewarded with the perfect celebratory meal.

Preheat the oven to 400°F (200°C).

Pour the olive oil into a large Dutch oven and add the chopped onions. Place the potatoes on top of the onions, then layer the beef, marrowbone, beans, and barley on top of the potatoes, in that order. Sprinkle with the paprika, cumin, and salt. Add the tomato paste and cover with 6 cups (1.5 L) of the broth or water.

Set the pot over medium heat and bring the mixture to a gentle simmer, then add the eggs and push them gently under the broth.

Cover the pot, transfer it to the oven, and cook for an hour. Top up the pot with 4 cups (1 L) of broth and continue to cook for 2 hours (you shouldn't need to add more broth during this time, so just set the timer for 2 hours).

At the 3-hour mark, add the remaining 4 cups (1 L) water. After approximately 1 more hour, all the ingredients should be cooked through and the broth just partly absorbed. A traditional cholent is left to cook for as long as 12 hours for religious reasons, but 4 hours is plenty to get a perfectly stewed dish, with fall-apart-tender meat.

When you're ready to serve, extract the marrow from the bone and mix it into the soup, then peel the eggs; you want to give half an egg, as well as half a potato, to every guest at the table. Serve the cholent hot, or let it cool to room temperature and set it aside for later.

This cholent keeps very well in the fridge for a few days, and it can be reheated as many times as needed.

NOTE

There is no need to presoak the beans for this recipe as they will soften over the long, slow cooking process. It's also possible to freeze the cholent for up to 2 months in an airtight container. Thaw overnight and reheat before serving.

Pasta e riso

PASTA AND RICE

TAGLIOLINI FREDDI ALL'EBRAICA
Pasta with Tomato Sauce

SERVES 4

—

**FOR THE
TOMATO SAUCE**

**10 medium
ripe tomatoes
(2⅔ pounds/1.2 kg)
or two 14.5–ounce
(410 g) cans whole
tomatoes or jars
tomato puree
(passata)**

**¼ cup (60 ml) extra-
virgin olive oil**

2 garlic cloves

**½ teaspoon kosher
salt, plus more to
taste**

Kosher salt

**1 pound (450 g)
dried tagliolini,
tagliatelle, or
capellini or a
quadruple recipe
Fresh Egg Pasta
(recipe follows),
cut into tagliatelle**

Tagliatelle, tagliolini (thin tagliatelle), and capellini (even-thinner pasta, similar to angel hair) are among the most popular pasta shapes in Jewish Italian cuisine. What makes this traditional recipe for pasta somewhat unusual is the fact that the pasta, which is tossed in a flavorful tomato sauce, is served at room temperature (like a pasta salad) the day after it's prepared, traditionally for Shabbat lunch.

The recipe for tomato sauce given here is my simplest go-to sauce for pasta, and it's as delicious as it is easy to make. What's great about the recipe is that you can prepare it in large quantities and use it for other dishes: it can accompany riso giallo (page 233), it makes a great accompaniment to supplì (page 64), it works well for stewing vegetables such as green beans (page 221) . . . the possibilities are endless.

———

To make the sauce, if using fresh tomatoes, blanch and peel them first: Bring a large saucepan of water to a boil. Use a sharp knife to score a cross in the bottom of each tomato. Working in batches, blanch the tomatoes in the boiling water for 30 to 60 seconds, remove them from the pan, and immediately transfer them to a bowl filled with ice and water. When the tomatoes are cool, take them out of the ice water and rub them with your fingers: the skins should come off easily. This step is not a must, but it does help to perfect the texture of the tomato sauce. Crush the tomatoes with a fork in a bowl, or puree them in a blender.

Pour the olive oil into a large sauté pan and place over medium heat. If you are a garlic lover, crush the garlic and add it to the skillet. If you are not a big fan, leave the garlic cloves whole. Sauté the garlic for 2 to 3 minutes, stirring often, until it is golden and well toasted. Once the garlic has flavored the oil, discard or leave it in the pan, as you prefer.

Add the fresh tomatoes or canned tomatoes or puree to the pan, along with the salt, bring to a simmer, and simmer for 20 minutes, stirring occasionally. (If you have a grease splatter screen, this would be a good occasion to use it, as the sauce will bubble up as it cooks.) The tomato sauce will thicken as time goes by: I like mine very thick, so I keep the cooking time quite long, but you can stop earlier if you prefer. Taste the sauce and add more salt as necessary.

In the meantime, bring a pot of water seasoned with 1 tablespoon salt to a rolling boil.

If you opted for store-bought pasta, add it to the pot and cook until al dente according to the package directions. If you have fresh pasta, drop it into the boiling water and cook for a minute or two, until it's soft but maintains some bite. Drain in a colander.

Add the pasta to the tomato sauce and toss well. Cook for a couple of minutes, then, if serving hot, transfer to a serving bowl and enjoy immediately.

Or, let the pasta cool to room temperature, lifting it up with two forks and stirring it back into the tomato sauce, then transfer to a bowl, cover, and refrigerate. Serve at room temperature.

VARIATIONS

There are multiple variations of this tomato sauce. Here are some common ones.

- Add 1 small onion, finely chopped, with the garlic and cook until translucent, about 5 minutes.

- Add ½ teaspoon dried oregano or dried basil to the sauce as it cooks.

- Add the leaves from a few sprigs of parsley, roughly chopped, to the finished sauce before tossing the pasta in it.

- Add 1 crushed chili pepper or a pinch of freshly ground black pepper when you add the salt to the sauce.

- continued -

PASSOVER PASTA • At Passover, Italian Jews don't want to miss out on their pasta. Families whose Italian roots date back for many generations make a special fresh pasta for Passover called *sfoglietti*, using certified kosher-for-Passover flour and eggs. In terms of making the dough, sfoglietti is prepared like regular egg pasta. However, the pasta sheets are cut into wide ribbons and are grilled in a metal grill basket over an open flame (or oven-baked at a very high temperature) to prevent them from rising at all, which would be forbidden on Passover. These burnt pasta ribbons are cooked like regular pasta in boiling water and served with a pasta sauce, or cooked in broth with vegetables for soup. If you want to give sfoglietti a go, note that the basic egg pasta recipe on the following pages will yield 32 sfoglietti, sized 1 by 3 inches (3 by 8 cm), which is a generous serving for one. Keep in mind, though, that unless you have access to special kosher for Passover flour, your sfoglietti will not be kosher for Passover, but they will still be very good at any time of the year.

Fresh Egg Pasta

SERVES 1

—

½ cup (65 g)
all-purpose flour,
plus more as
needed

Pinch of kosher salt

1 large (50 g) egg

Italians have a simple rule of thumb for making basic fresh egg pasta: start with 1 egg per person, and multiply according to the number of people you are feeding. Making fresh pasta can seem intimidating, and a bit messy too, but the result is totally worth the effort. Fresh homemade pasta is incomparably better than store-bought. Use this recipe for pumpkin-filled tortelli (page 129), meat-filled carcioncini (page 90), tagliatelle for the impressive Pharaoh's Wheel (page 118), or even dessert (see page 317) . . . just imagine the possibilities! NUMBERED STEPS PICTURED ON PAGE 105

———

On a clean work surface or in a medium bowl, combine the flour and salt and pile into a mound. Make a well in the center and crack the egg into the well [1]. Use a fork to incorporate the flour into the egg, starting from the edges and working your way in, then move on to using the tips of your fingers [2]. Once most of the flour has been absorbed, knead the dough with your hands [3] energetically for a couple of minutes: stretch it and pull it [4-6], then press it together again, and continue until it's smooth and pliable. Add flour as necessary so the dough doesn't stick to the counter. Or, if you have a pasta machine, let the machine do the kneading for you: set the machine to its widest setting, generally #8, and feed the rough dough through the rollers a few times [7], folding the pasta dough in half on itself every time it passes through the machine [8-9]. Repeat the process 5 times, or as needed, until the dough is even and silky.

Form the dough into a rough rectangle, wrap it tightly in plastic wrap, and allow it to sit for 15 minutes.

Thoroughly dust the counter with flour if you are planning on using a rolling pin instead of a pasta machine.

Rolling big pieces of dough is quite challenging, so work with a portion of the dough at a time. With a 1-egg recipe, you will have approximately 4 ounces (115 g) of dough, which you should be able to stretch into 3 rectangular sheets approximately 3 by 14 inches (8 by 36 cm). Divide the dough into 3 portions. Keep 2 portions wrapped in plastic wrap to prevent them from drying out while you work with the other portion.

- continued -

Roll out the dough with a rolling pin, or roll it through the increasingly narrow settings of your pasta machine. Lightly dust both sides of the pasta sheets with a little flour whenever it looks like they could get sticky. Go through each setting of the machine twice, to ensure perfectly even pasta sheets. Try to create evenly shaped rectangular sheets with straight sides. To achieve this, fold the uneven sides of the pasta sheet over themselves as you roll it through the machine, or as you roll them out with the rolling pin.

Roll the pasta sheet until it is thin, but not necessarily paper-thin [10]. If you'd like your pasta to have a nice bite and a rustic feel to it, stop at what on most pasta machines is setting #1, or when you have reached a thickness of approximately ⅛ inch (3 mm) if you are rolling it by hand. This thickness works very well for tagliatelle, lasagna noodles, and the like. For delicate filled pastas, try to go even thinner if you can. Repeat with the remaining dough.

Once you've rolled your pasta, shape it or cut it straightaway according to the recipe you are using it for, as it will dry out very quickly [11–12]. To gain a few minutes, you can lay a damp clean kitchen towel over the pasta sheets. If, however, you want to dry your cut pasta to save it for another day, lay it on a bed of semolina or flour and let it air-dry at room temperature, or dry it in a warm oven for 15 minutes. Store in a paper or plastic bag.

Pasta with Sour Grape Juice and Eggs

SERVES 4

———

Kosher salt

2 tablespoons extra-virgin olive oil

1 pound (450 g) dried tagliolini or tagliatelle or a quadruple recipe Fresh Egg Pasta (page 103), cut into tagliolini

1 large (50 g) egg plus 1 large (19 g) egg yolk

½ cup (120 ml) unsweetened white grape juice

Juice of ½ lemon (see Note)

1 cup (240 ml) vegetable, chicken, or beef broth, homemade (page 78) or store-bought

Thin egg pasta served at room temperature, almost like a pasta salad, is a common Shabbat dish, especially in the regions of Piedmont and Marche. Simple traditional preparations include pasta with good tomato sauce (see page 100) or with old-style bagna brusca, a condiment made with the juice of unripe grapes, called *agresto*, and eggs. This condiment probably evolved from a Sephardic sauce known as *agristada*, which features similar ingredients.

———

Bring a large saucepan of salted water to a boil. Preparing perfect cold pasta that remains fluffy, not sticky and gluey, for days relies on oil. So, add a tablespoon of the olive oil to the pot of water.

If using store-bought pasta, add it to the boiling water and cook until al dente according to the package directions. If using fresh pasta, cook it for a minute or two, until it is just tender but still has some bite. Drain the pasta in a colander and rinse it with cold water to stop the cooking, then toss it with the remaining tablespoon of olive oil. Set the pasta aside while you prepare the sauce.

Fill a large skillet with water and warm it up over medium heat to use as a water bath (double boiler) for the sauce.

In a small bowl, beat the egg and yolk well, then transfer them to a medium saucepan and whisk in the grape and lemon juices and broth. Place the saucepan in the skillet filled with boiling water and cook, whisking often, until the mixture thickens, about 10 minutes. Do not allow the sauce to boil, or the eggs will scramble.

Let the sauce cool to room temperature before tossing the cooled pasta with it. It can also be stored in the fridge for a day or two before you toss the pasta with it.

NOTE

Agresto was traditionally made with unripe grape juice. These days it's almost impossible to find juice made from unripe grapes, so lemon juice is added to regular grape juice to mimic the sour flavor of the unripe grape.

Spaghetti with Bottarga

SERVES 4

—

Kosher salt

¼ cup (60 ml) extra-virgin olive oil

2 garlic cloves

½ teaspoon crushed red pepper flakes (optional)

2 tablespoons grated bottarga, plus more to taste

1 pound (450 g) spaghetti

Freshly ground black pepper

¼ cup (15 g) chopped fresh parsley

Bottarga is a delicacy of salted, cured fish roe (generally from gray mullet or bluefin tuna). In the old days, mullet roe was mostly thrown away at the fish market, so the Sephardic Jews of Italy would gather the discarded roe to salt and dry on their balconies. Today, especially in Rome, Italian Jews still make abundant use of bottarga in their cuisine because it imparts a great salty, umami flavor to any dish: grate it over pizza bianca (page 328) or over vegetables, slice it for a panini, or sprinkle it over pasta.

———

Bring a large pot of water seasoned with 1 tablespoon salt to a rolling boil.

Pour the olive oil into a large skillet set over medium-low heat, add the garlic and the pepper flakes, if using, and cook until the garlic is golden, about a minute per side. Remove the garlic from the pan and discard it.

If you are making one of the Variations, add the ingredient of your choice to the skillet and cook for 5 to 10 minutes.

Stir in the bottarga, remove from the heat, and set aside.

Add the pasta to the boiling water and cook until al dente according to the package directions. Drain and transfer the pasta to the skillet with the sauce. Set the skillet over medium heat and toss the pasta with the sauce for 2 minutes, or until it is evenly coated. Add black pepper to taste and the chopped parsley, if desired, season with additional grated bottarga, and serve immediately.

VARIATIONS

If you like, add your choice of ingredients from the list below to the pan after removing the garlic from the oil.

• ½ pound (225 g) cherry tomatoes, halved

• 1 pound (450 g) dandelion greens

• 1 zucchini, thinly sliced

• ¼ cup (25 g) bread crumbs plus a pinch of grated lemon zest

Kosher Pasta Amatriciana

SERVES 4

—

2 tablespoons extra-virgin olive oil

5 ounces (140 g) Coppiette di Carne Secca (page 69) or turkey bacon, cut into strips

1¼ cups (100 g) thinly sliced onions

½ cup (120 ml) dry white wine

1 pound (450 g) canned chopped tomatoes

Kosher salt and freshly ground black pepper

1 dried chili pepper (optional)

1 pound (450 g) bucatini or spaghetti

The traditional Italian amatriciana sauce, from the region of Lazio, is made with tomato and guanciale, or pork jowl bacon, and tossed with bucatini or spaghetti. Jews don't eat guanciale, so to enjoy a good amatriciana, you can replace the guanciale with dried meat, such as coppiette, or with turkey bacon. The result is as tasty as the original, and healthier too!

———

Pour the olive oil into a large sauté pan set over medium heat, add the coppiette or bacon and onions, and cook until the meat is crisp, about 5 minutes. Add the wine and cook until it evaporates completely. Using a slotted spoon, transfer the meat and onions to a plate and set aside.

Pour the tomatoes into the pan, season them with salt and pepper to taste, add the chili pepper, if using, and cook over medium-low heat until the sauce is nice and thick, about 15 minutes.

Meanwhile, bring a large pot of water seasoned with 1 tablespoon salt to a rolling boil. Add the bucatini or spaghetti and cook until al dente according to the package directions; drain in a colander.

Add the pasta to the tomato sauce and increase the heat to medium. Add the meat and onions, mixing well. Serve immediately.

NOTE

The traditional recipe calls for grating Pecorino cheese onto the pasta right before serving. If you don't have any religious restrictions, by all means go ahead and finish the dish with cheese!

Orecchiette with Broccoli Rabe

SERVES 4

___

FOR THE PASTA

3⅓ cups (600 g) durum wheat flour, plus more for dusting

1¼ cups (300 ml) water

Pinch of kosher salt

FOR THE SAUCE

2¼ pounds (1 kg) broccoli rabe or turnip greens

5 tablespoons (75 ml) olive oil

2 garlic cloves, crushed

Crushed red pepper flakes

4 oil-packed canned anchovy fillets

Orecchiette (which translates as "small ears") is a pasta shape that most likely came to Italy from Provence, France, imported by the Jews who settled in Apulia as early as the twelfth century. The Jews of Provence celebrated Purim (see page 271) with a special pasta called *oznei Aman* ("Aman's ears") or *oznei galahim* ("ears of the priests"). This second name, which translates into Italian as *orecchie dei preti*, is still used in some small towns of Apulia to refer to orecchiette, which clearly proves the connection.

In this recipe, homemade orecchiette is dressed in the most traditional Italian way, with a satisfying mix of broccoli rabe, anchovies, garlic, and olive oil. If the task of shaping the orecchiette feels overwhelming, don't despair: instead, you can make spitadelle, a simplified version of orecchiette I came up with to help impatient people; see Note. If you want to make the dish with dried orecchiette instead, you'll need 1¼ pounds (550 g).

___

To prepare the pasta, in a medium bowl, mix together the flour, water, and salt, and knead well with your hands until you get a firm, smooth, and elastic dough; this will take about 5 minutes. Form the dough into a ball and let it rest for about 15 minutes, wrapped in plastic wrap.

Cut the dough into 6 portions. Working with one portion at a time, roll the dough into 10-inch (25 cm) ropes, then cut each rope into ½- to ¾-inch (1 to 2 cm) pieces. (Keep the remaining portions covered with plastic wrap as you work to prevent the dough from drying out.)

To shape the orecchiette, set out a butter or dinner knife and lightly dust a platter with durum wheat flour. Position the knife on top of a piece of dough, holding the knife at a 45-degree angle to your work surface, and press down gently on the dough, dragging the piece of dough toward you. The result should be a little curled-up roll. Unfurl the roll over your thumb to form a shape that resembles a seashell. The pasta shell will have a rough, uneven surface, which is what makes orecchiette great for grabbing any sauce you dress it with. Set the pasta shell aside on the prepared platter, and repeat with the remaining dough.

- continued -

Once your orecchiette are shaped, let them dry on the counter for at least an hour, and up to a day.

To make the sauce, wash and trim the broccoli rabe, removing the thicker parts of the stems.

Bring a large pot of salted water to a rolling boil. Add the orecchiette and cook for 5 minutes. Add the broccoli rabe, bring the water back to a steady simmer, and cook for approximately 10 minutes. You want the pasta to be cooked through but still a bit chewy to the bite, or al dente; you will know when the orecchiette are ready because they will float to the surface of the water.

In the meantime, pour the olive oil into a large skillet set over medium heat, add the garlic and red pepper flakes to taste, and heat until the garlic begins to color. Lower the heat, add the anchovies, and mash them with a spoon. Remove the skillet from the heat before the garlic starts brown.

Drain the pasta and the greens in a colander, reserving a cup or so of the cooking water.

Transfer the pasta and greens to the pan with the garlicky oil and toss over medium heat. Add a bit of cooking water to the pasta if it looks dry. Serve hot.

NOTE

To make spitadelle, divide the dough into 6 portions, roll each portion into a rope, and cut into pieces as for orecchiette. Spread out the pieces on a well-floured counter, sprinkle with additional flour, and bang each piece of dough with a meat mallet or the bottom of a heavy cup to flatten them into small, irregular disks. These little pasta disks are not going to be particularly good looking, so you might not prepare them for guests, but, like orecchiette, they are the perfect vessel for sauce because of their uneven surface and shape.

Kosher Carbonara, Two Ways

As is the case with amatriciana (page 108), the fact that observant Jews can't eat guanciale or pork jowl bacon doesn't deter us from enjoying our own versions of dishes our compatriots enjoy. Here pasta alla carbonara, a classic Roman dish of pasta dressed in creamy egg yolk sauce, guanciale, and grated cheese, is tweaked in two ways to become kosher: one version features dried beef, and the other is vegetarian, using zucchini. If you are after the meatiness of the original carbonara, the dried-beef version will work like a charm; if it's the egg-and-cheese combination you crave, the vegetarian version won't disappoint you.

Carbonara with Dried Beef (or Turkey Bacon)

SERVES 4

—

7 ounces (200 g) Coppiette di Carne Secca (page 69) or turkey bacon, cut into strips

1 tablespoon extra-virgin olive oil

Kosher salt

1 pound (450 g) spaghetti

1 large (50 g) egg plus 3 large (57 g) egg yolks

Freshly ground black pepper

In a large skillet, combine the dried meat or turkey bacon and olive oil and cook over medium heat for a couple of minutes, until the meat is crisp. Remove from the heat and keep warm.

Bring a large pot of water seasoned with 1 tablespoon salt to a rolling boil. Add the bucatini or spaghetti and cook until al dente according to the package directions; drain in a colander, reserving a few tablespoons of the cooking water.

Meanwhile, beat the eggs in a bowl with a fork, adding a generous pinch each of salt and pepper. Add a few tablespoons of the reserved cooking water to loosen the mixture.

Transfer the cooked pasta to the skillet with the dried meat and toss it with the beaten eggs. Serve immediately.

Carbonara with Zucchini

SERVES 4

—

4 medium zucchini

2 tablespoons extra-virgin olive oil

3 garlic cloves, minced

Kosher salt and freshly ground black pepper

1 pound (450 g) spaghetti

5 large (95 g) egg yolks

1 cup (100 g) grated Parmesan or Pecorino, plus more for serving

Slice the zucchini lengthwise in half, then cut into ½-inch-thick (1 cm) half-moons.

In a large skillet, heat the olive oil over medium heat. When the oil shimmers, add the zucchini and garlic and season with salt and pepper to taste. Cook, stirring occasionally, until the zucchini has caramelized and slightly browned, approximately 15 minutes (if the zucchini is ready before the pasta is cooked, keep warm over very low heat).

Meanwhile, bring a pot of water seasoned with 1 tablespoon salt to a rolling boil. Add the spaghetti and cook until al dente according to the package directions. Scoop out a few tablespoons of the cooking water and drain the pasta in a colander.

In a bowl, beat the egg yolks and cheese to form a smooth sauce, then add enough of the reserved cooking water to loosen the sauce.

Transfer the pasta to the skillet with the zucchini and toss with the sauce. Serve immediately, sprinkled with Parmesan.

Pasta with Onion and Anchovy

SERVES 4

—

Kosher salt

10 canned anchovy
(or sardine) fillets
packed in salt or
olive oil

6 tablespoons
(90 ml) extra-virgin
olive oil

3 big white onions,
thinly sliced

⅓ cup (80 ml) dry
white wine

Leaves from a few
sprigs of parsley,
chopped (optional)

1 pound (450 g)
bigoli or other
thick spaghetti

Freshly ground
black pepper

In Venice, where seafood is an essential part of the everyday diet, one of the best ways to indulge in carbs is with a humble plate of spaghetti in anchovy sauce. Bigoli is thick spaghetti with a rustic and rough texture, and it is such a staple of Venetian cuisine that the locals use the expression *andare a bigoli* ("go find bigoli") to refer to eating lunch. In spite of its truly Venetian identity and the fact that it is served by Christians on holidays such as Christmas Eve, Good Friday, and Ash Wednesday, this dish is believed to have a Jewish origin.

———

Bring a large pot of water seasoned with 1 tablespoon salt to a rolling boil. Meanwhile, if you are using salt-packed anchovies (or sardines), rinse them carefully in a colander under cold running water and set aside to drain.

Pour the olive oil into a large skillet set over medium-low heat, add the onions, and cook until very soft, about 15 minutes. Add a couple of tablespoons of the boiling water from the pot and cook until the onions are almost melted, about 5 more minutes.

Add the wine and anchovies to the skillet and mix well. You want the anchovies to dissolve into the onion sauce, so break them up carefully with the back of a wooden spoon. Remove the skillet from the heat, add the chopped parsley, if desired, and set aside.

Add the pasta to the boiling water and cook until al dente according to the package directions. Drain and transfer to the skillet with the sauce.

Set the skillet over medium heat and toss the pasta with the sauce for a couple of minutes, until it is evenly coated. Season with salt if needed and freshly ground black pepper and serve immediately.

RUOTA DEL FARAONE
Pharaoh's Wheel

SERVES 4 TO 6

½ cup (80 g) raisins

½ cup (70 g) pine nuts

Kosher salt

1 pound (450 g) dried tagliolini or tagliatelle or a quadruple recipe Fresh Egg Pasta (page 103), cut into tagliolini

½ cup (120 ml) goose fat, extra-virgin olive oil, or pan juices left from a roast (page 186), plus more for brushing

Freshly ground black pepper

½ Goose Prosciutto breast (page 49) or 10½ ounces (300 g) ground beef

Pinch of ground allspice, if using ground beef

Pharaoh's Wheel, also called *Frisensal de tagiadele* in Italian, is a baked pasta dish similar to a savory noodle kugel. The casserole consists of layers of fresh tagliatelle tossed in goose fat (or juices from a roast), with pine nuts, raisins, goose or beef sausage, and goose prosciutto. Each ingredient has symbolic meaning: the pasta is often baked in a round dish to resemble the wheels of Pharaoh's chariots; the noodles represent the waves of the Red Sea, the pine nuts the heads of the Egyptian horses, and the raisins or pieces of meat the Egyptians, submerged by the waves. Some families have a tradition of hiding an almond in the dish, and the lucky person who finds it in their serving makes a wish or receives a special treat.

———

Soak the raisins in a cup of hot water for 30 minutes; drain. In a small skillet, toast the pine nuts over low heat until golden, about 1 minute; remove from the heat.

Bring a large pot of salted water to a boil. If using store-bought pasta, add it to the boiling water and cook until al dente according to the package directions. If using fresh pasta, cook for a minute or two, until it is soft but still has some bite. Drain, reserving about ½ cup (120 ml) of the pasta water. Set aside.

In a large skillet, heat your fat of choice or the pan juices, then stir in the reserved cooking water. Add the pasta and toss well, then season with salt and pepper to taste. Set aside.

If using goose prosciutto, cut it into small cubes. If using ground beef, mix it with the allspice and a pinch each of salt and pepper, form into very small meatballs, and sear them in a lightly oiled medium skillet over medium heat.

Preheat the oven to 400°F (200°C). Brush a round baking dish, about 11 inches (28 cm) in diameter, with a little fat or oil.

Arrange a layer of pasta in the dish, followed by a layer of pine nuts, raisins, and prosciutto cubes or meatballs. Continue layering until you run out of ingredients, ending with raisins, meat, and pine nuts on top.

Bake the pasta for 30 minutes, or until golden. (You can also cook this dish on the stovetop in a Dutch oven, flipping it twice—turn it out onto a plate, then invert onto another plate and slide back into the pot— to ensure it's nice and crusty on both sides.) Serve warm.

NOTE

You can sauté ground meat to replace the meatballs if you like, but please don't use Bolognese sauce!

Dairy-Free Lasagna

SERVES 6 TO 8

FOR THE PAREVE BÉCHAMEL

½ cup (120 ml) extra-virgin olive oil

¾ cup plus 1 tablespoon (100 g) all-purpose flour

4 cups (1 L) vegetable broth, homemade (page 78) or store-bought

Pinch of grated nutmeg

Kosher salt

FOR THE RAGÙ

1 medium onion, chopped

1 celery rib, peeled and chopped

1 small carrot, peeled and chopped

¼ cup (60 ml) extra-virgin olive oil

2¼ pounds (1 kg) ground beef chuck (20% fat)

1 cup (240 ml) dry red wine

3⅛ cups (700 g) tomato puree (passata)

3 cups (720 ml) vegetable or beef broth, homemade (page 78) or store-bought, or water, plus more if needed

- ingredients continued -

A proper Italian lasagna mixes meat (sometimes pork) and milk. Has that discouraged Jews from enjoying lasagna and even making it a festive Shabbat dish? Of course not. All you need to do is tweak the recipe a bit to make lasagna kosher, using beef rather than pork and a béchamel made with olive oil and broth instead of butter and milk.

Making lasagna from scratch is a bit of a project, but it's all doable if you have the time. Commit to half a day of work, and you'll be rewarded with a truly delicious dish everyone will love. However, if you don't have much extra time, don't hesitate to use store-bought pasta. Buy ready-made lasagna noodles, and as long as the béchamel and the ragù are homemade, nobody will know the difference.

The lasagna can be assembled ahead and kept in the fridge overnight or frozen for up to 3 months, well wrapped in foil. Transfer it to the fridge to thaw for 24 hours before you plan on baking it.

To make the béchamel, in a large saucepan, warm the olive oil over medium heat for a minute. Add the flour and cook, whisking, until it forms a golden paste (called a roux), 3 to 4 minutes. Whisking constantly, add the broth in a slow, steady stream, then add the nutmeg and salt to taste. Bring to a gentle simmer, whisking, trying to remove lumps if there are any, and cook, whisking, until the sauce thickens, about 10 minutes. Make sure to whisk the sauce constantly so that it doesn't stick or burn on the bottom of the saucepan. The sauce should be thick enough to coat the back of a spoon, but it should not be as thick as pudding, as it will thicken further as it cools. Remove from the heat.

Cover the béchamel with plastic wrap and let cool to room temperature. (*The béchamel can be made ahead and kept in the fridge for a couple of days, or frozen in an airtight container for up to 3 months. Thaw it in the fridge and reheat it over low heat in a saucepan, stirring well, before using it.*)

To make the ragù, pulse the onion, celery, and carrot in a food processor until finely chopped to make a soffritto.

In a large saucepan, heat the olive oil over medium heat. Add the soffritto and cook, stirring occasionally, until the vegetables are very soft, about 5 minutes.

- continued -

1 bay leaf

Kosher salt

One 9–ounce (255 g) package oven-ready lasagna sheets or a quadruple recipe Fresh Egg Pasta (page 103)

2 tablespoons bread crumbs or matzo crumbs for topping

Add the beef and cook, stirring often, until it is lightly browned, about 10 minutes. Pour in the wine and cook, stirring constantly, until it evaporates, about 10 minutes. Add the tomato puree, broth or water, and bay leaf and stir well.

Reduce the heat to the lowest setting and cook, uncovered, for a couple of hours. If the liquid reduces too much, add another ½ cup (120 ml) broth or water. However, the ragù should be pretty thick when it's ready, not too liquid. Add salt to taste, if needed, and remove from the heat.

Discard the bay leaf and let the sauce cool to room temperature. (*The ragù can made ahead and stored in the fridge for a couple of days or frozen in an airtight container. Thaw and reheat before using.*)

Preheat the oven to 350°F (180°C).

If using fresh pasta dough, divide it into 4 portions and roll each portion into a large sheet approximately 9 by 12 inches (23 by 30 cm). Or roll into 12 smaller sheets sized 3 by 12 inches (8 by 30 cm), and use 3 of these sheets, arranged side by side in the baking dish, for each layer.

Coat the bottom of a 9-by-13-inch (23 by 33 cm) baking dish with a layer of béchamel. Put a layer of pasta on top of the béchamel, then spread more béchamel over the pasta and top with a generous layer of ragù. (Don't mix the béchamel and ragù together; leave them in separate layers.) Place another layer of pasta on top, then add another layer of béchamel and another of ragù. Repeat once more. Place the last layer of pasta on top and cover it with the remaining béchamel. Top with the remaining ragù, this time mixing the ragù and béchamel a bit with a spoon to obtain a marbled effect. Sprinkle the top of the lasagna with the bread or matzo crumbs so you'll have a crunchy top.

Bake for 40 minutes, or until the top is crunchy. Serve straightaway.

VARIATION

Italian Jews don't ever give up their lasagna, even for Passover. If you want to make lasagna for Passover, replace the egg pasta sheets with matzo, briefly soaked in beef broth, homemade (page 78) or store-bought, to soften them. To make the béchamel kosher for Passover, replace the all-purpose flour with potato starch or rice flour.

Baked Pasta with Cheese and Cinnamon

SERVES 4

FOR THE OPTIONAL BÉCHAMEL

4 tablespoons
(½ stick/57 g)
unsalted butter

Scant ½ cup (50 g)
all-purpose flour

2 cups (480 ml) milk

Pinch of grated
nutmeg

Kosher salt

A double recipe
Fresh Egg Pasta
(page 103)

FOR THE TOPPING

8 tablespoons
(1 stick/113 g)
unsalted butter,
softened, if not
using béchamel

4 ounces (115 g)
Parmesan or
Pecorino cheese,
grated

¼ cup (50 g) sugar

1 teaspoon ground
cinnamon

Kosher salt and
freshly ground
black pepper

Among the many creative dishes that our ancestors came up with, the most unexpected is this baked pasta with cheese and . . . cinnamon and sugar! It's an unusual combination, but a very interesting one. If you are not intimidated by savory dishes that have a hint of sweetness, you will surely enjoy this one: the cinnamon and sugar bring out and enhance the flavor of the cheese without overpowering it.

The traditional recipe is somewhat dry, so I have updated it for more modern palates, and I've included a creamy béchamel to enrich the dish. If you'd rather not make the béchamel, you can use butter in the dish instead. However, it is also perfectly possible to follow the original recipe, omitting the béchamel, and revert to the ancient version of the dish. Especially if you decide to omit the béchamel, please make sure to use the best-quality Parmesan or Pecorino you can find, because the cheese will single-handedly define the flavor of the dish.

This recipe belongs to the repertoire of holiday dishes for Shavuot, because the tight rolls of pasta are said to resemble the Torah scrolls.

If you are making the béchamel, in a large saucepan, melt the butter over medium heat. Add the flour and cook, whisking constantly, until it forms a golden paste (called a roux), 3 to 4 minutes. Whisking constantly, add the milk in a slow, steady stream, then add the nutmeg and salt to taste. Bring to a gentle simmer, whisking, trying to remove lumps if there are any, and continue to cook, whisking, until the sauce thickens, about 10 minutes. Make sure to whisk the sauce constantly so that it doesn't stick or burn on the bottom of the saucepan. The sauce should be thick enough to coat the back of a spoon, but it should not be as thick as pudding, as it will further thicken as it cools. (You should have about 2 cups/600 g béchamel.)

Remove the béchamel from the heat, cover with plastic wrap, and set aside until you're ready to use it.

- continued -

Divide the dough into 2 portions. Roll each portion out to just under ⅛ inch (3 mm) thick to make a 24-by-5-inch (60 by 13 cm) sheet. Cut each pasta sheet into 4 pieces sized 6 by 5 inches (15 by 13 cm). Repeat with the remaining portion of dough to make a total of 8 rectangular pieces.

Preheat the oven to 350°F (180°C). Coat the bottom of a 13-by-10-inch (33 by 25 cm) lasagna pan with about ½ cup (150 g) béchamel, or brush it with butter if not using béchamel.

In a medium bowl, combine the grated cheese with the sugar and cinnamon.

If using béchamel, spread about 2 tablespoons on top of each pasta rectangle. If not using béchamel, brush each rectangle with butter. For either option, sprinkle the pasta rectangles with about 1 tablespoon of the cheese mixture each, then season with a pinch each of salt and pepper.

Starting on a short side, roll up each pasta cylinder and arrange the rolls snugly in the prepared pan, seam side down. Brush the tops of the rolls with the remaining béchamel or butter and sprinkle with the remaining cheese mixture.

Bake, uncovered, for 15 minutes, or until a nice crust has formed on top. Serve hot.

LAGANE AL FORNO
Baked Pasta Casserole

SERVES 6

—

A triple recipe
Fresh Egg Pasta
(page 103)

¼ cup (60 ml) extra-
virgin olive oil, plus
more for greasing
the baking dish

⅓ cup (50 g) carrots,
peeled and diced

⅓ cup (50 g) onion,
diced

⅓ cup (50 g) celery,
diced

1⅔ pounds (750 g)
lean boneless
beef, preferably
top round, bottom
round, or eye of
round

Kosher salt

Freshly ground
black pepper

Pinch of ground
cloves

1 cup (240 ml) dry
white wine

3 quarts (2.8 L)
beef, chicken,
or vegetable
broth, homemade
(page 78) or store-
bought, or water

1 cup (130 g) peas,
fresh or frozen

2 garlic cloves

8 chicken livers

Lagane is an ancient Passover version of lasagna, in which sheets of toasted egg pasta (sfoglietti; see the sidebar on page 101) are layered with vegetables to form a rich, savory casserole. Interestingly, the same pasta and ingredients would also sometimes be turned into a soup, called *laganelle in brodo* ("small lagane in broth"; see the Variation). It is virtually impossible these days to truly replicate the original recipe, which featured ingredients that have gone out of favor (like unlaid eggs collected from the inside of a dead hen). It is, however, easy to make a recipe that is true to the spirit of the original with some minor changes. The original casserole was baked on the stove (which yielded an ugly burnt bottom most of the time), but this version bakes in the oven instead.

If you're not concerned about making the dish kosher for Passover, dried lasagna noodles can be substituted for the homemade sfoglietti.

———

Divide the pasta dough into 3 portions. Using a pasta machine or a rolling pin, roll it into thin sheets approximately 7 by 4 inches (18 by 10 cm). Immediately toast the sheets in a very hot oven, under the broiler, or in a metal grill basket over an open flame until dry and fairly browned overall, with some burnt spots.

Pour half of the olive oil into a large saucepan set over medium heat, add the carrot, onion, and celery, and cook for 10 minutes, or until the onions are soft and translucent. Add the beef and sear on all sides, about 5 minutes per side. Sprinkle the meat with ½ teaspoon salt, pepper to taste, and the ground cloves, then add the wine and simmer until it evaporates.

Cover the meat with 2 quarts (2 L) of the broth or water and bring to a simmer, then reduce the heat to medium-low and simmer for an hour.

Remove the meat from the pan (set the saucepan aside). Cut the meat into chunks and let it cool, then grind it coarsely in a food processor. Return the ground meat to the saucepan and set aside.

Meanwhile, bring a saucepan of salted water to a boil over medium heat. Add the peas and cook until tender, then drain and set aside.

2 hard-boiled eggs, peeled and chopped into little pieces

2 large (100 g) eggs, lightly beaten

Pinch of ground cinnamon

In a large cast-iron skillet or other heavy pan, heat the remaining olive oil over low heat. Add the garlic cloves and sauté until a light brown color; remove from the oil and discard.

Turn the heat up to high and, before the oil hits the smoke point, add the livers and sear them for about 30 seconds. Flip them over, season with a pinch each of salt and pepper, and sear the other side for another 30 seconds. You want to keep the searing time short to avoid overcooking the livers; it's sufficient to just brown them properly on both sides. Transfer to a plate to cool, then cut into bite-size pieces.

Preheat the oven to 350°F (180°C). Grease a 9-by-11-inch (23 by 28 cm) baking dish.

To assemble the casserole, set out all the ingredients you have prepared—beef, peas, livers, and boiled eggs, plus the pasta sheets— on the counter. Mix all the filling ingredients together. Then layer the filling and pasta in the prepared dish, alternating layers of filling and the lagane sheets, to make a tall pie. (Because the lagane sheets are hard, they will take up a lot of space in this phase, but they will soften and shrink when baked.)

Pour a ladleful of the remaining broth or water over the top layer of lagane to soak it thoroughly, and transfer the dish to the oven.

Bake the lagane for 1 hour, adding water or broth as needed to keep the pasta from drying out.

Remove the lagane from the oven. Pour the lightly beaten eggs evenly over the top, then sprinkle with the cinnamon and return the dish to the oven.

Bake for an additional 15 minutes, or until the lagane is golden and crispy on top and soft inside. Serve straightaway.

VARIATION

To make laganelle in brodo (see the headnote), cut the pasta sheets into 7-by-2-inch (18 by 5 cm) strips or break store-bought lasagna sheets into pieces. Cook them in boiling broth—approximately 1 cup (240 ml) per person—until they are soft, approximately 5 minutes.

Serve the laganelle in individual bowls with the broth, and set out all the other ingredients (beef, peas, liver, and hard-boiled eggs) on the table for guests to spoon over their soup as desired.

TORTELLI DI ZUCCA
Pumpkin-Filled Tortelli

**MAKES ABOUT 40
TORTELLI; SERVES 4**

—

FOR THE FILLING

One 1½-pound
(650 g) sugar
pumpkin

1 large (50 g) egg,
lightly beaten

1½ cups (150 g)
crumbled amaretti

⅔ cup (65 g) grated
Parmesan

Pinch of grated
nutmeg

A double recipe
Fresh Egg Pasta
(page 103)

All-purpose flour
for rolling

Cornmeal for
sprinkling

Kosher salt

FOR THE SAUCE

5 tablespoons (70 g)
butter

8 sage leaves

Grated Parmesan
cheese for serving

The city of Mantua and the surrounding region are known for their
famous tortelli di zucca, fresh pasta filled with pumpkin and ground
amaretti. While there is no absolute certainty about the origins of this
dish, the use of pumpkin paired with something sweet points in the
direction of the Jews. Mantua had a flourishing Jewish community
during the Renaissance, and the Jews who lived there then were
known to cook with pumpkin on a regular basis, particularly for Rosh
Hashanah, while the locals despised the humble pumpkin and took
ages to add it to their cuisine.

———

Preheat the oven to 400°F (200°C). Line a baking sheet with parchment
paper.

To prepare the filling, cut the pumpkin into 8 wedges and remove
the seeds and strings. Place the pumpkin slices on the prepared baking
sheet.

Roast for 30 minutes, or until the pulp is soft to the touch. Let the
pumpkin cool.

Scoop the pumpkin flesh into a food processor or a blender. Discard
the skin. Process the pulp to a smooth puree. Transfer to a bowl.

Add the egg, amaretti, Parmesan, and nutmeg to the pumpkin puree
and mix well. Cover the bowl with plastic wrap and set aside in the
fridge until needed.

For the tortelli, you want to roll the pasta extremely thin, practically
see-through. Divide the dough in half. On a floured surface, roll the first
piece of dough into a 9-by-13-inch (23 by 33 cm) sheet.

Using a teaspoon and your fingers, scoop up equally sized tiny balls
of filling and arrange them on the bottom half of the pasta sheet, leaving
a 1½-inch (4 cm) border of dough at the bottom edge and at the ends
of the dough, and spacing the balls of filling approximately 1½ inches
(4 cm) apart.

- continued -

Fold the top half of the pasta sheet over the filling and press out the air around each portion of filling. With a sharp knife or a crimped pastry wheel, cut the sheet into individual tortelli, either rectangular or round (a special cutter for round tortelli can be bought online; see Resources, page 340). Place the tortelli on a baking sheet dusted with a thin layer of cornmeal, which will help prevent sticking. Working quickly, repeat with the remaining dough and filling. The tortelli will be approximately 1½ by 2½ inches (4 by 6 cm).

Bring a large pot of water seasoned with 1 tablespoon salt to a rolling boil. Gently drop the tortelli into the water and cook for 3 to 4 minutes, until they float to the top.

In the meantime, for the sauce, in a medium nonstick skillet, melt the butter with the sage.

Drain the tortelli and toss them with the butter sauce. Arrange on plates or a platter and sprinkle with Parmesan cheese right before serving.

SCACCHI

Matzo Casserole with Meat and Vegetables

SERVES 4

—

3 matzo sheets

6 tablespoons (90 ml) extra-virgin olive oil

1 cup (50 g) carrots, peeled and finely chopped

1 cup (50 g) onion, finely chopped

1 cup (50 g) celery, peeled and finely chopped

One 1⅔-pound (750 g) lean beef roast, such as top round, bottom round, or eye of round

Pinch of ground cloves

Pinch of grated nutmeg

Kosher salt and freshly ground black pepper

1 cup (240 ml) dry white wine

3 medium artichokes (see Notes)

1 cup (150 g) peas, fresh or frozen

8 ounces (225 g) lean ground beef

1 garlic clove, crushed in a press or minced

1 large (19 g) egg yolk

Pinch of ground cinnamon

Scacchi is a rich, nourishing main course prepared for Passover in the Jewish communities of Tuscany. It's similar to Italian lasagna (page 121) and to Jewish Italian lagane (page 126), but it is made with matzo in place of pasta. This delicious casserole—with layers of matzo, vegetables, and meat—is practically a full meal on its own. Serve with a light salad.

———

In a medium bowl, soak the matzo briefly in hot water until soft but not mushy, then squeeze with your hands to remove all the excess water; set aside.

Pour 3 tablespoons of the olive oil into a Dutch oven or large saucepan set over medium heat, add the carrots, onion, and celery, and cook for 10 minutes, or until the onions are soft and translucent. Add the beef and sear on all sides until browned, 2 to 3 minutes per side.

Sprinkle the seared meat with the cloves, nutmeg, and salt and pepper to taste, then add the wine and cook until it evaporates.

Cover the meat with water and bring to a simmer. Reduce the heat to medium-low, partially cover the pot, and simmer for 1 hour.

Meanwhile, trim the spiky tops of the outer leaves of the artichokes with a sharp knife. Slice each artichoke into quarters and scoop out and discard the chokes with a sharp spoon, then slice each quarter lengthwise in half.

Bring a saucepan of salted water to a boil and cook the peas and artichokes for a few minutes, until they are soft but not mushy. Drain and set aside.

When it is done, lift the meat out of the pot and let it come to room temperature. Discard the broth, or reserve it for another recipe. Cut the meat into chunks with a chef's knife and coarsely grind it in a food processor; set it aside (see Notes).

Preheat the oven to 350°F (180°C). Oil an 8-by-12-inch (20 by 30 cm) baking dish.

In a medium bowl, gently mix the lean ground beef with the minced garlic, egg yolk, and cinnamon. Using moistened hands, form the meat mixture into 1-inch (3 cm) meatballs.

In a sauté pan or medium skillet, heat the remaining 3 tablespoons olive oil over medium-low heat. Add the meatballs and cook for about 5 minutes, turning occasionally, until they are golden brown. Remove from the heat.

Set all of the ingredients—softened matzo, peas and artichokes, ground cooked beef, and meatballs—out on your counter and layer them in the baking dish. The order doesn't really matter as long as you finish the casserole with a layer of ground beef.

Bake for 40 to 45 minutes, until the casserole has a crunchy top. Serve hot.

Leftover casserole keeps well in the fridge for a couple of days, covered with aluminum foil. It can be reheated in the oven as needed.

NOTES

- When artichokes are not in season, you can make this dish with steamed spinach or chard.

- Instead of braising and grinding the beef, some people instead prepare a ragù (see page 121); while it's not traditional, it's definitely a tasty option.

- You can cook this dish in a pot on the stove instead of in the oven. Layer the ingredients tightly in the pot, moisten them slightly with a ladleful of water or broth, and let the liquid evaporate over medium-low heat for about 10 minutes. The result is a bit softer than the baked version.

Risotto

SERVES 4

—

2 tablespoons extra-virgin olive oil

½ onion, finely chopped

1½ cups (300 g) Arborio rice

½ cup (120 ml) dry white wine

4 cups (1 L) vegetable broth, homemade (page 78) or store-bought

1 tablespoon unsalted butter

¼ cup (25 g) grated Parmesan cheese

Risotto is a quintessential Italian first course and, as such, it also belongs on the tables of Italian Jews all over the peninsula but especially in the regions of Piedmont and Lombardy. This recipe makes a basic risotto, but you can customize it to celebrate the holidays: with diced candied citron for Sukkot, raisins for Hanukkah, chopped pumpkin for Rosh Hashanah, and peas for Passover. All sorts of vegetables can be added at other times of the year, depending on what's in season. Simply prep the ingredients and add them to the rice while it's cooking.

———

Pour the olive oil into a large nonstick skillet set over medium heat, add the onion, and cook for 3 minutes, or until translucent. Add the rice and stir it with a wooden spoon for a couple of minutes, so that the grains are gently toasted in the oil.

Pour in the wine and simmer to evaporate it. Add a ladleful of the broth, lower the heat to medium-low, and cook, stirring, until the rice absorbs the broth. Once it does, add another ladleful of broth and cook, stirring, until it is absorbed. (If you want to add any vegetables or other ingredients, stir them into the rice at this point.) Continue cooking and adding broth, a ladleful at a time, for 20 to 30 minutes, until the rice grains are tender but not mushy. Turn off the heat, stir in the butter and Parmesan cheese, and mix well. Serve straightaway.

If there are leftovers, the best way to repurpose them is to make supplì (fried rice balls; see page 64).

VARIATION

This recipe can be made pareve by omitting the butter and cheese, but in that case, swap chicken or beef broth for the vegetable broth.

Tomato Sauce with Chicken Giblets for Risotto

SERVES 4

—

14 ounces (400 g) chicken gizzards and livers

Kosher salt

½ large onion

½ carrot, peeled

½ celery rib

1 garlic clove

¼ cup (60 ml) extra-virgin olive oil

½ cup (120 ml) dry red wine

2 cups (450 g) tomato puree (passata)

A few sprigs of marjoram

Historically, the butchers in Rome used to divide the meat of their cattle according to its buyers: the first *quarto*, the best part, was sold to the nobles, the second tier to the clergy, the third best to the bourgeoisie, and the fourth part to soldiers. Poor people could only afford the so-called *quinto quarto* (fifth quarter), the entrails. The Jews of Italy have traditionally relied on the humble quinto quarto to enrich their cuisine. This tomato sauce with chicken giblets is one example. Once you overcome the fear some people have of offal, you'll be surprised at how tasty it is in this simple tomato sauce for risotto and for supplì (page 64), as well as for fresh pasta. Ask your butcher to set aside some chicken livers and gizzards so you can try the dish: you'll be glad you did.

———

Rinse the gizzards well under cold water, cut them in half, and cut off and discard any fatty parts.

Bring a large saucepan of salted water to a rolling boil. Add the gizzards, partially cover, and boil for 1 hour. Drain the gizzards in a colander, rinse under cold water, and set aside to cool.

Rinse the livers and trim them if necessary. Cut the livers and gizzards into small, evenly sized pieces; set aside.

In a food processor, grind the onion, carrot, celery, and garlic to a coarse paste.

Pour the olive oil into a nonstick sauté pan set over medium heat, add the ground vegetables, and cook until softened, about 10 minutes. Add the livers and gizzards, pour in the wine, increase the heat to high, and cook for a minute or so to evaporate the wine.

Add the tomato puree, marjoram, and ½ teaspoon salt, reduce the heat to medium-low, and cook until the sauce reduces and thickens, about 30 minutes; if necessary, add a bit of water to keep the sauce from becoming too thick. Remove from the heat.

Rosh Hashanah and Yom Kippur

Rosh Hashanah is the Jewish New Year.
It is a holiday that relates to the individual and their relationship with God;
we begin to meditate on our actions and ask for God's forgiveness.

After the New Year, we have ten days to repent for our sins until Yom Kippur, the Day of Atonement, when we present ourselves before God to receive judgment. During Yom Kippur, work is forbidden and we must abstain from all food and drink for twenty-five hours.

Rosh Hashanah

On the Eve of Rosh Hashanah, various symbolic foods are blessed: for example, in the United States, it is customary to eat a slice of apple dipped in honey to wish for a sweet new year. Those symbolic foods differ, depending on the country. In Italy, you'll almost always find figs—rather than or in addition to apples and honey—on the Rosh Hashanah plate, as well as pumpkin, fennel, leeks, chard, dates, pomegranates, fish, and the head of a lamb. There are also some unexpected ingredients, such as green beans, quinces, and grapes, which are not often served elsewhere. All these foods, and the prayers recited over them, are supposed to bring prosperity and good luck in the coming year.

Many Italian Jewish families avoid spicy and sour dishes at the Rosh Hashanah celebrations, also with the hope to start the new year on a sweet note. The dinner meal always includes the same symbolic ingredients used in the blessings at the beginning of the evening. So pumpkin comes back in the guise of the filled pasta called *tortelli di zucca* (page 129), or fried (page 63) or sautéed and crushed (page 228). And there are many Jewish Italian regional specialties too: one classic Rosh Hashanah dish is triglie alla mosaica (page 167), red mullet in tomato sauce. For something sweet, a half-moon–shaped pie made with short-crust pastry and filled with almond paste (page 266) is one of many traditional ways to end the meal.

Yom Kippur

On the eve of Yom Kippur, Jews all over the world stock up on calories before fasting for twenty-five hours. Italian Jews are no exception.

At both the very end of the meal before the fast and at the meal after the fast, we eat some sort of pasta filled with meat and cooked in broth, such as carcioncini in brodo (page 90). Meatballs—especially the classic ngozzamoddi (page 150) with celery and tomato—are often prepared, as is meatloaf. Other dishes that are never missing, especially in Rome, are triglie con uvetta e pinoli (Red Mullet with Raisins and Pine Nuts, page 168) and torzelli (Fried Escarole, page 215). Among the traditional sweet break-the-fast dishes are bulo (page 333), a type of bread with raisins, and bruscatella, a bread-and-wine pudding served with a custard sauce.

Semolina Gnocchi

SERVES 6

—

4 cups (1 L) whole milk

1 teaspoon kosher salt

1¼ cups (250 g) semolina

1 heaping cup (120 g) grated Parmesan cheese

4 tablespoons (½ stick/57 g) unsalted butter

Freshly ground black pepper

2 large (38 g) egg yolks

There is an old Roman adage that says, "*Giovedì, gnocchi; venerdì, pesce; sabato, trippa,*" which translates as, "On Thursday, dumplings; on Friday, fish; on Saturday, tripe." Christians used to make very nutritious dumplings on Thursday to prepare themselves for Friday, the day they abstained from meat. Gnocchi alla romana, simple semolina dumplings baked with cheese, are one of the "Thursday gnocchi" often prepared in Rome and throughout the region of Lazio. Local Jews enjoyed gnocchi alla romana so much that they even turned them into a traditional first course for the holiday of Sukkot.

———

Pour the milk into a large saucepan, add half of the salt, and bring to a simmer. Reduce the heat to low and slowly and gradually add the semolina, stirring constantly with a wooden spoon. Increase the heat to medium and cook, stirring constantly, until the semolina thickens and begins to pull away from the sides of the saucepan, about 15 minutes. Remove from the heat and allow the mixture to cool for a couple of minutes.

Add two-thirds of the grated Parmesan and 2 tablespoons of the butter, stirring until the butter melts, then season with the remaining salt and pepper to taste. Add the egg yolks and mix well.

Turn out the mixture onto a clean work surface and spread it evenly into a rectangle with a thickness of just under ½ inch (1 cm). Let cool. (*The semolina can be prepared ahead and stored, covered with plastic wrap, in the refrigerator for up to 2 days.*)

Preheat the oven to 400°F (200°C). Grease a 12-by-8-inch (30 by 20 cm) or approximately 2-quart (2 L) baking dish with 1 tablespoon of the butter.

Using a 2-inch (5 cm) cookie cutter or a glass, cut out small disks from the semolina; you should have about 40 disks. Set the scraps aside.

Arrange the dough scraps in the bottom of the baking dish and sprinkle with a little of the Parmesan cheese. Arrange the semolina gnocchi in rows on top of the scraps, overlapping the slices slightly to resemble roof tiles.

Melt the remaining 1 tablespoon butter in a saucepan and brush it over the gnocchi, then sprinkle with the remaining Parmesan cheese.

Bake for about 15 minutes, or until the gnocchi are golden brown. Serve hot.

Leftovers keep well in the fridge, covered with foil, for a couple of days. Reheat in a 400°F (200°C) oven.

Venice and Veneto

Veneto is located in the northeast of Italy, along the Adriatic Sea. Its most famous tourist attraction is Venice, but the region also includes other popular destinations, such as Verona, Padua, Vicenza, Lake Garda, and even some ski resorts.

Venice has a particularly interesting Jewish history, as it was the site of the first Jewish ghetto. Actually, the word *ghetto* itself comes from the Venetian word *geto*, meaning "foundry," because of the presence of a foundry in the area that became the ghetto.

The ghetto expanded over time into three sections: the Ghetto Novo, the Ghetto Vecchio, and the Ghetto Novissimo. The Ghetto Novo, which was built in 1516, is home to three synagogues: the Scola Grande Tedesca, built by Ashkenazi Jews in 1528; the Scola Canton, constructed in the early 1530s; and the Scola Italiana, built in 1575. The Ghetto Vecchio was established in 1541, and today it features two restored synagogues: the Scola Spagnola and the Scola Levantina, both built in the mid–1500s and still in operation, in the summer and the winter, respectively. The Ghetto Novissimo was built in 1633 and included only housing blocks.

At its largest, at the end of the 1600s, Venice was home to between four thousand and five thousand people. Emancipation came in 1797, but with that freedom, the dispersal of the community began, and by the 1930s, there were fewer than two thousand Jews left. In the Fascist era, the Nazis started a systematic hunt for all Jews in Venice, and despite the heroic efforts of community leader Giuseppe Jona, hundreds were deported to death camps. Only eight residents returned after the war.

Today there are about four hundred Jews in Venice, a small population that is aging fast; however, the city still has a lively Jewish atmosphere. There are also about two hundred Jews in Padua, not far from Venice, another stunning Italian city well worth visiting.

Travelers who are interested in Jewish culture should not miss the Museum of Jewish Art, which opened in the Venetian Ghetto in 1955 and has a cozy bookshop and café, or the Renato Maestro Library and Archives, whose catalog includes twenty-five hundred Hebrew volumes dating from the sixteenth to nineteenth centuries, as well as eight thousand contemporary titles.

When it comes to food, the kosher options are limited by the size of the Jewish population. Other than the Middle Eastern restaurant called Gam, run by the Chabad, there is a tiny bakery, Panificio Volpe, where you can taste many traditional Jewish Venetian pastries, such as bisse (page 294) and azzime dolci (page 295).

For those who are comfortable eating non-kosher foods, any random Venetian bacaro—a place where cicchetti, or tasty nibbles, are served, alongside a glass of wine—will be a treat. The best ones are Osteria Anice Stellato, Ca' d'Oro alla Vedova, Cantina Do Mori, Al Timon, and Ristorante Vecia Cavana. In these restaurants, you can enjoy Jewish Venetian specialties such as bigoli in salsa (page 117) and sarde in saor (page 66), as well as other delicious local dishes.

CLOCKWISE FROM TOP: *The main square of the Ghetto; the old wooden dome of the Scuola Canton; a pastry from the local Jewish bakery; a sign that reads "small square of the synagogues."*

Pollame e pesce

POULTRY AND FISH

Chicken with Tomatoes and Peppers

SERVES 4

1 whole chicken, about 3 pounds (1.4 kg), or 3 pounds (1.4 kg) mixed chicken parts

3 large red bell peppers

¾ pound (300 g) ripe tomatoes (any type will do, including cherry tomatoes, if need be)

6 tablespoons (90 ml) olive oil

2 garlic cloves, crushed

½ cup (120 ml) dry white wine

½ cup (115 g) tomato passata

½ teaspoon kosher salt

Freshly ground black pepper

Thyme leaves for garnish (optional)

Cooking chicken can be tricky; sometimes the smallest mistake can lead to a sad, dry meal. This Roman recipe for chicken with peppers is easy, and you truly can't mess it up. The chicken is juicy and the sauce irresistible. The dish keeps well for days and can be reheated over and over again; it only gets better as the sauce thickens over time.

If using a whole chicken, cut it into serving pieces (or have the butcher do it for you). Refrigerate until ready to use.

Preheat the oven to 350°F (180°C). Line a baking sheet with parchment paper.

Cut the peppers in half, remove the seeds and membranes, and cut the peppers lengthwise into strips. Cut larger tomatoes into quarters, or cut cherry tomatoes in half.

Place the tomatoes and peppers on the prepared baking sheet, brush them with 2 tablespoons of the olive oil, and spread them out on the pan. Roast for 30 minutes, or until soft and caramelized on top. Remove from the heat. If you want to peel the peppers once they are cooled, it's easy, but it's not necessary.

Pour the remaining ¼ cup (60 ml) olive oil into a large skillet or sauté pan set over medium heat, add the garlic, and cook until golden. Working in batches, add the chicken pieces, skin side down, and sear for 5 minutes per side, or until golden. When all the chicken is seared, return the first batch(es) to the pan, add the wine, and let it evaporate.

Add the tomatoes and peppers to the pan, pour in the passata, and season everything with the salt and freshly ground pepper to taste. Add a cup (240 ml) of water to the pan and bring to a simmer, then reduce the heat to low, and cook the chicken for 45 minutes, or until cooked through. Whenever the pan starts to dry out, add another half a cup (120 ml) of water.

Serve the chicken hot, sprinkled with a few thyme leaves, if you like.

NOTES

- For children or other picky eaters, you can puree the tomatoes and peppers to make a sauce. Once the chicken is cooked, transfer the tomatoes, peppers, and pan juices to a blender and turn them into a smooth, creamy sauce to serve over the chicken.

- This dish can be prepared on the stovetop, if you want to avoid turning on your oven. Stew the tomatoes and peppers with the garlic in the olive oil over medium-low heat until soft, then turn the heat up to medium, add the chicken, and proceed as directed.

POLPETTONE DI POLLO
Chicken Meatloaf

SERVES 6

---

1 slice stale sourdough bread

14 ounces (400 g) ground chicken breast meat

2 large (100 g) eggs

Pinch of ground cinnamon

½ teaspoon kosher salt

Freshly ground black pepper

Fillings of your choice (see headnote), if desired

¼ cup (60 ml) extra-virgin olive oil, plus more for your hands

1 carrot, peeled

1 celery rib

1 garlic clove

1 cup (240 ml) dry white wine

Unlike a classic American meatloaf, a Jewish Italian meatloaf is not made in a loaf pan or baked on a sheet pan but cooked almost like a pot roast in a skillet on the stove, which gives it a crusty exterior and a soft center, less likely to dry out.

This meatloaf can be made with chicken, turkey, or veal and enriched with all sorts of ingredients. Traditional fillings often include hard-boiled eggs, chopped spinach, or pistachios. If you make this with turkey instead of chicken, it becomes a meatloaf to serve on the eve of Yom Kippur.

———

Soak the bread in a bowl of warm water until softened, then squeeze it well to remove the excess liquid. Transfer the bread to a bowl, add the chicken, eggs, cinnamon, salt, and pepper to taste and mix thoroughly with your hands.

Moisten your hands with a little olive oil and shape the meat mixture into a loaf on the counter, preferably long and not too large, to fit comfortably in the pan you'll be using. If you want to add any filling to the meatloaf (a few hard-boiled eggs, a cup of cooked spinach, ½ cup/50 g pistachios), this is the time to do so. You can leave these ingredients whole and arrange them in the middle of the meat mixture before shaping the meatloaf, or chop them and mix them into the meat before you shape it.

Finely chop the carrot, celery, and garlic, mix together, and set aside.

Pour the olive oil into a heavy nonstick saucepan just large enough to hold the meatloaf and heat over medium heat. Add the meatloaf and brown it on all sides, turning it with tongs, until a nice crust has formed, about 3 minutes per side.

Add the carrot and celery mixture to the pan, then pour in the wine and let it evaporate.

Cover the pan and cook the meatloaf over the lowest possible heat for about 1 hour, turning it every 15 minutes or so for even cooking and adding a bit of water if the pan seems to be drying out, until the meat is cooked through. Remove from the heat.

Let the meatloaf cool completely, then transfer it to a platter and cut into slices.

Collect the vegetables in the bottom of the saucepan, mix in a bit of water, and blend with an immersion blender (or in a regular blender) to make a sauce. Ladle the sauce over the meatloaf and serve.

Chicken Meatballs with Celery

SERVES 4 TO 6

—

1 pound (450 g) ground chicken (see Note)

1 large (50 g) egg

½ cup (50 g) bread crumbs or matzo flour

1 teaspoon kosher salt

6 tablespoons (90 ml) olive oil

6 celery ribs, peeled and cut into thin sticks

3 carrots, peeled and cut into chunks

1 cup (240 ml) dry white wine

½ cup (120 ml) chicken, beef, or vegetable broth, homemade (page 78) or store-bought, or water

Freshly ground black pepper

There are two dishes featuring chicken meatballs and celery in the Jewish Roman repertoire, and they differ essentially in terms of one ingredient—tomato—although the spices and some other ingredients vary a bit. This version, *in bianco*, which means "white," is more delicate than its tomato-based counterpart (see page 150). You can serve polpette in bianco on their own or with a side salad, but rice pilaf also works well with them, even though it's not Italian. To make a heartier meal, add a couple of cubed potatoes to the pan.

———

In a medium bowl, mix the ground chicken, egg, bread crumbs or matzo flour, and half of the salt together.

Using your hands, shape a generous tablespoon of the chicken mixture into a small oval meatball and place on a plate. Repeat with the remaining mixture.

In a large nonstick sauté pan or large saucepan, warm the olive oil over medium heat. Add the meatballs to the pan, working in batches if necessary to avoid crowding, and cook, turning them occasionally, until lightly colored on all sides, a few minutes or so. (If you browned the meatballs in batches, return them all to the pan.)

Add the celery, carrots, wine, broth, the remaining salt, and pepper to taste to the pan and bring to a boil, then reduce the heat to low. Partially cover the pan with the lid and cook for about 1 hour, stirring from time to time, until the vegetables are cooked through and the liquid is reduced to ¼ cup (60 ml). Serve hot.

The meatballs and their sauce keep well in the fridge, covered with plastic wrap or in an airtight container, for a couple of days. They can be reheated in a saucepan or in the microwave.

NOTE

You can make this recipe with half veal and half chicken, which will result in slightly more meaty, chewier polpette.

Chicken Meatballs with Celery in Tomato Sauce

SERVES 4 TO 6

—

6 celery ribs

3 carrots

⅓ cup (80 ml) extra-virgin olive oil

1 small onion, thinly sliced

1 garlic clove, minced

3 tablespoons tomato paste

½ cup (120 ml) water

One 14.5-ounce (410 g) can whole tomatoes

1 teaspoon ground cinnamon

1 teaspoon kosher salt

1 pound (450 g) ground chicken

½ cup (50 g) bread crumbs or matzo flour

Freshly ground black pepper

1 large (50 g) egg, beaten

The Italian name of this recipe is of uncertain origin. Some believe it comes from the verb *ingozzarsi*, which translates as something like "eating greedily" or "eating to excess," which is a fairly accurate description of what happens when people try this dish. Others think the name comes from *ozza*, the Roman dialect form of the word *ossa*, which means "bones" and might refer to the fact that the sauce was originally prepared with bone-in pieces of chicken. Whatever the origin, these scrumptious meatballs are often prepared for Rosh Hashanah and Yom Kippur, and they are always a hit. Serve ngozzamoddi on their own or with a side of salad or rice. Vegetarians can omit the chicken and enjoy the tomato sauce with just the celery and carrots. It's surprisingly satisfying, even without the meatballs.

———

With a potato peeler, peel off the stringy outer layer of the celery ribs, cut each rib crosswise in half, and then slice lengthwise in half, to obtain 24 thin sticks.

Peel the carrots and cut them into sticks that are 2 to 3 inches (5 to 8 cm) long and ½ inch (1 cm) thick. Set aside.

Pour the olive oil into a nonstick sauté pan or large saucepan set over medium heat, add the onion and garlic, and cook for 10 minutes, or until the onion is soft and translucent.

Add the tomato paste and water, bring to a simmer, and simmer for a minute. Add the celery, carrots, tomatoes, half of the cinnamon, and half of the salt, and crush the tomatoes with a wooden spoon. Reduce the heat to very low and cook for 30 minutes, or until the tomatoes fall apart into a sauce. Remove from the heat and set aside.

While the sauce simmers, prepare the meatballs: In a bowl, mix together the chicken, bread crumbs or matzo flour, the remaining cinnamon and salt, pepper to taste, and the egg. Transfer the mixture to the fridge and let it rest for 1 hour.

To make the meatballs, shape a generous tablespoon of the meat mixture into a small oval meatball with your hands and place on a plate. Repeat the process with the remaining meat mixture.

Return the tomato sauce to medium heat and bring to a simmer. Add the meatballs to the sauce and cover the pan. Wait patiently for a couple of minutes, without touching the meatballs, to avoid ruining their shape. Then add water just to cover the meatballs and cook, partially covered, for 30 minutes, or until the tomato sauce has thickened enough to coat the meatballs.

Serve hot, topping each portion of meatballs with a generous amount of sauce.

NOTE

If you don't mind starting with a whole large chicken (about 4½ pounds/2 kg) and doing a bit of butchering, you can prepare this dish the traditional way. Slice the meat from the breast, thighs, and drumsticks (discarding the skin) and grind it to make the meatballs. Set aside the heart, liver, and gizzards for sugo con rigaglie (see page 136), and use the carcass to enrich the sauce. The meatballs themselves are irresistible, but the bits and pieces of chicken in the sauce make the dish even tastier.

Fried Chicken

SERVES 4

—

FOR THE MARINADE

1 cup (240 ml) extra-virgin olive oil

1 cup (240 ml) fresh lemon juice, plus more for serving

½ cup (120 ml) water

1 garlic clove, smashed

½ teaspoon kosher salt

FOR THE CHICKEN

3 pounds (1.4 kg) mixed chicken pieces: drumsticks, thighs, wings, and/or breasts (see Note)

2 cups (250 g) all-purpose flour

1 tablespoon kosher salt

½ teaspoon freshly ground black pepper

2 large (100 g) eggs

Sunflower or peanut oil for deep-frying

Fresh lemon juice for drizzling

Most old Jewish Italian cookbooks include a recipe for fried chicken, a Tuscan Hanukkah specialty prepared to honor the miracle of the oil. It's no longer a tradition that many people really maintain, but it deserves to make a comeback—Hanukkah offers the perfect excuse to enjoy fried food, and this fried chicken is scrumptious!

———

To make the marinade, in a large bowl, combine the olive oil, lemon juice, water, garlic, and salt and stir well.

Place the chicken pieces in the bowl, turn them a couple of times to coat them well with the marinade, cover, and refrigerate for about an hour, turning them occasionally.

When ready to fry the chicken, preheat the oven to 350°F (180°C).

In a medium bowl, combine the flour, salt, and pepper. In a second bowl, whisk the eggs with a fork.

Take the chicken out of the marinade and pat it dry with paper towels. Coat each piece thoroughly with the flour mixture, transfer to the bowl of eggs, and coat completely, letting the excess drip off, then dip once more in the flour and shake off the excess. Set on a plate.

Pour 1½ to 2 inches (4 to 5 cm) of sunflower or peanut oil into a large deep skillet and heat over medium heat until a deep-fry thermometer reads 350°F (180°C). You can test the oil by dropping a small piece of food, such as a slice of apple, into it: if it sizzles nicely but doesn't bubble up too wildly, the oil is ready. (An apple is said to help diminish the smell of the frying oil, so I generally go for that, but any bit of food will do.)

Working in batches to avoid crowding, carefully place 2 or 3 pieces of chicken at a time in the oil and fry for about 3 minutes on each side, until the coating is a light golden color. Remove the chicken from the oil with tongs and place on a wire rack set on a baking sheet (line it with aluminum foil for easier cleanup). Allow the oil to return to the right temperature before frying the next batches.

When all the chicken is fried, slide the baking sheet into the oven and bake the chicken for 30 minutes, or until it's fully cooked through. Serve hot, with some lemon juice to go with it.

NOTE

The traditional way to make this recipe is to start with a whole chicken, carve it, and then fry the pieces bone-in and skin-on, but working with chicken parts simplifies the process.

Stuffed Turkey Meatloaf

This meatloaf is a very old specialty prepared by the Jews of Venice for Passover. It's a labor-of-love project that takes time; it requires that you remove the skin from a whole turkey and then stuff the skin with the breast meat and other ingredients before sewing it together into a roll and boiling the whole thing in turkey broth. I learned this recipe in Turin from my friend Marta Morello, who keeps up the old Passover tradition and makes this stuffed turkey meatloaf for her family every year. You can serve it as a main course or as a starter.

You'll need to source a whole turkey for this recipe, but you won't use the meat of the legs for the meatloaf, so you can save it for another use or add it to the stockpot (you can ask the butcher to cut off the legs for you, or just do it yourself). If your butcher can provide you with some extra turkey skin that would otherwise be discarded, get as much of it as you can, as that will allow you to make a larger meatloaf. NUMBERED STEPS PICTURED ON PAGE 157

SERVES 10 AS A STARTER OR A MAIN

—

1 whole turkey, 15 to 20 pounds (7 to 9 kg)

2 carrots

2 celery ribs

2 onions

2 garlic cloves

1 pound 6 ounces (600 g) ground beef or veal (see Notes)

2 large (100 g) eggs, lightly beaten

½ teaspoon grated nutmeg

Kosher salt and freshly ground black pepper

6 hard-boiled eggs, peeled

- ingredients continued -

Place the turkey on a work surface and, with a sharp knife, cut away the whole legs (if the butcher has not done this for you) and the wings; set aside. Turn the turkey breast side down and slit the skin down the backbone. Peel the skin away from both sides of the backbone (the maneuver resembles that of taking a shirt off a doll) and then from the breasts, trying to keep the skin as intact as possible. Remove the skin from the wings and legs (reserve the legs for another use); set the wings aside. Wash all the skin under running water, then remove as much fat as possible from it and set aside. (As an alternative to skinning the turkey whole, you can also break down the turkey into individual portions—breasts, legs, and wing—and skin those one at a time, although this will increase the time it will take to sew the skin back together [1–2]).

Slice off the 2 breasts from the turkey carcass. Save the carcass for the broth.

In a large stockpot, combine the carrots, celery, 1 onion, the turkey wings, the legs, if you are not reserving them for another use, and the carcass, [3] add water to cover completely, and bring to a simmer, then reduce the heat to medium-low and simmer for 1 hour. Remove from the heat and let the broth come to room temperature.

In the meantime, prepare the filling and the skin: Cut one of the turkey breasts into ½-inch-thick (1 cm) slices.

- continued -

• Thin butcher's
twine (or regular
cotton sewing
twine)

• Sterile needle

• Fish poacher
(optional)

Cut the other breast into 2 pieces: Cut off one-quarter of it and set aside. In a food processor, grind the remaining breast meat together with the remaining onion and 1 garlic clove.

Chop the remaining piece of breast meat into little pieces [4]. In a bowl, mix the ground breast meat, chopped breast, ground beef, beaten eggs, nutmeg, and salt and pepper to taste [5-6].

Now it's time to sew the skin: you want a large, roughly rectangular piece of skin about 10 by 16 inches (25 by 40 cm). If the skin is torn or you don't have a big enough piece, sew up any tears and/or sew smaller pieces together to get a large rectangle [7], like you would a quilt. Lay the skin on your clean work surface, with the inside up, and rub it with the remaining garlic clove.

Now assemble the turkey meatloaf: Arrange the turkey breast slices across the center of the rectangle of skin [8], leaving 1½ inches (4 cm) of skin empty at the top and at the bottom. Layer the slices to build in a bit of height.

Nestle the hard-boiled eggs [9], end to end, in one long line across the middle of the turkey slices. Cover the eggs and turkey slices with the mix of ground beef and turkey [10]. Once the filling is in place, fold [11] the long edges of the skin up and use your needle and twine to sew them together to form a tight (but not too tight, or the skin may burst while boiling) roll. Sew the ends together too, so that the filling can't escape [12].

Tie the roll with twine as you would a roast, if you like. Pierce the roll in multiple spots with a sterile needle to let the air escape.

If using a fish poacher, pour the reserved turkey broth into the pan and set the meatloaf on the rack in the pan. If using a large pot, set a wire rack in the pot, place the meatloaf on it, and pour the broth around the meatloaf. Bring the broth to a simmer over medium-low heat and cook the meatloaf for 1½ to 2 hours.

Lift the meatloaf out of the pan and transfer to a platter. Let cool to room temperature before slicing and serving. (Note that the skin is supposed to be peeled off and discarded, not eaten.)

The meatloaf can be stored in the fridge, tightly covered, for up to 2 days.

NOTES

• Ground turkey can be substituted for the ground beef or veal, if you prefer.

• Grilled chicken livers can also be added to the filling.

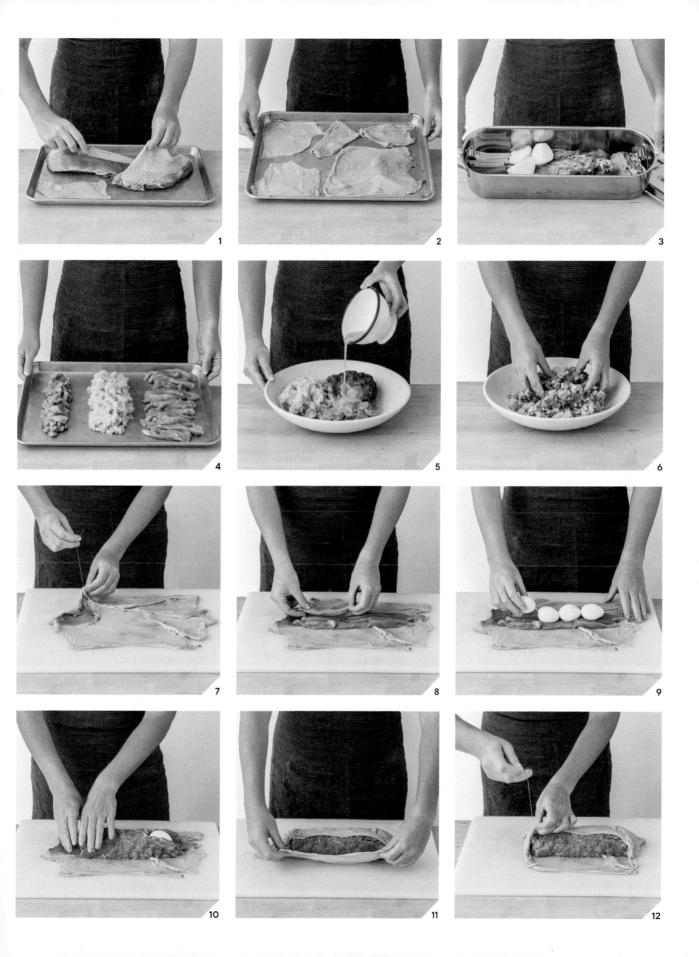

BRANZINO AL FORNO CON SALSA VERDE
Roasted Branzino with Salsa Verde

SERVES 4

—

FOR THE FISH

2 lemons

2 whole branzino
or seabass,
1⅛ to 1½ pounds
(500 to 700 g)
each, scaled and
gutted

1 small bunch thyme

4 garlic cloves

**FOR THE SALSA
VERDE**

2 hard-boiled egg
yolks

1 slice stale
sourdough bread,
crust removed

½ cup (120 ml) white
wine vinegar

¾ cup (180 ml)
extra-virgin
olive oil

2 oil-packed
anchovy fillets
or 1 teaspoon
anchovy paste

3⅔ cups (180 g)
chopped parsley

2 garlic cloves

1 teaspoon salt-
packed capers,
rinsed thoroughly
to remove the salt

Kosher salt

Here's an ideal dish to make when you don't feel like spending much time in the kitchen or when you've got friends coming over for an unplanned dinner. While the fish roasts unsupervised in the oven, all you need to do is whip up the salsa verde—a wonder condiment that makes virtually any dish taste better.

Salsa verde is a tangy, herb-packed green sauce from the region of Piedmont, which the local Jews have fully adopted, both to spice up weekday meals and to grace the Shabbat table. The traditional way to serve it is with boiled beef, but you can use it as a salad dressing, or drizzle it over fish.

———

Preheat the oven to 425°F (220°C).

Slice 1 lemon into thin rounds, to stuff the fish, and cut the other one into wedges, for serving.

Pat the fish dry with paper towels. Stuff the cavities with the lemon slices, the sprigs of thyme, and the garlic.

Transfer to a rimmed baking sheet and roast until the fish is just cooked through, 20 minutes or so, depending on the size of the fish.

Meanwhile, prepare the salsa verde: In a small bowl, mash the egg yolks with a fork. In another small bowl, soak the stale bread in the vinegar to soften it, then squeeze the excess vinegar back into the bowl and set it aside.

In the bowl of a food processor, pulse the mashed egg yolks, bread, olive oil, anchovies (or anchovy paste), parsley, garlic, and capers until mostly smooth. Adjust the thickness with the reserved vinegar, if desired. Season the sauce with salt to taste.

Fillet the fish and serve with the lemon wedges and salsa verde.

Leftover salsa verde keeps in a sealed jar in the fridge for 2 to 3 days.

BACCALÀ ALLA VICENTINA
Vicenza-Style Stockfish

SERVES 4

—

About 1⅛ pounds (500 g) stockfish or 2¼ pounds (1 kg) fresh cod fillet, skin on

1 cup (240 ml) extra-virgin olive oil

2 onions, finely chopped

One 4.4–ounce (125 g) can sardines in oil

Kosher salt and freshly ground black pepper

1 tablespoon all-purpose flour

¼ cup (20 g) grated Parmesan cheese

¾ cup (180 ml) milk

Leaves from a few sprigs of parsley, chopped

Polenta for serving

Baccalà alla vicentina is a chunky but delicate fish spread prepared by slow-cooking air-dried cod—stockfish—in milk. It works as both a starter and as a main course; it can be served chilled on small slices of bread, like a canapé, or warm with polenta for a full-fledged meal. Stockfish is a tricky ingredient because it requires a long soaking time (for this recipe, several days) before cooking, but you can substitute fresh cod here if necessary. Look for a thick fillet of stockfish or fresh cod, and make sure it still has the skin on (the stockfish will approximately double in weight when soaked).

In this recipe, the word *baccalà* refers to air-dried cod, but generally the term refers to salt cod (see pages 163 and 170). That's because they confused the two types of fish for ages in Vicenza, and the confusion remains in the name of the dish, though it's common knowledge in Italy that the fish used is actually air-dried cod.

———

If using stockfish, place it in a bowl, cover it with water, cover the bowl, and refrigerate for 3 days, changing the water every day. Drain the fish, pat dry, place on a plate, cover, and refrigerate overnight. (If using fresh cod, begin with the next step.)

Pour 2 tablespoons of the olive oil into a medium skillet set over medium heat, add the chopped onions, reduce the heat to low, and cook, stirring often, for 15 to 20 minutes, until the onions are soft and a dark amber color. Halfway through the cooking, add one-quarter of the sardines (reserve the remaining sardines for another dish) and mash them with a fork, mixing them well with the onions. When the onions are cooked, remove from the heat and set aside to cool.

Place the cod fillet skin side down on a work surface. Spread half of the onion-sardine mixture over the lower half of the fillet, just to coat it nicely, and sprinkle with salt, pepper, and half of the flour. Fold the top half of the fillet over itself, like a book, and then cut it into 2½-inch (6 cm) pieces. The pieces will look like small C-shaped sandwiches filled with onions.

Remove half of the remaining onion mixture from the pan and spread the rest of the mixture evenly over the bottom of the pan. Place the folded fish pieces in the pan so that they stand upright on top of the onion mixture, arranging them as snugly as possible so they won't open up during cooking. Cover with the remaining onion mixture and sprinkle with the remaining flour. Sprinkle the fish with the grated cheese and pour the milk and then the remaining ¾ cup (180 ml) olive oil over the top.

Partially cover the pan and cook over very low heat for 4 to 5 hours; the fish should be falling-apart tender.

Add the chopped parsley to the fish mixture and mash gently with a fork to make a coarse, chunky spread.

Serve hot or cold, as you prefer, with polenta on the side.

THE UNLIKELY COMBINATION OF FISH AND MILK · In 1431, a group of Italian mariners got lost at sea and ended up stranded in Norway, where the locals generously fed them a strange fish called stockfish. It was actually cod, air-dried for preservation. A few decades later, stockfish began to be exported to Italy, where the local Jews quickly took to it, as stockfish was not only kosher but also kept longer than fresh fish.

Most Italians think of Vicenza-style stockfish as a traditional Italian dish, but it's very likely that the Jews came up with it, as the mix of milk and fish in the ingredients seems to suggest. Italians would never have combined milk and fish: they generally ate fish on Friday, the day they abstained from meat and rich foods for religious observance, so milk would have been off the menu. The Jews, however, could freely mix fish and milk, according to the rules of kashrut.

Tuna Loaf

SERVES 4 TO 6

—

Two 5-ounce (140 g) cans yellowfin tuna packed in olive oil, drained

3 large (150 g) eggs

A spoonful of drained capers

2 tablespoons grated Parmesan cheese

4 oil-packed anchovy fillets (optional)

A few parsley leaves (optional)

Pinch of grated nutmeg

1½ cups (150 g) bread crumbs, or as needed

Mayonnaise for serving

Many Jewish families, especially Sephardic Jews, have a passion for canned tuna. We always have quite a bit of canned tuna stocked in our pantry, because it has a long shelf life and you never know when you might need it. When tuna doesn't end up in a pâté (page 71), you can turn it into a meatloaf, which makes a great cold starter or main dish. In this recipe, the tuna loaf is tightly sealed and cooked in boiling water, which makes it especially soft but firm enough to slice.

———

Bring a large pot of water to a boil over medium heat.

Meanwhile, in a food processor, combine the tuna, eggs, capers, Parmesan, anchovies, if using, parsley, and nutmeg and process until smooth. Add the bread crumbs and pulse to combine; the mixture should be thick enough to shape it easily into a roll.

Wrap the roll tightly in parchment paper, then wrap it tightly in aluminum foil, to make it waterproof.

Transfer the tuna loaf to the boiling water, making sure it's entirely submerged, and cook for 30 minutes, topping up the water if necessary. Remove the tuna loaf from the water and let it come to room temperature.

Unwrap the loaf, slice, and serve, with mayonnaise on the side.

Leftover tuna loaf (without mayonnaise) keeps well in the fridge, wrapped in plastic wrap, for up to 2 days.

BACCALÀ AL POMODORO
Salt Cod in Tomato Sauce

SERVES 6

—

2¼ pounds (1 kg) salt cod

3 tablespoons extra-virgin olive oil

1 onion, thinly sliced

One 14.5-ounce (410 g) can whole tomatoes

Kosher salt and freshly ground black pepper

1 cup (240 ml) dry white wine

A few sprigs of parsley

Baccalà al pomodoro ("with tomato sauce"), also known as *baccalà in guazzetto*, is a traditional Roman dish, one that the Jews of the Ghetto adopted for their holiday menus. There are countless variations on this dish, and you'll find some of them here (see below). It's important that you make sure to buy baccalà, which is salted cod, not stockfish, which is simply air-dried, and you will need to allow a couple of days for soaking and desalting the fish before cooking it.

———

Place the salt cod in a large bowl of cold water, cover with plastic wrap, and refrigerate for 2 days, draining it, rinsing it, and adding fresh water approximately every 8 hours. Drain.

Slice the fish into 6 large chunks, leaving any skin on.

Pour the olive oil into a large sauté pan set over medium-low heat, add the onion, and cook for 10 minutes, or until softened and translucent.

Add the canned tomatoes to the pan, crushing them with a spoon, bring to a simmer, and simmer for 15 minutes, until the tomatoes start to break down into a sauce. If you like your tomato sauce smooth, use an immersion blender to puree it (or pour into a regular blender and puree, then return to the pan).

Add the cod pieces and season with salt and pepper to taste, then pour in the wine, increase the heat to medium, and let the wine evaporate over medium heat.

Reduce the heat to medium-low, partially cover the pan, and cook the cod for 45 minutes, checking every once in a while to make sure that the sauce hasn't thickened too much (if it has, add a few tablespoons of water as needed). The cod should be very tender.

Tear the parsley leaves into pieces with your fingers and sprinkle over the fish before serving.

VARIATIONS

- For a more flavorful sauce, add a tiny bit of anchovy paste and a crushed garlic clove to the onions at the beginning of the recipe.

- For a sweet-and-sour twist, especially at the High Holidays, add a handful of raisins and pine nuts.

- For a Southern Italian version of this dish, mix in black olives and capers.

- To make this a more substantial meal, add some thinly sliced potatoes when you add the fish to the pan and let simmer for an additional 20 minutes, or until the potatoes are tender.

Baked Anchovies and Escarole

SERVES 4

—

2 bunches escarole or curly endive

¼ cup (60 ml) olive oil

2 garlic cloves, finely minced

1 pound (450 g) fresh anchovies, cleaned, deboned, and butterflied (you can have the fishmonger prepare the fish for you), skin left on (or use frozen anchovies)

¼ teaspoon kosher salt

⅛ teaspoon freshly ground black pepper

⅛ teaspoon crushed red pepper flakes (optional)

Crunchy bread for serving

When the Jews were confined to the Ghetto in Rome from 1555 to 1570, they had to live by the laws of the pope, some of which were pretty tyrannical. In 1661, the pope ruled that the only fish allowed for consumption by the Jews of the Ghetto would be small blue fish, namely, sardines and anchovies. Confronted with such limited choices, the women of the Ghetto, whose resources were also reduced due to poverty, made the most of the ingredients they had on hand. One example of their resourcefulness is this humble but extremely tasty dish, layering fresh anchovies and greens together with garlic and spicy red pepper.

———

Preheat the oven to 350°F (180°C).

Rinse, dry, and roughly chop the escarole (or endive).

Spread 1 tablespoon of the olive oil over the bottom of a 9-by-13-inch (23 by 33 cm) baking dish. Sprinkle some of the minced garlic over the oil. Arrange most of the escarole in the baking dish. Sprinkle the remaining garlic over the escarole, then arrange the anchovy fillets over the escarole, skin side up, and arrange the remaining escarole on top. Season with the salt, pepper, and red pepper flakes, if using. Pour the remaining 3 tablespoons olive oil evenly over the top.

Cover the baking dish tightly with aluminum foil, transfer it to the oven, and bake for 15 to 20 minutes, until the greens are tender and the anchovies are soft.

Serve immediately, with some crunchy bread alongside.

Sardine and Artichoke Casserole

SERVES 4

—

Juice of 1 lemon

6 artichokes

¼ cup (60 ml) extra-virgin olive oil

1⅛ pound (500 g) fresh sardines, cleaned, deboned, and butterflied (you can have the fishmonger prepare the fish), skin left on (or use frozen sardines)

Leaves from a few sprigs of parsley, coarsely chopped

¼ teaspoon kosher salt

⅛ teaspoon freshly ground black pepper

1 tablespoon bread crumbs or matzo meal

Sardines and artichokes layered together into a casserole and baked is another classic dish of the Roman Ghetto that features the humble blue fish that the pope dictated were the only option for the Jews in 1661. Little did the pope know that when good Roman artichokes are in season, combining them with sardines makes an exceptionally tasty, wholesome meal that leaves nothing to be desired. You can also serve this as a starter.

————

Fill a large bowl with water and add the lemon juice. Working with one artichoke at a time, trim off the top and the tough outer leaves with a sharp knife. Slice the artichoke into quarters, remove the choke with a sharp spoon, and discard. Slice the quarters in half again and drop the slices into the lemon water. Once all the artichokes are cut, drain the slices and set them aside.

Preheat the oven to 350°F (180°C).

Spread half of the olive oil over the bottom of a medium baking dish. Arrange half of the artichoke slices in the bottom of the dish, then arrange half of the sardines on top of the artichokes. Sprinkle with half of the parsley, season with half of the salt and pepper, and drizzle with the remaining oil. Make one more layer of artichokes and one more of sardines. Season with the remaining salt and pepper, sprinkle with the rest of the parsley, and scatter the bread crumbs or matzo meal on top.

Bake for 30 minutes, or until the topping is golden brown. Serve hot.

TRIGLIE ALLA MOSAICA
Mosaic Red Mullet

SERVES 4

—

5 tablespoons (75 ml) extra-virgin olive oil

4 garlic cloves, crushed

One 14-ounce (400 g) can small-diced tomatoes, with their juices, or 1 pound (450 g) fresh tomatoes, cut into small dice

1 teaspoon sugar

Kosher salt and freshly ground black pepper

2¼ pounds (1 kg) red mullet (see headnote), cleaned, scaled, and filleted (have the fishmonger do this, if you like)

Leaves from a few sprigs of parsley, coarsely chopped

Triglie alla mosaica is a traditional Jewish dish from the city of Livorno, typically served on Rosh Hashanah. The recipe originated in the Sephardic Jewish community that settled in Livorno after the Inquisition, but the dish became so well known in the region that it's often called simply *triglie alla livornese*, rather than *mosaica*. However, Jews still call the dish by its original name, to honor Moses and the miracle of the parting of the Red Sea, the memories this dish is meant to evoke.

The fish are gently cooked in a very slightly sweet tomato sauce and served as a simple main dish or rich starter. If red mullet is difficult to find, try bream, red snapper, sole, sand dab, or Pacific rock cod instead.

———

Pour the olive oil into a large nonstick sauté pan or skillet set over medium heat, add the garlic, and sauté for a couple of minutes, until golden.

Add the diced tomatoes and sugar, season with salt and pepper to taste, bring to a simmer, and simmer for 10 minutes.

Add the fish fillets to the pan in one layer and cook at a gentle simmer for 10 minutes, or until they are just cooked through. Don't try to flip or move the fillets as they cook, because they are very fragile and might break.

Use a slotted spatula to transfer the fillets to serving plates. Spoon the tomato sauce over the fish and sprinkle with the chopped parsley.

Red Mullet with Raisins and Pine Nuts

SERVES 4

—

1¾ pounds (800 g) red mullet, cleaned, scaled, and filleted (you can have the fishmonger do this, if you prefer)

6 tablespoons (90 ml) extra-virgin olive oil

½ cup (120 ml) white wine vinegar

Kosher salt

⅔ cup (85 g) pine nuts, lightly toasted in a skillet

1 cup (150 g) raisins, soaked in warm water to plump and drained

Freshly ground black pepper (optional)

Red mullet with raisins and pine nuts is a traditional Roman dish that Jews serve on the eve of the Yom Kippur fast. This makes it a fairly substantial meal on its own, but on that night, it is served as a starter and is just one of the many dishes that are part of the huge meal that precedes the fast. In both Jewish Roman and Venetian cuisine, sweet-and-sour fish dishes (as well as certain others featuring fish roe) have a symbolic meaning and are believed to bring good luck. If red mullet is difficult to find, try bream, red snapper, sole, sand dab, or Pacific rock cod.

———

Preheat the oven to 350°F (180°C).

Rinse the fish well and place them in a single layer in a Dutch oven. Cover the fish with the olive oil and vinegar. Sprinkle with salt, then add the pine nuts and raisins.

Partially cover the pot and cook the mullet over medium heat for 15 minutes.

Transfer the fish to the oven and bake for 15 minutes, or until cooked through and golden. As the red mullet bakes, baste it with the cooking liquid from time to time. Should the fish start to dry out, add a few tablespoons of water to the pot.

Serve the red mullet warm or at room temperature, sprinkled with black pepper, if you like.

Fried Cod Fillets

**SERVES 2 AS A MAIN
COURSE, 4 AS A
STARTER**

—

1 pound (450 g) salt
cod fillets

1 large (50 g) egg,
separated

1½ cups (190 g)
all-purpose flour

2 tablespoons white
wine vinegar

Kosher salt

1 cup (240 ml) water

Sunflower or peanut
oil for deep-frying

Baccalà, dried salted cod, is a staple of Roman cuisine. Toss pieces of the fish in a thick batter of eggs and flour and fry it. You can serve fried cod as a starter, with nothing but a squeeze of lemon to go with it, or have it as a main course with a side of vegetables or salad.

————

Place the salt cod in a large bowl of cold water, cover with plastic wrap, and refrigerate for 2 days, draining it, rinsing it, and adding fresh water approximately every 8 hours. Drain.

In the bowl of a stand mixer fitted with the whisk attachment, or in a medium bowl using a hand mixer, whip the egg white to soft peaks, about 1 minute; set aside.

In a large bowl, whisk together 1 cup (125 g) of the flour, the egg yolk, vinegar, a pinch of salt, and the water. Fold in the egg white to lighten the batter.

Pour 1½ to 2 inches (4 to 5 cm) of oil into a large saucepan and heat over medium heat until a deep-fry thermometer reads 350°F (180°C). You can test the oil by dropping a small piece of food, such as a slice of apple, into it: if it sizzles nicely but doesn't bubble up too wildly, the oil is ready. (An apple is said to help minimize the smell of the frying oil, so I generally go for that, but any bit of food will do.)

Place the remaining ½ cup (65 g) flour in a shallow bowl. Working in batches to avoid crowding the pan, toss the cod in the flour to coat it nicely, then dip it into the batter, and add it straight to the saucepan. Fry the fish for about 5 minutes, flipping the pieces as they cook, until golden and crispy.

Drain on paper towels and sprinkle with salt before serving.

Panfried Fish Roe with Vinegar

YIELD WILL VARY (SEE HEADNOTE)

—

Extra-virgin olive oil

Roe from shad, cod, yellowtail, grouper, or another big kosher fish

Kosher salt and freshly ground black pepper

White wine vinegar

Crunchy bread for serving

Panfried fish roe is a very flavorful traditional Roman dish. This recipe involves a bit of a treasure hunt—because sourcing fish roe is not easy—but it is a breeze to make. Ask your local fishmonger to set aside for you any available roe from kosher fish such as shad, cod, yellowtail, or grouper. The bigger the sacs of roe, the better. This unusual dish is a good one to try for those who don't generally consume fish eggs or roe, because it is cooked and served hot. Try it with a fresh salad and some crunchy bread like ossi (page 327).

The number of servings will depend on the size and quantity of eggs you get. In principle, ½ pound (225 g) per person as a main or ¼ pound (110 g) per person as a starter should be plenty.

————

Choose a nonstick skillet that's large enough to accommodate all the roe in one layer and pour in enough olive oil to coat the bottom. Warm the oil for a minute over medium heat, then gently drop the roe sacs into the skillet, trying to keep them whole as much as possible. Sprinkle a pinch each of salt and pepper over the roe and pour in some vinegar. The quantity of vinegar doesn't really matter, because it will eventually evaporate, so just add it a couple of tablespoons at a time, as needed, to cook the roe and prevent it from sticking to the skillet. Let the roe sacs sear on one side, then turn them carefully. They should be fully cooked in a couple of minutes or so, depending on their size.

Serve immediately, with some crunchy bread alongside.

LATTE ISN'T ALWAYS MILK • If you speak a bit of Italian, you might wonder about the *latte*—"milk"—in the Italian name of this dish. It doesn't refer to cow's milk. This dish was originally prepared using the gonads of male fish, called *lattume*, as well; hence the dialect name *ova e latte*.

CACIUCCO LIVORNESE ALLA GIUDIA
Fish Stew

SERVES 4 TO 6

—

3 pounds (1.4 kg)
assorted fish, such
as mullet, grouper,
snapper, sea
bream, cod, and/
or porgy, cleaned
and scaled, larger
fish cut into steaks
(heads and tails
reserved), smaller
fish left whole (see
headnote)

FOR THE BROTH

2 quarts (2 L) water

⅓ cup (80 ml) dry
white wine

1 celery rib

1 onion, quartered

1 garlic clove

Scant ½ teaspoon
kosher salt

½ teaspoon black
peppercorns

Reserved fish heads
and tails (from
above)

FOR THE STEW

1 garlic clove

1 small fresh hot
chile, halved and
seeded

1 celery rib

1 onion

¼ cup (60 ml) extra-
virgin olive oil

Kosher salt

One 14.5-ounce
(410 g) can whole
tomatoes

The city of Livorno is well known for caciucco, a flavorful stew prepared with all sorts of seafood, cooked in a rich tomato sauce. The origins of the dish are hard to determine, as there are many legends surrounding it. The word *caciucco* seems to come from the Turkish word *kaçukli*, meaning "small bits and pieces," which would describe the variety of small fish and seafood in the dish. And who would have cooked a Turkish soup with inexpensive bits and pieces of fish in Livorno at the end of the sixteenth century? The Sephardic Jews. Some culinary historians believe that the dish must have originally been a humble kosher fish soup and then transformed into a nonkosher seafood stew later on. This is a kosher version of caciucco—the way it was probably prepared centuries ago—that includes a typical selection of fish and no crustaceans or shellfish.

You can have the fishmonger prepare the fish for you. Ask him to clean and scale all the fish and cut bigger fish into steaks, reserving the heads and tails; smaller fish can be left whole.

———

Refrigerate the fish while you make the broth; have the heads and tails ready for the broth.

To make the broth, in a stockpot or other large pot, combine the water, wine, celery, onion, garlic, salt, and black peppercorns, along with the reserved fish heads and tails. Bring the liquid to a boil over medium-high heat, then reduce the heat to medium and simmer for 40 minutes. Remove from the heat.

Strain the broth through a fine-mesh sieve into a saucepan; discard the solids. Set the broth aside.

To make the stew, in a food processor, finely grind the garlic, chile, celery, and onion together.

In a sauté pan or large skillet, heat the olive oil over medium heat for a few seconds. Add the ground vegetables and season with salt, then reduce the heat to low and cook for 5 minutes. Add the canned tomatoes, breaking them down with a fork, then add the tomato paste and cook for 20 minutes, to make a chunky sauce.

Add the vinegar and saffron and stir briefly. Add the fish and wine, increase the heat to medium, and simmer for a couple of minutes to evaporate the wine.

1 tablespoon tomato
 paste

1 tablespoon white
 wine vinegar

Pinch of saffron
 threads

½ cup (120 ml) dry
 white wine

Leaves from a few
 sprigs of parsley,
 chopped

FOR THE BREAD

4 slices stale
 sourdough bread

1 garlic clove

2 tablespoons extra-
 virgin olive oil

Add a few ladlefuls of the fish broth, enough to cover the fish, and cook for 30 minutes, or until the fish is cooked through, adding more broth as needed to keep the fish covered (you don't want the finished stew to be too thin, so add the broth a little at a time). Add the chopped parsley, adjust the salt to taste if necessary, and remove from the heat.

While the fish cooks, toast the bread slices and rub them well with the garlic clove. Drizzle with the olive oil and place a slice in each soup plate.

Just before serving, fillet the whole fish and return the fillets to the saucepan.

Ladle the fish stew over the garlic bread and serve hot.

Roman Fish Soup

SERVES 6

6½ cups (1.5 L) water

1 large yellow onion, quartered

1 carrot, halved

1 celery rib, halved

4½ pounds (2 kg) assorted fish (red snapper, striped bass, cod, haddock, tuna, and/ or fresh sardines), cleaned, scaled, skinned, and filleted if necessary, heads, tails, and bones reserved (see headnote)

5 tablespoons (75 ml) olive oil

2 garlic cloves, minced

3 cups (675 g) tomato puree (passata)

Pinch of crushed red pepper flakes

¾ cup (180 ml) dry white wine

¼ teaspoon kosher salt

Freshly ground black pepper

Crunchy bread for serving

Zuppa di pesce was once a specialty of only the coastal towns near Rome, but it became common in the capital—where it is still known as a local favorite—through the influence of the Jews. The Jews of the Roman Ghetto prepared the dish out of necessity and poverty, using fish scraps from the nearby fish market, and made it into a delicacy. This soup becomes a full meal when pasta is added to the broth or when it's served with crunchy bread, which can be used to scoop up the last drops of the sauce.

Ask your fishmonger to fillet the fish for you, removing the skin as well, and to reserve the heads, tails, and bones for you, as you will need them to make the fish broth.

In a stockpot or other large pot, bring the water to a rolling boil over medium-high heat. Add the onion, carrot, and celery, plus all the fish heads, tails, and bones you have, and bring to a simmer, then reduce the heat to low and simmer for a minimum of an hour, to make a flavorful, rich broth. Remove from the heat.

Strain the broth through a fine-mesh sieve into a large saucepan; discard the solids. Set the broth aside.

In a large saucepan, warm the olive oil over medium heat. Add the garlic and cook until golden, 2 to 3 minutes. Pour in the tomato puree, add the red pepper flakes, and bring to a simmer, then let simmer uncovered, stirring occasionally, for about 5 minutes.

Add the fish fillets to the pan, raise the heat to high, and pour in the wine. Season with salt and pepper to taste and cook for a couple of minutes to evaporate the alcohol, then reduce the heat to medium-low.

Cook until the tomato sauce has thickened, at least 15 minutes.

Pour the fish broth over the fish in the tomato sauce and mix gently to blend well. Serve the soup hot, with a side of crunchy bread.

The soup is best when just made, but leftovers can be stored in the refrigerator, in a bowl covered with plastic wrap or in an airtight container, for a day or two.

Manzo, vitello e agnello

BEEF, VEAL, AND LAMB

Meat Patties with Garlic and Herbs

SERVES 4 TO 6

—

1½ pounds (700 g) fatty ground beef

3 tablespoons coarsely chopped parsley, or to taste

3 garlic cloves, crushed

½ teaspoon kosher salt

Freshly ground black pepper

⅓ cup (80 ml) extra-virgin olive oil

Tomato Sauce (see page 100) for serving, warmed (optional)

Pinzette, Roman meat patties spiced with garlic and herbs and cooked in olive oil or tomato sauce, are a very homey food that comes together quickly and that everyone in your family will enjoy. They are similar to American burgers, but with a lot more flavor. They can be served as a simple main course with a salad or a side of roasted vegetables.

———

In a big bowl, mix together the ground beef, parsley, garlic, salt, and pepper to taste. Wet your hands with water and form the meat into patties: the traditional shape is the size of a flat open palm, but it's also perfectly acceptable to make smaller patties, which will cook faster. You'll want to serve 1 large or 2 smaller patties per person. Place the patties—6 to 8, depending on size—on a plate as you finish them.

In a large nonstick skillet, warm the olive oil over medium heat until hot. Add the patties, in batches if necessary to avoid overcrowding the skillet, and cook for a couple of minutes on each side, until evenly browned. Cover the pan and let the patties cook for a couple more minutes, until an instant-read thermometer inserted into one patty reads 160°F (71°C) and the juices run clear.

Serve as is, or with the tomato sauce spooned over them.

CUSCUSSÙ LIVORNESE
Couscous with Meatballs and Vegetables

SERVES 4

—

FOR THE COUSCOUS

1 cup (170 g) semolina

¼ cup (60 ml) sunflower or peanut oil

1 cup (240 ml) water

½ teaspoon kosher salt

FOR THE BEANS

⅔ cup (100 g) dried Great Northern or cannellini beans

1 cup (240 ml) beef, chicken, or vegetable broth, homemade (page 78) or store-bought

2 garlic cloves, peeled, one left whole, the other crushed

1 teaspoon kosher salt

1 tablespoon extra-virgin olive oil

1 onion, finely chopped

Half a 14-ounce (400 g) can small-diced tomatoes (reserve the rest of the can for the vegetables, below)

- ingredients continued -

Culinary historians believe that couscous was brought to Italy by the Sephardic Jews who left Morocco and Tunisia to settle in Sicily in the late fifteenth century. Called *cuscussù* in Sicilian dialect, the humble couscous became a classic accompaniment to fish soup at the tables of Sicilian Jews. It was only around the early eighteenth century that couscous arrived in Tuscany, where it was served as a side for meatballs or vegetable soups and quickly became a Shabbat staple. Today couscous is widely recognized as a dish of North African origin, but in Italy, couscous was considered Jewish food for many centuries.

This dish takes a long time to prepare but is worth every minute. If you don't have the time to make the couscous itself from scratch, you can use about 1 cup (195 g) instant couscous and cook it according to the instructions on the package.

———

To make the couscous, pour the semolina into a large shallow bowl and rub in 3 tablespoons of the oil with your fingers until thoroughly absorbed.

In a medium nonstick saucepan, combine the water, the remaining tablespoon of oil, and the salt and bring to a boil. Pour in the semolina and stir once with a spoon, then reduce the heat to low and cook for 15 minutes.

Remove the couscous from the heat and transfer it to a couscous sieve or a coarse-mesh sieve set over a bowl. Sift the couscous into the bowl to obtain a very light, fluffy texture. Set aside to cool.

To cook the beans, bring a large saucepan of water to a boil. Add the beans, reduce the heat to medium, and let them simmer for 2 minutes, then remove from the heat, cover, and let stand for 1 hour.

Transfer the beans to a colander, then rinse and drain them. Put the beans back in the saucepan, cover with the broth, and add the crushed garlic and salt. Bring to a simmer and cook for an hour, adding water if necessary, until tender.

In the meantime, pour the olive oil into a nonstick sauté pan set over medium-low heat, add the onion and the remaining garlic clove, and cook for 5 minutes, or until golden. Add the diced tomatoes and simmer for 5 minutes, then remove from the heat.

- continued -

FOR THE MEATBALLS

2 slices stale
  sourdough bread

½ pound (250 g)
  fatty ground beef

½ onion, thinly
  chopped

1 tablespoon
  chopped parsley

1 large (50 g) egg

Kosher salt and
  freshly ground
  black pepper

FOR THE VEGETABLES

3 tablespoons extra-
  virgin olive oil

1 onion, chopped

2 carrots, peeled
  and cut into
  chunks

2 zucchini, cut into
  chunks

1 celery rib, cut into
  chunks

⅔ cup (100 g) green
  peas, fresh or frozen

½ cabbage, thinly
  sliced

One 14-ounce
  (400 g) can small-
  diced tomatoes

½ cup (115 g) tomato
  puree (passata)

Kosher salt and
  freshly ground
  black pepper

When the beans are fully cooked, drain them and add them to the tomato mixture. Stir and set aside.

To prepare the meatballs, in a medium bowl, soak the bread in water to cover, then remove it from the water and squeeze out the excess liquid.

In another medium bowl, mix the ground meat, bread, onion, parsley, egg, and a pinch each of salt and pepper together. Wet your hands and make small meatballs the size of a walnut, transferring them to a plate as you shape them; you should get about 12 meatballs. Cover and refrigerate.

To cook the vegetables, pour the olive oil into a large nonstick sauté pan set over medium heat, add the onion, and cook for 2 to 3 minutes, until translucent. Add the carrots, zucchini, celery, peas, cabbage, diced tomatoes, and tomato puree and season with salt and pepper to taste. Cook for 25 minutes, or until the vegetables are soft. If necessary, add a little water, a bit at a time, to the pan.

Meanwhile, bring the pot of beans back to a simmer, add the meatballs, and simmer for 10 minutes, or until cooked through, adding a bit of water if necessary.

Place the couscous in the center of a large serving plate and cover it with the beans and meatballs, then distribute the vegetables all around in a crown. Serve, making sure each person at the table gets an even portion of all the components of the dish (couscous, beans, meatballs, and vegetables).

All the components of the dish keep well if stored separately in the fridge in individual airtight containers. Once the dish is assembled, it does not keep well, because the couscous will become soggy as it absorbs moisture from the other ingredients.

Meatballs with Spinach in Tomato Sauce

SERVES 4

1 pound (450 g) fresh spinach, cleaned, or one 10-ounce (285 g) package frozen spinach

2 cups (480 ml) beef, chicken, or vegetable broth, homemade (page 78) or store-bought

1 slice stale sourdough bread

1¼ pounds (550 g) ground beef (see Notes)

1 large (50 g) egg, lightly beaten

½ teaspoon kosher salt, or more to taste

Freshly ground black pepper

Pinch of grated nutmeg

¼ cup (60 ml) extra-virgin olive oil

1 cup (225 g) tomato puree (passata)

These meatballs are just one example of the thriftiness and creativity of the Jewish women in the Roman Ghetto: while the Romans made their meatballs with ground beef only, the Jews saved money by using less meat and adding spinach. This dish is also a great way to get children to eat a healthy dose of veggies, because the spinach is nicely hidden inside the tasty meatballs, and you can't really tell it's there when the meatballs are enrobed in the thick tomato sauce.

Bring a stockpot or other large pot of water to a boil. Add the spinach and cook for a few minutes, until tender, then drain in a colander. When the spinach has cooled, squeeze out the excess water and chop it in a food processor.

Pour the broth into a medium bowl. Add the bread and soak it in the broth to soften, then squeeze it well to remove the excess liquid.

In a large bowl, mix the beef, bread, and spinach together, then add the egg, salt, pepper to taste, and nutmeg and mix well.

With slightly wet hands, shape the mixture into meatballs the size of a walnut and place them on a plate; you should get about 30 meatballs. Let them rest in the fridge for about 5 minutes.

In a large sauté pan or skillet, heat the olive oil over medium heat for a minute or so. Working in batches to avoid crowding the pan, add the meatballs and fry them on all sides until golden, a couple of minutes.

Return all the meatballs to the pan, add the tomato puree, and cook for 15 to 20 minutes, until the tomato sauce has thickened slightly. Adjust the salt if needed and serve.

Leftover meatballs keep well keep in the fridge, in a bowl covered with plastic wrap or in an airtight container, for a couple of days. They can be reheated in a skillet or in the microwave.

NOTES

• If you prefer, you can skip frying the meatballs and just cook them in the tomato sauce. In that case, add a cup (240 ml) of water to the puree and let it come to a gentle simmer before you add the meatballs. They will take about 20 minutes to cook through.

• If you have any meat left over from preparing a pot of beef broth (page 78), you can finely grind it and use it in this recipe.

Slow-Cooked Pot Roast

SERVES 6

3 tablespoons extra-virgin olive oil

1 large onion, thinly sliced

One 2¼-pound (1 kg) beef round or chuck roast, sinew removed

One 14.5–ounce (410 g) can tomato puree (passata) or whole tomatoes

1 cup (240 ml) dry red wine (optional)

1 teaspoon kosher salt, or more to taste

½ cup (120 ml) water

Freshly ground black pepper

Stracotto, which translates as "overcooked," is a classic entry on the Shabbat menu for most Roman Jewish families, but it also works great as a make-ahead dinner option for busy weekdays. One of the reasons people love this recipe is that it actually makes two meals: slow-cooking a beef pot roast for hours in a simple but flavorful tomato sauce yields not only falling-apart tender meat but also a delicious meaty tomato sauce for a hearty plate of pasta the next day. The beef in this recipe is left to stew slowly for 3 hours; if you need to save time, you can use a pressure cooker (see the Variation).

———

Pour the olive oil into a Dutch oven set over medium heat, add the onion, and cook until translucent, about 5 minutes.

Add the beef and brown it evenly on all sides, turning it with tongs.

Pour the tomato puree and wine, if using, over the browned meat and season with the salt. Add the water, partially cover the pot, reduce the heat to low, and let simmer for about 3 hours. Every hour or so, baste the meat with its cooking liquid or turn it over. Add some water if the tomato sauce thickens too quickly. When the roast is done, add pepper to taste and, if necessary, a bit more salt to the sauce.

Lift the meat out onto a cutting board and carve it into thick slices. Arrange the meat on plates or a platter, spoon the sauce over it, and serve.

Leftover sliced meat will keep well in the fridge, in an airtight container, for up to a week. Leftover tomato sauce can be used to dress pasta, both short (such as rigatoni) and long (such as spaghetti).

NOTE

You can speed up the cooking process by using a pressure cooker and substituting small chunks of boneless beef for the roast. That turns the dish into more of a stew, but the flavor will be unchanged. Follow the recipe, using the pressure cooker, to the point of adding the water. Then make sure to cover the meat completely with water, close your pressure cooker according to the manufacturer's instructions, and let the pressure cooker heat up over medium heat until it whistles or reaches full pressure. Lower the heat to the minimum and cook for 30 minutes. Remove the pressure cooker from the heat, reduce the pressure according to the manufacturer's instructions, and remove the lid. Return the pot to the stove, uncovered, and let the tomato sauce thicken enough to coat the back of a spoon before serving.

VARIATION

You can make an even richer version of this dish by using short ribs on the bone instead of beef round or chuck.

COPPIETTUCCE
Slow-Cooked Beef in Tomato Sauce

SERVES 4

—

3 tablespoons extra-
virgin olive oil

1 garlic clove,
crushed in a press
or minced

1½ pounds (700 g)
rump cap or
boneless chuck
roast, fat trimmed
and sliced ⅓ inch
(8 mm) thick

½ teaspoon kosher
salt

Freshly ground
black pepper

¼ cup (60 ml) dry
red wine

2¼ cups (500 g)
tomato puree
(passata)

2 bay leaves

½ cup (120 ml) water

Coppiettucce are delicious slices of beef slow-cooked in tomato sauce, a dish that closely resembles Italian beef pizzaiola. Coppiettucce make for a very simple main course that comes together relatively quickly and is sure to please adults and kids alike. It is usually served with a side of fresh salad or roasted vegetables. If you visit Rome, be careful not to confuse coppiettucce with the similarly named coppiette (page 69), which are slices of dried meat.

———

In a large skillet, heat the olive oil over medium heat. When the oil begins to shimmer, stir in the garlic and let it brown a little.

Working in batches, add the beef and sear until lightly browned on both sides, about a minute per side; when all the beef has been seared, return the first batch(es) to the pan. Add the salt and pepper to taste and pour in the wine.

Once the wine has evaporated, add the tomato puree and bay leaves. Pour in the water and stir briefly to make sure all the slices of meat are coated with sauce. Partially cover, reduce the heat to low, and cook for approximately 25 minutes, turning the slices halfway through. Uncover the pan, raise the heat to medium, and cook for an additional 5 minutes, or until the meat is cooked through. Depending on the thickness of the meat slices, the cooking time may be slightly longer. In that case, add water a few tablespoons at a time if necessary while the meat finishes cooking.

Serve immediately.

BRASATO RACHELE
Beef Stew with Squash

SERVES 4 TO 6

—

1 kabocha or butternut squash (about 1 pound/ 450 g)

5 tablespoons (75 ml) extra-virgin olive oil

2 onions, thinly sliced

2¼ pounds (1 kg) boneless beef sirloin, cut into ½-inch (1 cm) cubes

1 cup (240 ml) dry white wine

½ teaspoon kosher salt, or more to taste

About 2 cups (500 ml) beef, chicken, or vegetable broth, homemade (page 78) or store-bought

Freshly ground black pepper

As it often happens with dishes that have been passed down from generation to generation, nobody today has a clue who Rachele was (other than perhaps the Biblical matriarch), but her recipe for a delicious beef stew with squash lives on. The stew is often prepared for Rosh Hashanah because squash symbolizes hope for a sweet year ahead.

———

Peel and halve the squash. Remove all the seeds and fibers, then cut the squash into ½-inch (1 cm) cubes.

Pour the olive oil into a Dutch oven set over medium heat, add the onions, and cook until soft and translucent, about 5 minutes. Add the meat and brown it well on all sides, about 10 minutes.

Add the wine, squash, salt, and enough broth to cover all the ingredients. Bring the liquid to a boil, then cover the pan, reduce the heat to low, and simmer gently until the meat is tender and the squash is falling apart into a puree, 1 to 1½ hours. Season with more salt if necessary and pepper to taste and serve.

VARIATIONS

- The Jews of Veneto prepare a similar dish, stufadin de zuca zala, with only a couple of small tweaks: veal is used instead of beef, rosemary is added, and a sweet wine like Marsala is substituted for the dry one.

- You can also cook the beef in one piece and then slice it to serve, which is how brasato is traditionally prepared in Italy, but I find that the stew pieces come out juicier and tastier than a whole roast.

Beef Stew in Carrot and Wine Sauce

SERVES 4

———

2¼ pounds (1 kg) boneless beef chuck, cut into 1½-inch (4 cm) cubes (see Note)

1½ cups (360 ml) dry red wine

⅓ cup (80 ml) extra-virgin olive oil

¾ cup (165 g) tomato puree (passata)

2 carrots, peeled and cut in half

2 celery ribs, cut in half

1 small onion, quartered

Pinch of ground cloves

1 teaspoon kosher salt, plus more to taste

Freshly ground black pepper

Among the Shabbat dishes that the Jews of Piedmont have borrowed from their local Italian neighbors, brasato is one of the most delicious, and the most fitting for the holiday. This rich beef stew can simmer for hours on end and be reheated as needed, and it only gets better with time, so it works well as a dinner option for those who like to prepare their weekday meals ahead of schedule. Serve it with the Shabbat yellow rice (page 233), for a festive dinner. You can slow-cook the dish in a Dutch oven, or make it in a pressure cooker to save time.

————

In a Dutch oven, combine the beef, wine, olive oil, tomato puree, carrots, celery, onion, cloves, salt, and pepper to taste. Pour in enough water to cover all the ingredients and bring to a simmer over medium heat, then reduce the heat to medium-low, partially cover, and cook, adding water if needed to keep the ingredients covered, for 2 to 2½ hours, until the meat is tender.

With a slotted spoon, lift the beef from the pot and set aside on a platter.

Using an immersion blender, blend the contents of the pot to obtain a smooth, liquid sauce. Or transfer the ingredients to a regular blender and blend to a sauce, then return to the pot.

Place the meat back in the pot, bring just to a simmer, and simmer for a few minutes, until the sauce thickens enough to coat the meat. Adjust the salt to taste and serve.

NOTE

You can cook the beef in one piece and then slice it to serve, which is how brasato is traditionally presented in Italy, but I find that the stew pieces come out juicier and tastier than a whole roast.

Brisket with Beans and Chard

SERVES 6 TO 8

—

6 tablespoons
   (90 ml) extra-virgin
   olive oil

2¼ pounds (1 kg)
   fresh chard or
   spinach, trimmed

3 cups (550 g) dried
   cannellini beans,
   soaked overnight
   in water to cover

2¼ pounds (1 kg)
   brisket

1⅛ pounds (500 g)
   lean ground beef

5 tablespoons (30 g)
   bread crumbs, or
   more if needed

2 large (100 g) eggs,
   beaten

Kosher salt and
   freshly ground
   black pepper

1 cup (240 ml) water

4 to 6 beef sausages

2 hard-boiled
   eggs, peeled and
   quartered

Other than the candles and challah on the table, nothing contributes more to the Shabbat atmosphere than a pot of stew simmering in the kitchen. And every Jewish community in the world has a slow-cooked stew with beans in its culinary tradition. This recipe comes from Florence, home to one of the oldest continuous Jewish communities in Europe. It is a slightly laborious recipe, as it also includes meatballs and sausages, but you'll be rewarded with the most delicate, fall-apart meat you have ever tasted.

———

Pour 2 tablespoons of the olive oil into a large nonstick skillet set over medium heat, add the chard or spinach, and cook for 3 minutes. When the leaves begin to wilt, cover the skillet, increase the heat to medium-high, and cook for about 4 minutes. Remove from the heat and set aside.

In a large Dutch oven, heat 2 more tablespoons of the olive oil over medium heat. Add the beans, cover with water, and bring to a simmer, then reduce the heat slightly and let the beans simmer for an hour.

Add the greens and then the brisket and cook over very low heat for least 3 hours, or up to 6 hours, adding water as needed to keep the ingredients from drying out.

In the meantime, prepare the meatballs: In a medium bowl, mix the ground beef, bread crumbs, beaten eggs, ½ teaspoon salt, and a pinch of pepper together. You should have a mixture that can be shaped into small balls; if it is too soft to shape, mix in more bread crumbs.

With wet hands, shape the mixture into meatballs about the size of a walnut and place on a plate. You should have about 25 meatballs.

In a medium saucepan, combine the water and the remaining 2 tablespoons olive oil and bring to a simmer over medium heat.

Add the meatballs to the simmering liquid and cook for a few minutes, just so that they will retain their shape. Drain.

When the brisket is cooked, lift it from the pot, transfer it to a cutting board, and cut it into large chunks.

Add the meatballs and sausages to the pot, season with salt and pepper to taste, and stir gently to mix everything together. Let cook for about 10 minutes, and return the brisket to the pot.

To serve, arrange some chard and beans in the bottom of each serving dish and top with some of the brisket, plus slices of sausage, as desired, and some meatballs. Garnish with the hard-boiled eggs and serve.

Beef-Stuffed Cabbage Rolls

SERVES 4 TO 6

—

1 Savoy cabbage

Kosher salt

1 onion

Leaves from a few sprigs of parsley

1 pound (450 g) fatty ground beef

2 tablespoons bread crumbs or matzo crumbs

Kosher salt and freshly ground black pepper

Pinch of grated nutmeg

2 cups (480 ml) beef, chicken, or vegetable broth, homemade (page 78) or store-bought

In Northern Italy, Jews and Christians alike prepare stuffed cabbage rolls in the winter, as they make great comfort food for cold days. Christians use ground pork and grated cheese in the filling, while Jews use ground beef. Capunet is often served for the holidays of Sukkot and Simchat Torah, as the little rolls, when served in pairs, look like a Torah scroll.

Serve the capunet on its own or with a side of risotto (page 135).

———

Peel away and discard the outer leaves of the cabbage if they are anything but perfect. Bring a large pot of water to a rolling boil, then add 1 tablespoon salt and the cabbage and blanch for 3 to 4 minutes. Drain the cabbage, pat it dry with a clean kitchen towel, and let cool to room temperature.

In the meantime, finely chop the onion and parsley. Transfer to a bowl, add the ground beef, bread crumbs, a generous pinch each of salt and pepper, and the nutmeg, and mix well with your hands.

With your fingers, carefully peel off the cabbage leaves, trying your best to avoid tearing them. Should some of the leaves have large, thick center ribs, trim them away with a knife.

Put one leaf on your clean work surface, rib side up, and place some of the meat filling at the base of the leaf, leaving enough room on either side of the leaf so that you can comfortably fold it over without the filling spilling out. Fold the left and right sides of the leaf over the meat mixture, then fold up the bottom of the leaf over the filling and roll up into a compact cylinder; the tighter the roll, the better. Repeat with the remaining leaves.

If you have any leftover meat, you can shape it into small balls and add them to the saucepan with the cabbage rolls. If, on the other hand, you have leftover cabbage leaves, layer them in the bottom of the saucepan before adding the cabbage rolls.

Gently place all the cabbage rolls, seam side down, in a single layer in a large saucepan, arranging them snugly one against the other to minimize the chance of their opening while cooking.

Cover the rolls with the broth and let them cook over very low heat for 1½ hours, adding more water a bit at a time, if necessary.

Serve the capunet hot or at room temperature.

Leftovers can be kept in the fridge, in an airtight container, for a couple of days. They can be reheated in a saucepan or in the microwave.

CODA ALLA VACCINARA
Stewed Oxtail

SERVES 4

—

4½ pounds (2 kg) oxtail pieces

3 tablespoons extra-virgin olive oil

1 carrot, peeled and finely diced

1 small onion, peeled and finely diced

4 celery ribs, 2 finely diced, 2 cut into chunks

1 bay leaf

1½ teaspoons dried marjoram

½ cup (120 ml) dry white wine

3⅓ cups (750 g) tomato puree (passata)

½ teaspoon kosher salt

Freshly ground black pepper

2 tablespoons raisins

2 heaping tablespoons pine nuts

¼ teaspoon unsweetened cocoa powder

A typical dish of Roman *cucina povera* ("cooking of the poor"), oxtail is part of what we call the *quinto quarto* (the "fifth quarter"; see page 136), the less desirable cuts of meat that are left after all the better ones have been sold. Although it's inexpensive, oxtail becomes a deliciously rich main dish when slow-cooked for a long time. Thanks to the long unattended cooking time it requires, stewed oxtail has turned into a favorite Shabbat dish.

Like stracotto (page 186), this dish will actually make two meals: serve it one day, and then pull the meat off the leftover oxtails the next day and turn it into a chunky Bolognese sauce to go with pasta, or tuck the meat inside fried rice balls (page 64).

———

Put the oxtail pieces in a colander and rinse several times under cold water, until the water runs clear.

Bring about 3 quarts (2.8 L) water to a boil in a stockpot or other large pot and add the oxtail. Remove the pot from the heat and leave the meat in the water for 10 minutes, then drain.

Pour the olive oil into a large pot set over medium heat, add the carrot, onion, and finely diced celery, and cook, stirring frequently, until soft, about 10 minutes. Add the oxtail and sear the pieces on all sides until browned, about 5 minutes.

Add the bay leaf and marjoram, then pour in the wine and let it evaporate, stirring often. Add the tomato puree and season with the salt and pepper to taste. Add water to cover the meat and bring to a simmer, then reduce the heat to low and cook over low heat for about 2½ hours, until the meat is falling off the bone.

In the meantime, bring a medium saucepan of water to a boil. Add the chunks of celery and cook for a few minutes, until soft, then drain.

Add the cooked celery, raisins, and pine nuts to the cooked oxtails. Transfer a few ladlefuls of the sauce to a small bowl and add the cocoa, stirring until it is dissolved, then add to the pot with the meat, stirring well, and cook for 10 more minutes. Serve.

Leftovers keep well in the fridge, in a bowl covered with plastic wrap or in an airtight container, for a couple of days. They can be reheated in a saucepan or in the microwave.

Sukkot and Simchat Torah

Sukkot is the celebration of the harvest. It marks the end of the agricultural season, when farmers, after a year of work struggling against the elements of nature, finally have their granaries, warehouses, and cellars filled with the harvest. At the end of Sukkot, we celebrate the holiday of Simchat Torah, the day when the weekly reading of the Bible starts over from the very beginning of the book.

Sukkot

On Sukkot, Jews recall the huts where our ancestors lived for forty years in the desert, after fleeing from Egypt. The huts are a symbol of the precariousness of life but also, above all, of the protection God has given to the people of Israel.

The most important requirement of this holiday is to spend time in a sukkah, a replica of the huts the Jews lived in during their years in the desert: people gather in the sukkah to eat their meals and, where possible, even to sleep.

Unlike in the United States, though, where many people live in houses with a yard and can build their own sukkah there, in Italy we generally live in apartment buildings. Most Jews therefore have a very communal experience of Sukkot, as we gather to celebrate the holiday in shared huts located outside local synagogues or other Jewish institutions.

In Italy, women prepare and bring to the sukkah trays of food to distribute to friends and neighbors. This is why many traditional Sukkot specialties—such as the fried cookie bites called castagnole (page 313), the fried chickpeas called *ceci spassatempi* (page 57), and the traditional hand pies called *buricche* (page 43)—seem designed for packing and for sharing.

Other traditional Sukkot dishes include risotto with candied citron (page 135) and chicken in tomato and bell pepper sauce (page 144), as well as the classic labor-intensive-but-amazing capunet (page 195), beef-stuffed cabbage rolls.

Simchat Torah

While the food prepared for this holiday pretty much overlaps with the foods prepared for Sukkot (cabbage rolls being the most notable example), there is a cute tradition that distinguishes Simchat Torah: while the men dance and pray joyfully around the Torah scrolls, the women throw candies and chocolates from their section of the synagogue over toward the men's section, and children run to collect them. The "crop" is often quite rich, comparable to that of Halloween for American kids.

SCALOPPINE CON LA LATTUGA
Veal Scaloppine with Lettuce

SERVES 4

—

1 head butterhead or Bibb lettuce

3 tablespoons all-purpose flour

1 pound (450 g) thin veal cutlets

6 tablespoons (90 ml) extra-virgin olive oil

1 cup (240 ml) beef, chicken, or vegetable broth, homemade (page 78) or store-bought

⅓ teaspoon kosher salt

Freshly ground black pepper

Roman Jews seem to have a fascination with cooking salad greens, maybe because salad has always been readily available and very inexpensive in Italian farmers' markets. This dish, which is traditionally prepared for Sukkot, is a great way to use up any lettuce that has been sitting in your fridge a little too long; layered with veal cutlets, the greens have a second chance to shine, even if they're past their prime.

———

Separate the lettuce leaves, discarding any outer ones that look unappealing. Wash and pat dry.

Spread the flour in a shallow bowl. Dredge the veal slices in the flour, shaking off the excess, and put on a plate.

Pour ¼ cup (60 ml) of the olive oil into a large skillet set over medium heat. Add the veal slices, in batches to avoid crowding, and cook on both sides for a few minutes, until browned. Transfer the veal to a plate as it is browned, and set aside to cool.

Preheat the oven to 400°F (200°C).

Grease a deep baking dish with 1 tablespoon of the remaining olive oil and arrange half of the veal cutlets in a single layer in it, fitting them snugly into the dish. Cover the veal cutlets with half of the lettuce, then top with the remaining veal cutlets, followed by a layer of the remaining lettuce. Ladle the broth on top. Season with the remaining tablespoon of olive oil, the salt, and pepper to taste. Bake for about 20 minutes, until heated through. Serve hot.

ARROTOLATO DI VITELLO RIPIENO
Veal Roulade

SERVES 6

—

¼ cup (60 ml) extra-virgin olive oil

6 large (300 g) eggs

Kosher salt

5 chicken livers

One 3-pound (1.4 kg) boneless veal breast roast

Freshly ground black pepper

3 medium zucchini, thinly sliced lengthwise

1 garlic clove

This roulade is a breast of veal roast stuffed with zucchini and chicken livers. Like other traditional holiday dishes, it can be served hot or cold, accompanied by roasted vegetables or a salad. The recipe may be a vestige of the days when people didn't worry about their cholesterol (eggs *and* liver in a single meal), but it is nutritious and satisfying. Make it on special occasions when you want to indulge.

———

Preheat the broiler.

In a medium nonstick skillet, heat 1 tablespoon of the olive oil over medium heat. Break the eggs into the pan, season with salt, and scramble the eggs. When they are fully set, remove from the heat and let cool.

Place the chicken livers on the broiler pan, season with salt, and broil for 5 to 7 minutes. Turn the livers over and broil for another 5 to 7 minutes, or until cooked through and no longer pink inside. Set the livers aside to cool, then cut them into ½-inch (1 cm) chunks.

Place a sheet of heavy-duty plastic wrap on a large work surface, place the veal breast on top, and cover with more plastic wrap. Using a mallet, pound the veal breast until it is an even thickness of ½ inch (1 cm) or thinner. (You could also have your butcher do this for you.) Season the veal with salt and pepper to taste.

Layer the sliced zucchini on top of the veal, leaving a border of about 1 inch (3 cm) on all sides. Cover the zucchini with the scrambled eggs and arrange the chicken livers on top of everything.

Gently roll the meat up into a cylinder and tie the roll securely at 1-inch (3 cm) intervals with kitchen string.

In a Dutch oven or a large nonstick saucepan, heat the remaining 3 tablespoons olive oil over medium heat. Add the garlic and cook for a minute or two to flavor the oil. Add the roulade and sear on all sides until nicely browned, 1 to 2 minutes per side.

Add a cup (240 ml) of water to the pot and let simmer over medium-low heat for 40 minutes.

Transfer the roulade to a cutting board, cover it loosely with aluminum foil, and let rest for about 10 minutes.

Using a sharp knife, cut the veal crosswise into slices about ½ inch (1 cm) thick, removing the strings as you cut. Arrange the slices on a platter and serve hot or at room temperature.

ARROSTO DI VITELLO CON PATATE
Veal Roast with Potatoes

SERVES 4

2¼ pounds (1 kg) potatoes

6 tablespoons (90 ml) extra-virgin olive oil

2 sprigs rosemary

2 garlic cloves, peeled

Kosher salt and freshly ground black pepper

One 1⅓-pound (600 g) boneless lean veal roast

5 tablespoons (75 ml) dry white wine

When the holiday season comes around and you have to prepare multiple festive meals, one of the simplest make-ahead dishes is a veal roast. It's a wonderful option for a celebratory dinner, not only because it is tender and delicious but also because it freezes very well. The veal can be prepared days or weeks ahead, sliced, and stored in the freezer, then thawed on the day it needs to be served. Just reheat the pan juices, pour them over the slices of veal, and bring straight to the table.

———

Preheat the oven to 400°F (200°C).

Peel the potatoes and cut into cubes. Place them in a bowl, add 3 tablespoons of the olive oil, 1 rosemary sprig, the garlic, and salt and pepper to taste, and toss until the potatoes are well coated.

Transfer the potatoes to a roasting pan and spread out into one layer. Bake the potatoes for 20 minutes.

Meanwhile, tie the veal roast with twine if the butcher has not already done so. Slip the remaining sprig of rosemary under the twine to secure it to the roast.

In a large saucepan or a pot, heat the remaining 3 tablespoons olive oil over high heat. Add the veal roast and sear for a minute or so on each side to brown nicely.

Once the meat is browned on all sides, pour in the wine and let it evaporate for a couple of minutes.

Transfer the roast to the roasting pan, placing it in the middle of the potatoes. Pour the meat juices from the saucepan over the roast.

Roast the veal for 35 minutes, or until an instant-read thermometer inserted in the center reads 149°F (65°C). Let the roast rest for 10 to 15 minutes before slicing and serving with the potatoes.

Leftovers keep well in the fridge, in a bowl covered with plastic wrap or in an airtight container, for a couple of days. They can be reheated on the stovetop or in a microwave.

NOTE

If you are planning to freeze the veal after roasting, cook it on its own and then make the potatoes separately on the day you are serving the dish.

Veal with Lemon, Parsley, and Anchovy Sauce

SERVES 6

—

½ cup (65 g) all-purpose flour

One 3-pound (1.4 kg) boneless veal shoulder roast

3 tablespoons extra-virgin olive oil

2 garlic cloves

1 cup (240 ml) dry white wine

4 carrots, peeled and cut into big chunks

1 onion, roughly chopped

6 oil-packed anchovy fillets

Juice of ½ lemon

Leaves from a few sprigs of parsley, chopped

Kosher salt

Many generations of Italian Jews are familiar with this recipe, but nobody today knows if there was at some point in history an actual Rebecca who came up with the dish or if it is an homage to the famous Rebecca of the Bible, one of the matriarchs of Israel. The veal roast features a sauce made with lemon, parsley, and anchovy, a combination reminiscent of the Piedmontese salsa verde (see page 159), which goes well with many foods, whether meat or fish.

———

Place the flour in a large shallow dish and roll the veal roast in it to coat it completely.

In a Dutch oven or other large heavy pot, heat the olive oil over medium-high heat. Add the garlic cloves and let them sizzle for a minute or so, then add the meat and sear it for 1 to 2 minutes on each side, until it is nicely golden brown all over. Remove the roast to a plate.

With the heat still on medium-high, pour in the wine to deglaze the pot, scraping the browned bits up from the bottom with a whisk and stirring well for a minute. Place the roast back in the pot and pour in enough water to cover the meat halfway.

Add the carrots, onion, anchovies, lemon juice, and parsley. Add a pinch or so of salt, but don't overdo it; the anchovies will be salty enough. Bring to a simmer, then reduce the heat to low, cover the pot, and let the roast simmer for 2 hours, or until the meat is tender and fully cooked—a thermometer inserted in the center should read 160°F (71°C). Remove the meat from the pot and set it aside on a platter.

Use an immersion blender to blend the liquid and vegetables into a sauce (or transfer to an upright blender and blend well).

Slice the roast as thin as possible and serve with the sauce poured over the top.

MIXING MEAT AND FISH • This recipe can spark controversy about whether it is kosher, because it includes both veal and anchovies. Many Orthodox communities in Europe and the United States don't mix meat and fish. Until some years ago, Italian Jews were allowed to eat meat and fish together in the same dish. But, in recent years, the Rabbinate has decided to uphold the prohibition, so religious Italian Jews have had to stop eating dishes that mix meat and fish. You decide if this dish is right for you.

ALBONDIGA
Veal Meatloaf

SERVES 6 TO 8

—

3⅓ pounds (1.5 kg) ground veal

2 tablespoons raisins, soaked in warm water to plump, drained, and squeezed dry

1 tablespoon chopped tarragon

2 teaspoons ground fennel

¼ teaspoon ground cloves

½ teaspoon ground cinnamon

½ teaspoon kosher salt

4 hard-boiled-egg yolks

1 cup (240 ml) water

Rounded ¼ teaspoon grated nutmeg

Pinch of saffron threads

Crunchy bread for serving

Although *albondigas* is the Spanish word for "meatballs," the Jews of Ferrara used *albondiga* as the term for a single large meatloaf. This recipe calls for flavorful herbs and spices to complement the veal, which results in a very unusual, tasty meatloaf. Serve with crunchy bread and, if you like, a fresh salad on the side.

———

In a large bowl, mix the ground veal, raisins, tarragon, fennel, cloves, cinnamon, and salt together.

Place the mixture on a work surface and divide it in half. Shape each portion into a log. With your fingers, make 4 indentations in each log, spacing them evenly, then place the egg yolks in the indentations in one log. Place the other log, indentation side down, on top of the first one and press them together to form a meatloaf, with the egg yolks stuffed inside.

In a Dutch oven, bring the water to a boil over medium heat, then add the nutmeg and saffron. Place the meatloaf in the pot, reduce the heat to low, cover, and cook for 1½ hours, or until cooked through and firm.

Serve the meatloaf warm, with crunchy bread.

Lamb Roast with Potatoes

SERVES 4 TO 6

—

One 4-pound
(1.8 kg) leg of
lamb (or use lamb
shoulder)

Leaves from 1 bunch
rosemary

3 garlic cloves

Leaves from 1 bunch
sage

½ cup plus
2 tablespoons
(150 ml) extra-
virgin olive oil

1 teaspoon kosher
salt

Freshly ground
black pepper

2½ pounds (1.1 kg)
potatoes

1 cup (240 ml) dry
white wine

You can find this roast in virtually every restaurant in Rome. While it is not a Jewish dish by origin, it has become a classic Passover main course because it features lamb, one of the foods commonly served on the holiday. It is also much appreciated as a Shabbat meal option, since the roasted lamb can be reheated easily.

———

Using a sharp knife, make deep cuts at 1-inch (3 cm) intervals across the lamb, cutting through almost to the bone. Set aside.

Reserve a few rosemary leaves for roasting the lamb. Finely mince the garlic, the remaining rosemary, and sage, then transfer to a small bowl and add half of the olive oil. Rub the mixture all over the lamb, pushing the herbs deep into the cuts. Season the meat with ½ teaspoon of the salt and black pepper to taste. Let the lamb rest while you prepare the potatoes. (*The lamb can rest overnight, covered, in the fridge. Remove the lamb from the refrigerator 1 hour before cooking.*)

Preheat the oven to 350°F (180°C). Line a baking sheet with aluminum foil.

Peel the potatoes and chop into small chunks. Place the potatoes on the prepared pan, sprinkle them with the remaining ½ teaspoon salt, drizzle with the remaining olive oil, and toss to coat. Sprinkle with the reserved rosemary.

Place the leg of lamb on the baking sheet, arranging the potatoes around it, and roast for about 1 hour, until a thermometer inserted into the center of the roast reads 149 to 160°F (65 to 71°C). Halfway through the cooking time, after roughly 30 minutes, pour the wine over the lamb and turn the potatoes with a spoon so they brown evenly.

When the lamb is done, remove it from the oven, cover it with aluminum foil, and let it rest for 15 to 20 minutes.

Carve the lamb into thick slices and serve with the potatoes; drizzle the pan juices over the meat.

Passover Lamb with Artichokes and Fava Beans

SERVES 4

—

½ cup plus 2 tablespoons (150 ml) extra-virgin olive oil

1 onion, minced

5 garlic cloves, minced

2¼ pounds (1 kg) mixed cuts of lamb

½ cup (120 ml) dry white wine

Kosher salt

Freshly ground black pepper

2 lemons, halved

10 medium artichokes

20 to 30 fresh fava beans in the pod (see headnote)

Delicate fava beans and hearty artichokes are both at the peak of their season in Italy when it's Passover time. If fresh fava beans are not available, frozen shelled beans work too. If you have fresh fava beans, consider removing the individual beans from their skins. It's not essential, but the dish looks much neater.

———

Pour the olive oil into a Dutch oven set over medium-high heat, add the onion and garlic, and cook until tender, 4 to 5 minutes.

Working in batches, add the lamb and sear, turning occasionally, until browned all over; transfer the lamb to a plate as it is browned.

Return all the lamb to the pot and add the wine, ½ teaspoon salt, and pepper to taste. Simmer to let the wine evaporate, then add enough cold water to cover the meat. Bring to a simmer, then reduce the heat to low, partially cover the pot, and simmer until the meat is just tender, 30 to 45 minutes.

Meanwhile, fill a large bowl with water and squeeze in the juice of 1 lemon. Working with one artichoke at a time, remove the tough outer leaves, then cut off the top and peel the stem. Quarter the artichoke lengthwise, remove the choke with a sharp teaspoon, and place in the lemon water. Set the artichokes aside.

Bring a pot of salted water to a boil. Add the fava beans and blanch for 1 minute, then drain and let cool.

To shell the fava beans, break through the pod of each one at the dimpled point at the inside curve of the bean with a knife, then squeeze the other end of the shell to pop out the favas. If desired, split the skins and pop out the beans.

When the lamb is just tender, increase the heat to medium and bring the liquid to a boil. Drain the artichokes and add the artichokes and fava beans to the pot. Squeeze in the juice of the remaining lemon and cook until the artichokes are tender, approximately 15 minutes. Remove the pot from the heat.

Season the dish generously with salt and pepper and let rest for a few minutes before serving.

Leftovers can be saved in the fridge, tightly covered, then reheated and served the next day.

Turin and Piedmont

Piedmont, the northwestern Italian region west of Lombardy, bordered on three sides by the Alps, has an interesting Jewish history. The capital city of Turin is where most of the Jewish community currently resides. It's the third-largest Jewish population in Italy, with approximately twelve hundred residents. But there are also myriad cute little towns in the countryside, such as Casale Monferrato, Vercelli, Alessandria, Asti, Carmagnola, Cherasco, Cuneo, Ivrea, Mondovì, and Saluzzo, that were once home to small Jewish congregations. It's possible, with a bit of planning, to visit the old synagogues and cemeteries in these towns.

The first evidence of a Jewish presence in Piedmont dates back to the early fifteenth century, and it seems to be linked to the expulsion of the Jews from France in 1394. The earliest traces of Jews in Turin date back to 1424, when, according to local regulations at the time, the Statuta Sabaudiae of Amedeo VIII, there was a rigid separation between Jews and Christians. Jews had to wear a distinctive yellow symbol, but they did enjoy religious freedom.

In the sixteenth century, growth of the Piedmontese Jewish communities was driven by the expulsion of the Jews from Spain. Coming from the coastal regions of southern France, from Provence, and, through more complicated itineraries, from Germany, large groups of Jews arrived in Piedmont in search of both safety and business opportunities.

The Counter-Reformation marked the start of a sharp worsening of the situation of the Jews in Piedmont. In 1679, Maria Giovanna Battista di Savoia-Nemours decreed that all the Jews of Turin had to take up residence in a specific area, thus creating the first Piedmontese ghetto. After the War of the Spanish Succession in 1723, the strict rules of Vittorio Amedeo II further worsened the socioeconomic situation of the Jews in Piedmont, who fell into a state of misery.

The gates of the ghetto were not demolished until the Napoleonic occupation in 1800, and the emancipation of the Jews followed nearly fifty years later. After emancipation, the Jews of Turin celebrated by starting the construction of a grand new synagogue. That building was never in fact used as a synagogue, but it was later turned into the impressive Mole Antonelliana, one of the major sights of the city.

In the twentieth century, the passing of the racial laws in 1938 and then the tragedy of the Shoah took a heavy toll on the Jews of Piedmont; almost four hundred Jews were transported from Turin alone.

Today the Turin community runs the only Jewish school in the country, a unique model of cultural integration in the multiethnic quarter of San Salvario, where children of all religions are admitted to study.

Visit San Salvario to enjoy scrumptious kosher baked goods from Bertino bakery or great ice cream from Mara dei Boschi. Not far from the Jewish neighborhood, those who don't

CLOCKWISE FROM TOP LEFT: *The facade of the synagogue in Vercelli; the facade of the synagogue in Turin; the interior of the synagogue in Casale Monferrato.*

keep kosher should check out the restaurants Scannabue and Osteria dell'Oca. In most restaurants in town, you can find local specialties such as bagna cauda (page 35), bonet (page 243), and brasato (pages 189 and 191).

Travelers to Turin can explore the synagogue, the semi-preserved ghetto, and the sixteenth-century cemeteries. However, and more important,

you can also take a day trip to Casale Monferrato and Vercelli, to visit the stunning synagogues these two towns boast. Casale Monferrato has a Piedmontese Baroque temple, in use since 1599, adjacent to the Museum of Jewish Art and Ancient History, while Vercelli has an enormous synagogue with a domed ceiling and stained-glass windows that date back to 1878.

Contorni

SIDES

Roasted Tomatoes

SERVES 4

---

12 ripe tomatoes, preferably Casalino (see Notes)

½ cup (120 ml) extra-virgin olive oil

¼ teaspoon kosher salt, plus more to taste

Freshly ground black pepper

1 to 2 tablespoons finely minced garlic

Leaves from a few sprigs of parsley, roughly chopped (see Notes)

A special variety of tomato, called Casalino, hails from Southern Italy, especially the region between Naples and Rome. If you are able to get your hands on some Casalino tomatoes, just know that you will never want to eat any other variety of tomato again. These tomatoes are irresistible raw, but they are also the key ingredient in this delicious side dish of simple roasted tomatoes.

Preheat the oven to 400°F (200°C).

Cut the tomatoes crosswise in half. Use your fingers to dig out and discard most of the seeds.

Pour half of the olive oil into the bottom of a baking dish, then place the tomato halves cut side up in the dish, arranging them close to one another. Drizzle with the remaining olive oil and sprinkle with the salt and pepper to taste. Sprinkle the garlic and parsley on top.

Bake for 25 to 30 minutes, until the tomatoes are slightly charred and very soft. Serve hot or at room temperature.

Although the tomatoes will keep in the fridge, covered, for a few days, they are best served straight from the oven. To use up any leftovers, try sandwiching them with sliced mozzarella for a Caprese-style panini.

NOTES

• Casalino tomatoes should be easy to spot among the fancy heirloom tomatoes at the farmers' market, because they look like very small beefsteak tomatoes, pleated tightly and irregularly ruffled; they have thick skin and a very firm pulp. For a substitute, in terms of flavor, look for tomatoes that are sweet but pleasantly tangy and tart, almost salty (because of the qualities of the soil where they grow, usually sandy places near the sea). Most of the time, Casalino tomatoes are sold slightly unripe and a bit green, which is particularly desirable if you want to eat them in a salad.

• Basil or oregano can be substituted for the parsley.

TORZELLI
Fried Escarole

SERVES 4

—

4 heads escarole (or curly endive)

6 tablespoons (90 ml) extra-virgin olive oil

Kosher salt and freshly ground black pepper

If you are not a salad or greens lover, give fried escarole (or curly endive, which will work too!) a chance to make you change your mind. Frying the greens takes away some of their bitterness and gives them a pleasant crispiness. If you want to bake the escarole instead of frying it, see the Variations.

Fried escarole is usually served for Rosh Hashanah, along with Red Mullet with Raisins and Pine Nuts (page 168), but because it's fried, it also makes for a great Hanukkah side dish.

———

Bring a large pot of water to a boil over high heat. Add the whole escarole (or curly endive) heads and blanch for about 1 minute, just long enough to soften the leaves slightly. Drain and let cool.

Cut the heads of escarole in half or into quarters, depending on the size. Squeeze out the excess water with your hands and set the escarole aside to drain and dry on a clean kitchen towel.

In a large skillet, warm ¼ cup (60 ml) of the olive oil in a large skillet over high heat. Place the escarole halves in the pan cut sides down (work in batches if necessary, then return all the escarole to the pan) and cook for 10 minutes, or until golden brown.

When the escarole is cooked, season with salt and pepper to taste and drizzle with the remaining 2 tablespoons olive oil. Serve warm.

VARIATIONS

- To bake the escarole, preheat the oven to 350°F (180°C). Pour ¼ cup (60 ml) extra-virgin olive oil into a baking dish. Place the escarole cut side down in the dish and bake until golden brown, about 10 minutes.

- Some people make a deep-fried version of this dish: In a shallow bowl, beat 2 large (100 g) eggs with ¼ cup (60 ml) water; spread some flour in another shallow bowl. Coat the escarole in the egg mixture and then in flour before frying in abundant olive oil.

Hanukkah

Hanukkah, the eight-day Festival of Lights, usually falls around the
time when Christians are celebrating Christmas. During Hanukkah,
we honor a miracle that occurred thousands of years ago,
in 165 BCE, in Israel.

Jerusalem was then under the rule of Antiochus IV Epiphanes of Syria, a cruel and tyrannical ruler.

Judas Maccabeus became the leader of a Jewish rebellion against Antiochus that reconquered the temple, which had been taken over and profaned by the king's army. Entering the temple to rededicate it, the Jews had to light the menorah, but they found only a small amount of oil, enough to last for just one day. However, that oil burned for eight days.

In memory of the miracle of the oil, at Hanukkah we light candles in our homes for eight consecutive evenings, and we eat foods fried in oil. Italian Jews don't generally eat latke —panfried grated-potato pancakes—on Hanukkah, as American Jews do, because those fritters are more of an Ashkenazi tradition. However, we do eat bomboloni (page 276), decadent doughnuts stuffed with pastry cream that are very similar to the Israeli sufganiyot.

Other Hanukkah dishes include golden fried chicken (page 152), the fried vegetables called *pezzetti fritti* (page 63), and concia (page 46), a Roman starter of fried zucchini with garlic and herbs.

As for nonfried foods, a typical Italian Hanukkah meal might be risotto with raisins (page 135), while crostata di ricotta e visciole (page 263)—ricotta and sour cherry tart—makes a great Hanukkah dessert. In many families, there is a custom of braiding challah bread (page 323) in the shape of an elaborate hanukiah, the nine-branch candelabra used to light candles during the holiday.

Dandelion Greens with Bottarga

SERVES 4

2¼ pounds (1 kg) dandelion greens

¼ cup (60 ml) extra-virgin olive oil

2 garlic cloves, crushed

½ teaspoon crushed red pepper flakes (optional)

1 teaspoon kosher salt

Juice of ½ lemon

3 tablespoons grated bottarga (see Resources, page 340)

Salty cured bottarga makes everything taste better, be it pasta (page 107) or vegetables. In this recipe, it's paired with dandelion greens to make a peppery, pleasantly bitter side dish. Dandelion greens are often considered just a salad ingredient, but they are great cooked too. Here they are turned into a side dish that also doubles as a sandwich filling for crunchy bread, such as ossi (page 327), or topping for pizza bianca (page 328).

Wash the dandelion greens well under cold running water. Bring a big pot of water to a boil over high heat. Drop the dandelion greens into the pot, reduce the heat to medium, and cook for 10 minutes. Drain in a colander and let cool to room temperature.

Squeeze the dandelion greens, trying to pack them tightly in your hands, to remove excess water.

Pour the olive oil into a large skillet set over medium-low heat, add the garlic and red pepper flakes, if using, and cook until the garlic is golden. Add the dandelion greens, season with the salt, and cook for about 10 minutes, stirring often.

Right before serving, stir the lemon juice into the greens and sprinkle the grated bottarga over the top. Serve warm.

Spinach with Pine Nuts and Raisins

SERVES 4

—

½ cup (60 g) raisins

2 pounds (900 g) fresh spinach, trimmed

3 tablespoons extra-virgin olive oil

½ onion, finely chopped

2 tablespoons pine nuts

Kosher salt and freshly ground black pepper

Among the many ingredients that have been paired with the unmistakably Jewish combination of pine nuts and raisins, spinach is one of the favorites. This dish, which is considered a Jewish Venetian specialty, makes a great starter or side dish for the holidays. It is often served on Rosh Hashanah, because raisins and pine nuts are supposed to bring abundance and good luck for the coming year. The same custom exists for many Roman Jewish families.

————

Drop the raisins into a small bowl filled with warm water and let soak until plumped.

Put the spinach in a large saucepan, add ½ cup (120 ml) water, cover, and cook over low heat for a few minutes, until wilted. (Italians tend to cook food longer than people do in the United States or the United Kingdom, so it's OK if the spinach is really cooked and even a bit mushy.) Drain in a colander, let cool, and then squeeze well to remove the excess water. Set aside.

In a medium saucepan, heat the olive oil over medium heat. Add the onion and cook until tender and translucent, about 5 minutes.

In the meantime, in a small skillet, toast the pine nuts over medium heat until they are gently browned, about a minute; be careful not to burn them. Remove from the heat and set aside.

Drain the raisins and pat dry.

Add the spinach, pine nuts, and raisins to the onions, season with salt and pepper to taste, and stir well to combine. Serve warm or at room temperature.

FAGIOLINI A CORALLO
Green Beans in Tomato Sauce

SERVES 6

---

2 pounds (900 g)
Romano beans
(see headnote)

6 tablespoons
(90 ml) extra-virgin
olive oil

1 onion, thinly sliced

1 pound (450 g)
canned whole
tomatoes

Kosher salt and
freshly ground
black pepper

Leaves from a few
sprigs of parsley,
chopped (optional)

Fagiolini a corallo, which translates as "coral beans," are long, flat beans (called Romano beans in the United States and piattoni in Italy) cooked in tomato sauce. They are called *corallo* in this dish because they resemble red and green coral when cooked. Serve this as part of your dinner when these beans are in season (during the spring and summer), or swap in regular fresh or frozen green beans any time of year.

———

Trim the ends of the beans and pull off any strings.

Pour the olive oil into a large nonstick saucepan set over medium heat, add the onion, and cook until soft and translucent, about 10 minutes. Add the tomatoes, breaking them up with a wooden spoon, and cook for 10 minutes, stirring occasionally.

Add the beans, season with salt and pepper, reduce the heat to low, cover, and cook for about 25 minutes, adding a few tablespoons of water if the sauce thickens too much, until the beans are soft.

Sprinkle the chopped parsley over the beans, if desired, and serve.

CAROTE SOFEGAE
Sweet-and-Sour Braised Carrots

SERVES 4

—

¼ cup (60 ml) extra-virgin olive oil

1 onion, thinly sliced

12 to 15 medium carrots, peeled and sliced into coins

Kosher salt and freshly ground black pepper

A handful of raisins, soaked in hot water to plump and drained

A handful of pine nuts

¼ cup (60 ml) red wine vinegar

Carote sofegae, which translates as "suffocated carrots," is a traditional Jewish Venetian side dish that is cooked very slowly. The sweet-and-sour preparation includes raisins and pine nuts—signature Jewish Italian ingredients—as well as vinegar. Carrot dishes like this have been eaten by Jews since the Middle Ages, especially for the holiday of Rosh Hashanah: the carrots were believed to bring prosperity for the New Year, as they resemble gold coins.

———

Pour the olive oil into a large nonstick saucepan set over medium heat, add the onion, and cook for 5 minutes, then add a few tablespoons of water and cook for 5 more minutes, until the onion is soft.

Add the carrots to the pan, season with salt and pepper, and stir. Reduce the heat to the lowest setting, add ¼ cup (60 ml) water, cover, and cook, stirring once, until the carrots begin to soften, about 10 minutes.

Increase the heat to medium and cook the carrots, uncovered, for 15 minutes, or until they start turning golden. Add the raisins and pine nuts and cook for about 10 more minutes, pouring in a bit of additional water if needed, until the carrots are very soft.

Add the vinegar and simmer for 2 minutes. Serve the carrots hot or at room temperature.

NOTE

In the Jewish Italian culinary tradition, there are a variety of vegetables that are braised with vinegar like these carrots, such as eggplant, Savoy cabbage, collard greens, and green beans. Feel free to use this technique to experiment!

Eggplant and Vegetable Stew

3 eggplants

Kosher salt

1½ onions

2 celery ribs

5 cherry tomatoes

¼ cup (60 ml) extra-virgin olive oil

2 garlic cloves, smashed

1 cup (200 g) chopped ripe tomatoes or canned diced tomatoes, with their liquid

2 tablespoons mixed black and green olives, pitted

1 tablespoon capers

½ cup (120 ml) white wine vinegar

1 tablespoon sugar

Sunflower or peanut oil for deep-frying

Freshly ground black pepper

5 basil leaves

Caponata is somewhere between a cooked salad and a vegetarian stew that vaguely resembles ratatouille. It's one of the most ancient preparations of Sicilian cuisine, and it likely has Jewish origins, indicated by the presence of eggplant in the dish. As you slowly cook the eggplant with tomatoes, celery, olives, capers, and herbs, it all turns into a savory, briny mix, one that tastes even better the next day.

———

Cut the eggplants into ¾-inch (2 cm) cubes. Transfer them to a colander, salt generously, weight them down with a plate, and let drain for 30 minutes in the kitchen sink.

Cut the half onion into very thin slices. Cut the whole onion into chunks roughly the same size as the eggplant cubes. Cut the celery into chunks and cut the cherry tomatoes in half.

Pour the olive oil into a large nonstick skillet set over medium heat, add the sliced onion and garlic, and cook for about 3 minutes, until the garlic is slightly browned. Add the celery, tomatoes (both cherry and chopped), olives, capers, and the chopped onion to the pan and cook for 10 minutes, until the vegetables begin to soften. Add the vinegar and sugar and cook for another 10 minutes. Remove from the heat.

Remove the plate covering the eggplant and squeeze the eggplant in the colander to remove any remaining liquid.

Pour 1 inch (3 cm) of sunflower or peanut oil into a large saucepan and warm over medium heat until a deep-fry thermometer reads 350°F (180°C). You can test the oil by dropping a small piece of food, such as a slice of apple, into it: if it sizzles nicely but doesn't bubble up too wildly, the oil is ready. (An apple is said to help minimize the smell of the frying oil, so I generally go for that, but any bit of food will do.)

Add only as many eggplant cubes to the pan as will fit in a single layer without crowding and fry until golden, turning often. Remove the eggplant with a slotted spoon and spread out on a paper towel–lined plate to drain. Cook the remaining eggplant cubes in the same manner, adding more oil if needed.

- continued -

Once the fried eggplant has drained, add it to the pot of vegetables. Season with ½ teaspoon salt and pepper to taste, adding a bit of water if the vegetables look dry, and cook the caponata over medium heat, stirring frequently, for 5 minutes.

Stir in the basil leaves, remove from the heat, and let the caponata cool to room temperature before serving.

Caponata keeps well in the fridge, in a bowl covered with plastic wrap or in an airtight container, for 3 to 5 days; it can also be frozen. Leftovers can also be used to dress pasta, in which case, add either grated Parmesan cheese or mozzarella, torn into small pieces, to the caponata.

CONTORNO DI PISELLI E CARCIOFI
Peas and Artichokes

SERVES 4

—

8 artichokes

½ lemon

5 tablespoons (75 ml) extra-virgin olive oil

1 onion, finely chopped

4¼ cups (600 g) peas

Leaves from a few sprigs of parsley, finely chopped

Kosher salt and freshly ground black pepper

Peas and artichokes is a simple vegetarian side dish that is often seen on the tables of Jews whose families came from Urbino, in the Marche region. The sweetness of the peas complements the bitterness of the artichokes, creating a perfectly balanced side to any meal. The dish is typically prepared in the spring, when peas and artichokes are in season, but you can use frozen artichoke quarters and frozen peas if necessary.

———

Cut off the dry tip of the stem of one artichoke and peel it with a vegetable peeler. Cut off the top one-third of the artichoke leaves and squeeze a bit of lemon juice over the cut areas to prevent browning. Using kitchen shears, trim off the remaining thistles on the points of the outer leaves. Gently open up the artichoke by pressing on it to open out the leaves and rinse it very well under cold water. Repeat with the remaining artichokes. Cut the artichokes into quarters (or eighths, if you prefer) and remove and discard the hairy chokes.

In a large saucepan, heat 3 tablespoons of the olive oil over medium heat. Add the artichokes and sear for a couple of minutes, stirring them gently so the quarters don't break apart. Add water to cover, bring to a simmer, and braise the artichokes until tender, 20 to 25 minutes. Drain.

In the meantime, pour the remaining 2 tablespoons olive oil into a medium saucepan set over medium heat, add the onion, and cook for a few minutes, until translucent, then stir in the peas. Add water to cover and simmer until all the water has evaporated and the peas are tender.

Mix the artichoke quarters into the peas. Add the parsley and stir well, then season with salt and pepper to taste. Serve warm or at room temperature.

ZUCCA SFRANTA
Herbed Pumpkin Spread

SERVES 4 TO 6

—

One 3-pound (1.4 kg) sugar pumpkin or kabocha squash

3 tablespoons extra-virgin olive oil

1 onion, thinly sliced

A handful of basil leaves, torn into pieces

Leaves from 2 sprigs parsley, coarsely chopped

Scant 1 teaspoon kosher salt

Freshly ground black pepper

Crunchy bread for serving

Pumpkins and squash are specialties of Emilia-Romagna, where the locals harvest great quantities of them in the fall, so it's no wonder those seasonal ingredients are used in this dish to celebrate the end of the Yom Kippur fast.

The spread can be served both as a side dish and as a starter, with some crunchy bread or crackers to go with it.

———

Cut the pumpkin or squash in half. Scoop out and discard the seeds and fibers. Cut the pumpkin (or squash) into thick slices and peel each slice with a vegetable peeler. Chop the slices into cubes.

Transfer the pumpkin to a deep nonstick skillet, add 2 cups (480 ml) water, and set over medium heat. Add the olive oil, onion, basil, parsley, salt, and pepper to taste, cover, and cook for 25 to 30 minutes, stirring occasionally, until the pumpkin is falling apart and can be mashed with a fork. Add a little additional water if necessary to finish the cooking.

Mash the pumpkin to a coarse but creamy spread and serve hot or at room temperature, with crunchy bread alongside.

VARIATION

This dish can be made savory or sweet. In Venice, the sweet version goes by the name of *succa desfada*. It includes candied citron and is prepared for Rosh Hashanah.

Stuffed Tomatoes with Rice

SERVES 4

—

4 large beefsteak tomatoes or large tomatoes on the vine

1¼ cups (300 ml) extra-virgin olive oil

Kosher salt

2 medium potatoes

Three 10-ounce (285 g) cans tomato puree (passata)

1 bunch basil, leaves removed and torn into pieces

¾ cup (150 g) Arborio rice (see Note)

There is written evidence in the form of a *carme*—a poem—about Jewish cuisine dating to as far back as the beginning of the nineteenth century that the Jews of Rome were renowned for this specialty, tomatoes stuffed with rice. To this day, especially in the summer, these tomatoes often grace the Shabbat tables of Roman Jewish families.

———

Slice off the tops of the tomatoes and refrigerate the tops to use later. Scoop out the insides of the tomatoes, reserving the pulp, seeds, and juices. Put a tablespoon of olive oil and a pinch of salt inside each tomato and set aside in the fridge.

Transfer the reserved tomato pulp and juices to a blender. Blend well to obtain a smooth liquid.

Peel the potatoes and cut into small cubes. Place them in a 10-by-13-inch (25 by 33 cm) baking dish, or any baking dish large enough to accommodate the tomatoes and potatoes comfortably. Toss the potatoes with 2 tablespoons of the olive oil to coat them nicely.

In a big bowl, mix the blended tomato mixture, tomato puree, ½ teaspoon salt, the basil, rice, and the remaining olive oil. Let sit for a minimum of 30 minutes on the counter, or up to overnight in the fridge; the rice will soften and expand over time.

Preheat the oven to 350°F (180°C).

Remove the tomatoes from the fridge and fill with the rice-tomato mixture. Cover with the reserved tomato tops.

Place the stuffed tomatoes on top of the potatoes and bake for approximately 40 minutes, until the tomatoes are gently browned on top and the potatoes are golden. If you like your tomatoes slightly charred, turn on the broiler and broil for about 5 minutes.

NOTE

To reduce anxiety over the timing needed for the rice to cook to perfection, you can use parboiled rice (such as Ben's Original), which will prevent the rice from being under- or overcooked.

RISO GIALLO DEL SABATO
Yellow Rice for Shabbat

SERVES 4

—

3 tablespoons extra-virgin olive oil

1 large onion, cut into very small dice

2 cups (400 g) Carnaroli or Arborio rice

1 cup (240 ml) dry white wine

½ teaspoon kosher salt

4 cups (1 L) chicken broth, homemade (page 78) or store-bought, or as needed

3 pinches saffron threads or 1 packet saffron powder

This rice, a specialty of the cities of Ferrara and Venice, is usually prepared for Shabbat, and it is believed to be the predecessor of risotto alla milanese. It is similar to traditional Italian risotto, but it differs slightly as it lacks cheese and butter. It makes a perfect side dish to most roasts and stews. In particular, it nicely complements both stracotto (page 186) and brasato (pages 189 and 191).

———

Pour the olive oil into a large saucepan set over medium heat, add the diced onion, and cook until softened and translucent, about 5 minutes.

Stir in the rice and cook, stirring, for about 3 minutes, to toast it nicely. Add the wine, season with the salt, and stir constantly until the wine has evaporated, about 5 minutes.

Add half of the broth and the saffron, turn the heat to high, and bring the broth to a simmer, then lower the heat to maintain a steady simmer. Once the broth has evaporated, add the remaining broth and continue stirring until the rice is very creamy; taste a couple grains of rice to be sure it is cooked perfectly—it should be soft but not at all mushy. If the rice is still a bit crunchy, add more water a little at a time and continue to cook and stir for another couple of minutes. When the rice is done, remove it from the heat.

Transfer the rice to a baking dish and let it come to room temperature, then cover and refrigerate. The rice can be reheated on a hot plate as needed on Friday night or at Saturday lunchtime, and it can also be served at room temperature with a spoonful of plain tomato sauce (see page 100) or with pan juices from a roast (page 186).

THE GOLDEN STEM · The city of Milan is home to the famous risotto alla milanese, a delicious creamy rice dish that gets its golden color from saffron. However, some culinary historians believe that the true origins of the dish are found elsewhere. While saffron was known to the population of Italy at the time of the Roman Empire, it had almost fallen into oblivion until the Middle Ages. The rediscovery of saffron in Europe in the late fifteenth century can generally be attributed to the Spanish presence in the Mediterranean in that period, but it is likely that some of the precious gold stamens were brought to Italy by Sephardic Jews who were expelled from Spain and settled in Lombardy and Veneto, in the northern part of the country.

Rome and Lazio

Rome has the longest continuously inhabited Jewish settlement in the world; in fact, Jews have been a fixture of Roman culture for well over two millennia. The first Jews came to Rome from Israel in 161 BCE to ask for Rome's protection in Judea against the Syrian King Antiochus; some of them then settled there, creating the first-ever community of the Diaspora.

Relations between the Jewish immigrants and Roman emperors varied, but they were often favorable. According to the Latin writer Svetonio, the Jews of Rome were treated kindly by Caesar, and when he was assassinated, in 44 BCE, they stood vigil at his tomb. His successor, Augustus, scheduled grain distributions so that they would not conflict with the Jewish Shabbat.

Despite the favors they enjoyed in the capital, though, the Jews in Palestine often clashed with the Roman Empire. Indeed, many Roman Jews were originally captured as slaves during the Roman-Jewish Wars in Palestine from 66 to 73 CE and 132 to 135 CE. In 212, the emperor Caracalla allowed Jews in Rome to become Italian citizens, which solidified their foothold in the region. As many as twelve synagogues were built in Rome over the first and second centuries, though none has survived until today.

The prosperity enjoyed by the Jews in Rome ended when Constantine the Great converted to Christianity in the fourth century CE and began limiting the rights of Jewish citizens who refused to convert. Jewish synagogues were systematically destroyed, and by the Middle Ages, any gains Jews had made in the Roman Empire had vanished.

As Rome was the seat of the Catholic papacy, the Jews became subject to the whims of the popes. Some popes were sympathetic (such as Leo X, who did not require Jews to wear identifying badges and sanctioned a Hebrew printing press), but others levied taxes and imposed restrictions on civil rights.

In 1555, Pope Paul IV forced the Jews to be segregated into ghettos. The Roman Ghetto was established in the area called Portico d'Ottavia, and it lasted for more than three hundred years.

In 1870, when Italy was united under King Victor Emmanuel, the ghettos were dismantled and Jews were given full citizenship. By the beginning of the twentieth century, the population of Jews was well integrated into Roman culture. And by the 1930s, almost forty-eight thousand Jews were living in Rome.

The subsequent Nazi occupation of Rome was catastrophic: more than a thousand citizens were deported in October 1943, and many more were subsequently rounded up and sent to their deaths. There was a mass murder in the Fosse Ardeatine quarry in 1944. Despite these tremendous losses, however, about 80 percent of Roman Jews survived the Holocaust.

Today Rome has a Jewish population of about fifteen thousand and more than a dozen synagogues. One of them, the synagogue of Ostia Antica, is among the oldest in the world, dating back to the fourth century.

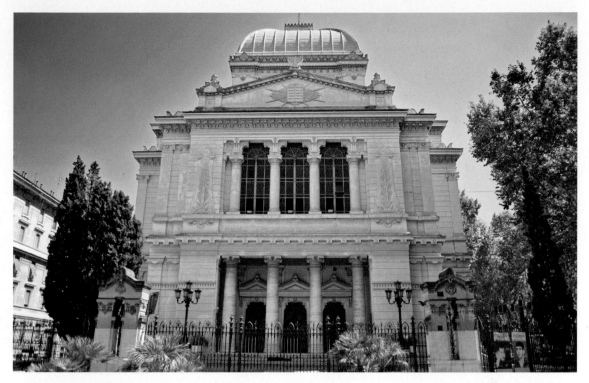

The Great Synagogue of Rome

Most of Roman Jewish life centers around what the locals call the Piazza, the former Ghetto. Around the corner from the amazing synagogue of Tempio Maggiore and the Jewish Museum, tourists can walk through a small maze of streets to find a Jewish school, a kosher butcher, a Judaica store, and a number of irresistible kosher restaurants and bakeries. While some Jews have moved to other parts of town, the Ghetto is still the beating heart of the Jewish community of Rome, a place to hang out, pray, shop, and, more important, eat.

In the Ghetto, you can enjoy a delicious kosher meal featuring all the traditional foods of *cucina ebraica romanesca* (Jewish Roman cuisine) in the many restaurants around the piazza, such as Bellacarne, Ba Ghetto, and Taverna del Ghetto. Some of the notable dishes they serve include carciofi alla giudia (page 59), concia (page 46), aliciotti con indivia (page 165), pezzetti fritti (page 63), abbacchio (page 205), and pomodori a mezzo (page 212).

Make sure to stop at Boccione, a tiny nondescript pastry shop that has been run by the same family for the last three hundred years. Boccione is where I stock up on delicious cookies, such as pizza de beridde (page 284) and ginetti (page 289), and amazing cakes and other pastries (including the crostata di ricotta e visciole, page 263).

For a casual kosher meal, you can get a great burger at Fonzie or a slice of crunchy pizza bianca (page 328) at Antico Forno Urbani. Or venture outside the Ghetto to dine at Little Tripoli, which serves the foods that the Jews of Libya brought with them to Rome, such as spicy hraimi (page 72).

If you don't keep kosher, try Felice al Testaccio, for amazing traditional pastas and abbacchio (page 205); Flavio Al Velavevodetto, for equally great pasta, as well as excellent meat dishes such as coda alla vaccinara (page 196) and pollo ai peperoni (see page 144); and, last but not least, the bakery and restaurant of the Roscioli brothers, whose high-quality ingredients make most items on the menu truly outstanding.

Dolci

DESSERTS

Quince, Two Ways

In the Jewish Italian culinary tradition, quinces appear on our table twice a year. They are prepared for Rosh Hashanah, as one of the foods that receive a blessing during the seder, and for Sukkot, when they are eaten under the sukkah, usually in the form of jelly or jam, along with the traditional bollo buns (page 333), sweet rolls with raisins.

You can serve the candied quinces and the quince jelly on their own, with ice cream as a dessert, or to complement a cheese board.

Candied Quinces

**MAKES ABOUT
12 PIECES**

—

1 pound (450 g)
quinces
(about 3 big ones)

2 cups (480 ml)
water

1¼ cups (250 g)
sugar

1 teaspoon fresh
lemon juice

Peel the quinces (save the skin to make jelly; recipe follows), cut them into quarters, and remove the cores. (Quinces can be really difficult to cut up. Should that be the case, blanch them in boiling water for about 2 minutes to soften them before slicing them.)

In a medium saucepan, combine the water and sugar and heat over medium heat, stirring gently, until the sugar dissolves. Add the quinces and lemon juice, reduce the heat to low, and simmer the quinces in their sugar syrup for about 2 hours. Don't stir while the quinces cook, but gently rotate the pot occasionally to ensure the quinces are evenly coated in syrup.

When the quinces are ready, they will have turned a deep red, and the sugar syrup will have reduced to a thick liquid. Candied quinces should be chewy and somewhat wobbly. If they don't seem to be ready and the syrup seems too thick, add a few tablespoons of water and cook for a bit longer. Remove from the heat and let cool.

The candied quinces can be stored in their syrup in an airtight container in the refrigerator for up to a week.

Quince Jelly

**MAKES FIVE
8-OUNCE (240 ML)
JARS**

—

3½ pounds (1.6 kg)
quinces

7 cups (1.7 L) water

About 4½ cups
(900 g) sugar

Wash the quinces, then core and quarter them; leave the skin on. (Quinces can be really difficult to cut up. Should that be the case, blanch them in boiling water for about 2 minutes to soften them before slicing them.)

Put the quinces in a large saucepan and add the water. If you have reserved quince skins left from making candied quinces (opposite), add them to the saucepan. Bring to a boil over high heat, reduce the heat to low, cover, and simmer for 45 minutes to 1 hour, until the quince pieces are soft.

Line a large sieve with a clean kitchen towel and set it over a bowl. With a potato masher, mash the quinces until they have the consistency of slightly runny applesauce.

Transfer the mashed quince to the lined sieve, then squeeze the mash to release as much juice as possible (do this in batches if necessary). Let the quinces drain for 3 to 4 hours.

Measure the amount of juice you have gathered, and measure out an equal amount of sugar, approximately as listed in the ingredients. Discard the mashed quince or save it for another use.

In a large heavy saucepan, combine the juice and sugar and bring to a boil over medium heat, stirring constantly until the sugar is dissolved. Attach a candy thermometer to the side of the pan. As the jelly cooks, skim off the foam that comes to the surface with a slotted spoon. When the temperature reaches approximately 212°F (100°C), pour the jelly into sterile jars and seal, following the instructions below.

The jelly will keep for 6 months to a year in properly sealed sterile jars. If you do not want to can the jelly, it is best consumed within a week; keep refrigerated.

TO PRESERVE JELLY: Preheat the oven to 325°F (160°C). Wash the jars in hot soapy water and rinse, but don't dry. Place the jars on a baking sheet and leave them in the oven for 10 minutes. Meanwhile, soak the lids in boiling water for a few minutes.

- Ladle the hot jelly into the jars, leaving about a ¼-inch (6 mm) headspace at the top.

- While they are still hot, cover the jars with their lids. Flip the closed jars upside down and let come to room temperature.

- A properly sealed jar lid will not spring up when you press down on the center of it. If the lid springs up when you lift your finger, the jar will need to be boiled before it can be stored safely.

Charoset

MAKES ⅔ POUND
(1.2 KG)

2 cups (200 g)
walnuts

1½ cups (200 g)
blanched whole
almonds

1½ cups (200 g)
hazelnuts

¾ cup (100 g) pine
nuts

½ cup (50 g)
pistachios

1¼ cups (300 g)
pitted dried dates

⅔ cup (100 g)
golden raisins

1 Golden Delicious
apple, peeled,
quartered, and
cored

Vegetable oil if
needed

Pinch of grated
nutmeg

Scant ½ cup (100 ml)
orange juice

Every Jewish family has its own way of preparing charoset, the sweet paste made of fruits and nuts that is eaten at the Passover Seder, so there are probably as many recipes for it as there are Jews out there. This is my family recipe, along with variations for other versions of charoset that are popular in Italy.

This recipe makes a large amount, but don't let that stop you. After Passover, you can eat leftover charoset as a protein snack, adding pantry ingredients such as oats or cookie crumbs to turn the paste into balls.

———

Combine the walnuts, almonds, hazelnuts, pine nuts, and pistachios in a food processor and grind to a coarse powder. Transfer to a large bowl and set aside.

Put the dates and raisins in a bowl filled with hot water and let soften for 10 minutes, then drain. In the meantime, puree the apple in the food processor.

Once the dates and raisins have softened, add them to the food processor with the apple puree and process to make a smooth paste. If the dates are too sticky, add a bit of vegetable oil to ease the processing.

Add the fruit puree to the ground nuts and mix together, then add the nutmeg and stir well. Stir in the orange juice a little at a time to make a thick paste; it should be thick enough to hold a shape.

The charoset can be transferred to a jar or rolled into small balls for serving. It can be stored in the refrigerator for up to a week.

VARIATIONS

- Some families, especially in Piedmont, add boiled chestnuts as well as chopped hard-boiled eggs to their charoset.

- Some versions of charoset include pears in addition to apples.

- Common spice additions include cinnamon, ginger, and cloves.

- Some recipes call for mixing the paste with dry or sweet white wine instead of orange juice.

BRUSCATELLA E ZABAIONE
Bread Pudding with Zabaione

SERVES 4

—

FOR THE BREAD

8 to 10 slices stale sandwich bread, preferably challah (page 323)

1 tablespoon sugar

1 tablespoon ground cinnamon

Pinch of ground cloves

1 cup (240 ml) strong red wine (such as Barolo, Barbera, or Dolcetto)

FOR THE CUSTARD

8 large (152 g) egg yolks

½ cup plus 2 tablespoons (150 ml) dry Marsala (or other dessert wine)

½ cup (100 g) sugar

Bruscatella is a very humble dish that the Jews of Central and Northern Italy prepare to break the Yom Kippur fast. It is a simple bread pudding, sprinkled with sugar and cinnamon and soaked in sweet wine. Zabaione (sometimes spelled zabaglione), a creamy custard similar in taste to eggnog, turns the humble pudding—which is not even baked!—into an irresistible dessert.

————

Toast the bread slices in a toaster or a low oven until crisp. Remove from the heat.

In a small bowl, mix together the sugar, cinnamon, and cloves.

Arrange 4 slices of the toast in a baking dish, sprinkle them with half of the cinnamon-sugar mixture, and moisten them with ½ cup (120 ml) of the wine. Make a second layer using the remaining ingredients and same procedure. Let the soaked bread rest for the duration of the fast (or overnight).

To make the custard, combine the egg yolks, wine, and sugar in a large heatproof bowl. To prepare a bain-marie, set the bowl over a large saucepan filled with simmering water.

Using a handheld mixer on low speed, or a whisk, beat the egg mixture until it thickens slightly, 5 to 8 minutes. If you have a digital thermometer, the custard should reach 149 to 158°F (65 to 70°C). Be careful not to overheat the custard, because at around 169°F (76°C), the eggs will scramble and the zabaione will curdle!

Once the zabaione is ready, remove the bowl from the heat and let cool to room temperature. (*The zabaione can be made in advance and refrigerated until ready to serve.*)

Serve 2 slices of soaked bread per person on small dessert plates, and top each with a generous spoonful of zabaione.

Zabaione keeps well in the fridge in a bowl covered with plastic wrap or in an airtight container for a couple of days, but bruscatella should be served straightaway after its resting time.

BONET

Chocolate and Amaretti Flan

SERVES 10

—

FOR THE CARAMEL

¾ cup (150 g) sugar

1 tablespoon water

FOR THE CUSTARD

2 cups (480 ml) whole milk

⅔ cup (50 g) unsweetened cocoa powder

4 large (200 g) eggs

½ cup (100 g) sugar

4 teaspoons amaretto (optional)

Heaping ½ cup (60 g) crumbled store-bought amaretti

This delicious chocolate and amaretti flan is a perfect make-ahead dessert for Shabbat, but you can also have it for a refreshing Passover treat, as it's entirely flourless. It hails from the Piedmont region in Northern Italy, where it's served in most restaurants to end a meal on a sweet note.

————

Preheat the oven to 300°F (150°C). Set out ten 4- or 5-ounce (120 or 150 ml) ramekins.

To make the caramel, in a small heavy saucepan, heat the sugar with the water over medium-low heat; stir gently and briefly with a whisk to dissolve the sugar, then leave the sugar alone to turn into an amber syrup. (A candy thermometer should read 338°F/170°C.)

As soon as the caramel is ready, quickly divide it among the ramekins, tilting the ramekins so that the bottoms and lower part of the sides are covered. Transfer to a roasting pan and set aside.

To make the custard, pour the milk into a medium saucepan, then sift in the cocoa; whisk well to remove all lumps. Bring the milk to a simmer over low heat.

In the meantime, in a large bowl, using a handheld mixer, beat the eggs and sugar together until fluffy, about 3 minutes. Slowly pour the warm milk into the egg mixture, beating constantly. If using the liqueur, add it now. Add the crumbled amaretti and mix well.

Divide the custard evenly among the ramekins. Pour enough boiling water into the roasting pan to come one-third to halfway up the sides of the ramekins.

Slide the pan into the oven and bake for 30 for 35 minutes. The tops of the flans should feel set when you touch the center with a finger, but the flans should still jiggle slightly when shaken. Remove the ramekins from the water bath and let cool.

Cover the top of each ramekin with plastic wrap and put the flans in the fridge for at least 4 hours, or overnight, to set completely.

To serve, remove the plastic wrap, run a knife around the edges of each ramekin, and carefully turn the flan out onto a plate. If you don't feel confident enough to flip the ramekins, by all means just serve the flans in their ramekins instead.

Bonet keeps well in the fridge, covered with plastic wrap, for 2 to 3 days.

MOUSSE AL CIOCCOLATO
Chocolate Mousse

SERVES 10

—

10½ ounces (300 g) dark chocolate, preferably 60 to 70% cacao

6 large (300 g) eggs (see Note), separated

Chocolate shavings, for decoration (optional)

One of my go-to recipes for a quick and satisfying pareve (dairy-free) dessert is my grandmother's chocolate mousse. I don't like recipes that call for milk substitutes to make a recipe pareve, because the results often end up being a disappointment. Instead, you can make this chocolate mousse with just two ingredients: fresh eggs and good-quality dark chocolate. The mousse can be easily turned into a flourless chocolate cake as well; see page 259.

Pick a chocolate that's dark but not too dark, like one with a 60 to 70% cacao content. A lower percentage will still work; a higher one will not work well. This mousse is rich, so it's best served in small portions.

———

Break up or chop the chocolate and place it in a heatproof bowl. Set the bowl over a saucepan of barely simmering water and allow the chocolate to melt, stirring occasionally. Once the chocolate has melted, remove it from the heat and let cool until tepid.

In the meantime, put the egg yolks in a large bowl. In the bowl of a stand mixer fitted with the whisk attachment, or in a large bowl, using a handheld mixer, whip the egg whites to very firm peaks, about 5 minutes.

When the chocolate has cooled, pour it into the bowl with the egg yolks and whisk well. Using a rubber spatula, stir in about one-third of the egg whites to lighten the mixture. Carefully spoon another third of the egg whites on top of the chocolate mixture and gently fold them in (do not stir). Add the remaining whites, folding just until the egg whites are incorporated.

Spoon the mixture into ten 4- or 5-ounce (120 or 150 ml) ramekins or small coffee cups. Refrigerate for at least 2 hours, or overnight, until set.

Serve the mousse cold, decorated with chocolate shavings, if desired.

NOTE

If you're pregnant or want to avoid eating uncooked eggs for another reason, you can buy pasteurized egg whites and use regular egg yolks but "pasteurize" them at home with the chocolate. It's easy: just cook the egg and chocolate mixture over very low heat, stirring constantly, until a candy thermometer reads 149°F (65°C), then set aside to cool before proceeding. To get pasteurized egg whites to form stiff peaks, add a splash of lemon juice or a pinch of cream of tartar to the bowl.

Passover Chocolate Mousse Cake

MAKES ONE 10-INCH (25 CM) ROUND CAKE; SERVES 8 TO 10

—

10½ ounces (300 g) dark chocolate, preferably 60 to 70% cacao

6 tablespoons (90 g) unsalted butter or margarine

6 large (300 g) eggs (see Note, page 245), separated

¼ cup plus 3 tablespoons (90 g) sugar

Chocolate shavings, for decoration (optional)

With a small tweak of the ingredients—that is, the addition of butter (or margarine) and some sugar—the chocolate mousse on page 245 can be turned into a superb flourless chocolate mousse cake. I have yet to find someone who doesn't go crazy for this cake at the first bite.

What makes the cake so special is its texture: the egg whites make the base of the cake fluffy, like a chocolate pillow, and the top of the cake is rich and creamy, thanks to the egg yolks.

———

Preheat the oven to 350°F (180°C). Line the bottom of a 9-inch (23 cm) springform pan with parchment paper.

Break up or chop the chocolate and place it in a heatproof bowl with the butter or margarine. Set the bowl over a saucepan of barely simmering water and allow the chocolate and butter to melt, stirring occasionally. When everything has melted, remove from the heat and let cool to room temperature.

In the meantime, put the egg yolks in a large bowl. In the bowl of a stand mixer fitted with the whisk attachment, or in a large bowl, using a handheld mixer, whip the egg whites to very firm peaks, about 5 minutes.

When the melted chocolate mixture has cooled, add it to the egg yolks, along with the sugar, and whisk well.

Using a rubber spatula, stir about one-third or less of the egg whites into the chocolate mixture to lighten it. Carefully spoon another third of the egg whites on top of the chocolate mixture and gently fold them in. Add the remaining whites and fold them in just until incorporated.

Transfer half of the batter to another bowl and set aside in the refrigerator.

Pour the remaining batter into the prepared pan and bake for 20 minutes: it will turn into a soft, moist cake. Remove from the oven and let cool completely in the pan.

When the cake has reached room temperature, pour the reserved chocolate mousse on top of it. Refrigerate the mousse cake, uncovered, for at least 2 hours, or overnight, until set.

When you're ready to serve, run a sharp thin-bladed knife around the cake's edges and then remove the sides of the springform pan. Peel the paper from the bottom, and place the cake on a serving platter. Serve cold, decorated with chocolate shavings, if desired.

Leftover cake will keep in the refrigerator, wrapped in aluminum foil, for a couple of days.

TORTA DELLO SHABBAT DI SANDRA
Sandra's Shabbat Cake

MAKES 1 LOAF CAKE OR RECTANGULAR CAKE; SERVES 6

—

4 large (200 g) eggs

2 cups (400 g) sugar

2½ cups (315 g) all-purpose flour

½ cup (75 g) potato starch

½ cup (120 ml) sunflower or peanut oil

½ cup (120 ml) milk, orange juice, or water

Scant 1 tablespoon (12 g) baking powder

Whenever I have a Shabbat dinner at the home of the Chief Rabbi of Milan, Rav Arbib, I have to save room for dessert, or, more specifically, for this simple yet scrumptious sponge cake that his wife, Sandra, prepares for guests.

One of the reasons I love the cake is that it comes together with a simple but memorable combination of ingredients. The base unit of measure is 1 cup (240 ml). All the ingredients are also given in weights here as well, but if you use a cup measure, you'll be able to easily remember the formula (4 eggs, 3 cups starch—all-purpose flour plus potato starch—2 cups sugar, and 1 cup liquid, plus a tablespoon of baking powder) and put the cake together in a flash.

—

Preheat the oven to 350°F (180°C). Line the bottom of a loaf pan or a rectangular baking pan with parchment paper. Any size of baking pan will work as long as it can accommodate the batter and allow room for expansion, as the cake will rise a lot in the oven.

In the bowl of a stand mixer fitted with the paddle attachment, or in a large bowl, using a handheld mixer, blend the eggs and sugar for a few seconds. Add the flour, potato starch, oil, milk (or juice or water), and baking powder and beat until creamy.

Pour the batter into the prepared pan and bake for 45 minutes, or until the top is golden and a toothpick inserted in the center comes out clean. Allow the cake to cool to room temperature before serving.

The cake keeps, well wrapped, for a week.

VARIATIONS

- This cake is very versatile: you can fold fresh fruit, such as sliced apples or fresh berries, into the batter, or add almond extract or lemon zest for an aromatic twist.

- You can also make a wonderful marble cake (see photo) by adding 3 tablespoons unsweetened cocoa powder and 1 tablespoon milk (or other liquid) to half of the batter and then swirling the batters together in the baking pan.

Vanilla and Chocolate Roulade

—

**5 large (250 g) eggs,
separated**

**5 tablespoons (65 g)
granulated sugar**

**5 tablespoons (40 g)
all-purpose flour
(or 2½ tablespoons
each flour and
unsweetened
cocoa powder for
a chocolate roll)**

**About ⅓ cup (80 g)
chocolate hazelnut
spread or jam,
1¼ cups (300 ml)
heavy cream,
whipped to soft
peaks, or another
filling of your
choice**

**Confectioners'
sugar for rolling
and for sprinkling**

Rotolo, a fluffy sponge cake roll, is easy to prepare. It can be either vanilla or chocolate and filled in different ways, such as with sweetened whipped cream or pastry cream, or—more commonly—store-bought chocolate hazelnut spread. While rotolo is surely not the most sophisticated dessert, it's a big crowd-pleaser and foolproof to make.

————

Preheat the oven to 350°F (180°C). Line a large baking sheet with parchment paper.

In the bowl of a stand mixer fitted with the whisk attachment, or in a large bowl, using a handheld mixer, whip the egg whites until they form stiff peaks, about 5 minutes. Gradually add the granulated sugar and whip for 1 more minute, or until you have stiff, glossy peaks.

Add the egg yolks and whip until they are incorporated. Sift the flour (or the flour and cocoa) over the mixture and whip until smooth.

Spread the batter evenly in the prepared pan. Gently bang the pan on the counter to level the batter. Bake for 10 minutes, or until the top of the cake springs back when touched with your finger.

If you are using a filling that can be spread on the cake while it is still hot, such as hazelnut spread, you can skip the next step; just cover the cake with the filling and roll it up (discard the parchment). Cover the cake once it has cooled.

If you're using a cold filling, such as whipped cream or pastry cream, proceed as follows: Lay a clean kitchen towel on your work surface and sprinkle it with confectioners' sugar. When the cake comes out of the oven, immediately invert it onto the towel. Peel off the parchment paper, then delicately roll the cake up from the short side, with the towel inside it. Allow the cake to cool completely, rolled up in the towel. At this point, you can fill the cooled cake or store it in the fridge for later.

- continued -

To fill the cooled cake, unroll it carefully and remove the towel. Spread the filling evenly, leaving about a 1-inch (3 cm) border on all sides, and roll up the cake again. Place the cake on a platter, seam side down, and refrigerate until just a few minutes before serving.

Serve the cake sprinkled with confectioners' sugar.

The cake will keep, well wrapped in aluminum foil, for at least several days, or as long as a week, depending on the filling.

VARIATIONS

- Make a two-layer roll: Reduce the amount of flour by 1 tablespoon. Divide the batter between two bowls. Add a scant tablespoon of unsweetened cocoa powder to one of the bowls and a scant tablespoon of flour to the other and whisk gently until smooth. Spread the white batter in the pan and bake for 5 minutes. Spread the cocoa batter on top of the white cake and bake for 8 minutes, or until the top of the cake springs back when touched with your finger.

- Make girelle, a kids' favorite in Italy: Prepare the two-layer roll. Spread some melted chocolate or hazelnut spread over it, leaving a border, and roll it up. Cut the roll into thick slices and dip one side of each slice in melted chocolate, then let stand on a wire rack until the chocolate has set.

- To serve the roulade on Passover, substitute potato starch or matzo cake meal for the flour.

TORTA DI TU B'SHVAT
Tu B'Shvat Cake

MAKES ONE 9-INCH
(23 CM) CAKE;
SERVES 8

—

1 heaping cup
(110 g) blanched
whole almonds

1¾ ounces (50 g)
dark chocolate,
coarsely chopped

2 cups (250 g) pitted
soft dates, plus
(optional) halved
pitted dates for
decoration

2 large (100 g) eggs

⅔ cup plus
2 teaspoons
(140 g) sugar

1¼ cups (150 g)
all-purpose flour

1 teaspoon (4 g)
baking powder

2 tablespoons honey

2 tablespoons milk
or orange juice if
needed

Whipped cream for
serving (optional)

Jews all over Europe celebrate Tu B'Shvat by eating the seven crops for which the Biblical land of Israel was renowned—wheat, barley, olives, dates, grapes, figs, and pomegranates—as well as other types of dried fruits and nuts. This recipe, which yields a dense, soft fruitcake enriched with dates, almonds, and chocolate chunks, is a fitting way to welcome the holiday.

———

Preheat the oven to 350°F (180°C). Line the bottom of a 9-inch (23 cm) cake pan with parchment paper.

In a food processor, coarsely grind the almonds and chocolate together.

With a knife, chop the 2 cups dates into very small pieces.

In the bowl of a stand mixer fitted with the whisk attachment, or in a large bowl, using a handheld mixer, whip the eggs and sugar for 5 minutes, until light and fluffy. Using a rubber spatula, fold in the flour, baking powder, and honey. Add the almond mixture and dates and stir well. If stirring is really difficult—this will depend mostly on the type of dates you use—add up to 2 tablespoons of milk or orange juice, as needed.

Pour the batter into the prepared pan and smooth it with a spatula. If you'd like, decorate the top of the cake with a few date halves.

Bake the cake for about 40 minutes; a toothpick inserted in the center should come out clean. Remove from the oven and let cool completely. Slice the cake and serve plain or with whipped cream on the side.

This rich, dense cake will keep very well for up to a week, wrapped in aluminum foil, at room temperature.

Pumpkin Cake

**MAKES ONE
9-BY-13-INCH
(23 BY 33 CM)
RECTANGULAR
CAKE OR 10½-INCH
(27 CM) TUBE CAKE;
SERVES 10**

—

1 cup (240 ml)
sunflower or
peanut oil, plus
more for greasing
the pan

One 2-pound
(900 g) kabocha
squash or sugar
pumpkin or one
15-ounce (425 g)
can pumpkin puree

2 cups (250 g) all-
purpose flour

2 teaspoons (9 g)
baking powder

1 teaspoon (6 g)
baking soda

1 teaspoon ground
cinnamon

4 large (200 g) eggs

1 cup (200 g) packed
brown sugar

½ cup (100 g)
granulated sugar

1 teaspoon pure
vanilla extract

When celebrating Rosh Hashanah or the end of the Yom Kippur fast, the Jews of Emilia-Romagna use a special ingredient in their dishes: *zucca barucca*, which is the dialect name for a variety of squash grown in Italy that closely resembles kabocha. While most dictionaries say that barucca is a play on the Italian word *verruca*, which means "wart," the Jews think that the name comes from the Hebrew word *baruch*, which means "holy." What better way to celebrate the High Holidays than with a cake made with "holy" pumpkin?

———

Preheat the oven to 350°F (180°C). Grease a 9-by-13-inch (23 by 33 cm) cake pan or 10½-inch (27 cm) tube pan with oil.

If using a squash or a sugar pumpkin, line a baking sheet with parchment paper. Cut the squash in half, scoop out the seeds and fibers with a sharp spoon, and discard. Cut the squash into thick slices and peel each slice with a vegetable peeler. Cut each slice into cubes and transfer the cubes to the prepared baking sheet.

Bake the squash until tender, about 45 minutes. Transfer it to a blender (leave the oven on) and puree until smooth. You should have 2 scant cups (425 g).

In a large bowl, whisk the flour, baking powder, baking soda, and cinnamon together; set aside.

In another large bowl, whisk the oil, eggs, brown sugar, granulated sugar, the reserved squash puree or the canned pumpkin, and vanilla together until combined.

Pour the wet ingredients into the dry ingredients and whisk everything together until completely combined.

Spread the batter in the prepared pan and bake for approximately 45 minutes. The cake is done when a toothpick inserted in the center comes out clean. If you find that the top or edges of the cake are browning too quickly, cover loosely with aluminum foil.

Let the cake cool on a wire rack before slicing and serving.

The cake keeps well in the fridge, wrapped in aluminum foil, for up to a week.

A WELL-TRAVELED CAKE · While the origins of this cake are most likely Portuguese, it had a first wave of popularity in Italy in 1660, in Livorno, when a local Jewish baker served it to the grand duke of the region, who greatly enjoyed it. Many years later, the cake had a second wave of fame, thanks to the Jews of Italian origin who fled Libya in the 1960s: they, too, had preserved the ancient recipe for the cake, and they brought it to the Italian communities where they settled, driving a rediscovery of the dessert.

BOCCA DI DAMA
Passover Almond Cake

MAKES ONE 10-INCH
(25 CM) ROUND CAKE;
SERVES 6 TO 8

—

FOR THE CAKE

6 large (300 g) eggs,
separated, plus
2 large (60 g) egg
whites

2 cups (220 g)
almond flour or
finely ground
almonds

1½ cups (300 g)
granulated sugar

Sliced almonds for
sprinkling

FOR THE ICING

⅔ cup (80 g)
confectioners'
sugar

2 large (60 g) egg
whites

Bocca di dama, which translates as "mouth of a lady," is a fluffy, delicate sponge cake made with almond flour and eggs. Since it doesn't contain wheat flour and it doesn't rely on baking powder for rising, it's generally considered a classic Passover dessert, but it's absolutely delightful year-round as well, and it's gluten-free too.

————

Preheat the oven to 350°F (180°C). Line the bottom of a 10-inch (25 cm) springform pan with parchment paper.

To make the cake, in a large bowl, using a handheld mixer, beat the 6 (180 g) egg whites on medium speed for about 5 minutes, until stiff peaks form.

In another large bowl, using the handheld mixer (no need to clean the beaters), beat together the almond flour or ground almonds, egg yolks, granulated sugar, and the remaining 2 (60 g) egg whites on medium speed until well combined, about 5 minutes.

Using a rubber spatula, gently fold the beaten egg whites into the almond mixture until just combined, then scrape the batter into the prepared pan.

Bake the cake for about 35 minutes, until golden; a wooden skewer inserted into the center should come out clean. If the top of the cake starts to brown too fast, cover it loosely with foil.

Let the cake cool in the pan for 10 minutes. Run a knife around the edges of the pan and gently remove the springform ring. Let cool completely.

In a small skillet, toast the sliced almonds over medium heat for 2 to 3 minutes, until just browned. Remove from the heat and let cool.

To prepare the icing, in a large bowl, using a handheld mixer, whip the confectioners' sugar with the egg whites on high speed to make a light, glossy icing.

Preheat the broiler (or use a kitchen torch).

Cover the cake with the icing, then sprinkle the sliced almonds on top. Place the cake under the broiler for 3 to 5 minutes, until the top of the cake is golden (or use the kitchen torch). Let cool.

Lift the cake carefully from the bottom of the springform pan and peel off the parchment paper, then transfer to a serving plate.

The frosted cake keeps well in the fridge, wrapped in aluminum foil, for a couple of days. If left unfrosted, the cake keeps well at room temperature for up to a week.

Margherita Sponge Cake

MAKES ONE 8-INCH (20 CM) ROUND CAKE; SERVES 8 TO 10

——

1 tablespoon butter or margarine, softened, for greasing the pan

4 large (200 g) eggs

Scant ⅔ cup (120 g) granulated sugar

¾ cup (120 g) potato starch, sifted

Confectioners' sugar for sprinkling (optional)

Torta Margherita is a three-ingredient, gluten-free, dairy-free sponge cake, known to virtually every baker in Italy for its simplicity and delightful pillowy texture. On Passover, among Jews, it's the preferred flourless recipe to prepare for breakfast and snacks. This recipe is adapted from the historic book *Science in the Kitchen and the Art of Eating Well*, by the greatest culinary writer of Italy, Pellegrino Artusi.

————

Preheat the oven to 350°F (180°C). Grease an 8-inch (20 cm) round cake pan with the butter or margarine and line the bottom with parchment paper.

Separate the eggs, placing the whites and yolks in two separate large bowls. Set the whites aside in the refrigerator.

Using a handheld mixer, beat the yolks with the granulated sugar for 5 minutes, or until very pale and creamy, then add the potato starch and beat until thoroughly incorporated.

With clean beaters, beat the egg whites to stiff peaks, about 5 minutes. Gently fold them into the batter.

Spoon the batter into the prepared pan, spreading it evenly. Bake the cake for about 40 minutes, until golden on the top and firm to the touch. Remove from the oven and let cool completely.

Run a knife around the edges of the cake to loosen it, then flip it onto a serving platter. Sprinkle the cake with confectioners' sugar, if desired, and serve.

Flourless Chocolate Cake

MAKES ONE 9-INCH (23 CM) ROUND CAKE; SERVES 8

—

8 tablespoons (1 stick/113 g) unsalted butter, cut into chunks, plus more for greasing the pan

7 ounces (200 g) dark chocolate, preferably 60% cacao

4 large (200 g) eggs

¾ cup (150 g) granulated sugar

⅓ cup (50 g) potato starch or cornstarch

1 tablespoon confectioners' sugar for garnish

Tenerina means "tender," a word that describes very well the texture of this flourless chocolate cake. It has a light, meringue-like top crust and a rich, fall-apart-soft chocolate center.

This recipe was created in the city of Ferrara in the twentieth century to honor Elena Petrovich, queen of Montenegro and wife of the king of Italy. The lively Jewish community of Ferrara adopted the decadent flourless cake to celebrate Passover.

———

Preheat the oven to 350°F (180°C). Butter a 9-inch (23 cm) cake pan and line the bottom with parchment paper.

Place a metal bowl over a pot of simmering water. Finely chop the chocolate, place it in the bowl, and stir with a heatproof spatula to encourage the chocolate to melt. When the chocolate is almost melted, add the butter and let it melt too. Stir to combine. Remove the bowl from the heat and place on a kitchen towel to cool.

Separate the eggs, placing the whites and yolks in two separate large bowls.

Using a handheld mixer, whip the egg whites with half of the granulated sugar until stiff peaks form, about 5 minutes.

With the mixer (no need to clean the beaters), whip the egg yolks with the remaining sugar until pale and fluffy, about 5 minutes.

Pour the chocolate mixture over the egg yolks and beat until smooth, about a minute. Using a rubber spatula, gently fold in about one-quarter of the egg whites, then carefully add the rest of the egg whites. Being careful not to deflate the batter, fold in the potato starch or cornstarch.

Pour the batter into the prepared pan and bake for 30 minutes, or until the cake has risen and the top cracks a bit. Remove the pan from the oven and let the cake come to room temperature. As it cools, the cake will sink a bit.

Run a knife around the edges of the cake, invert it onto a wire rack, and peel off the parchment paper, then invert onto a serving plate. Sift the confectioners' sugar over the top and serve.

The cake keeps well in the fridge, wrapped in aluminum foil, for up to a week.

Ricotta Cheesecake

MAKES ONE 8-INCH
(20 CM) ROUND CAKE;
SERVES 8

—

2 cups (500 g)
ricotta cheese
(preferably from
sheep's milk rather
than cow's milk)

Softened butter for
greasing the pan

1 tablespoon bread
crumbs

¾ cup (150 g) sugar

1 teaspoon ground
cinnamon

3 large (150 g) eggs

⅓ cup (50 g) raisins,
soaked in hot
water to plump and
drained

Whipped cream for
serving (optional)

Cassola is a very simple Roman ricotta cake that is traditionally prepared for the holiday of Shavuot. Roman Jews likely learned to make ricotta from the Sicilian Jews, skilled cheese producers, who fled Southern Italy at the end of the fifteenth century. These days we eat ricotta cheesecake as a dessert, sweetened with sugar and cinnamon, but a few generations ago people ate it as a snack—sandwiched between slices of crunchy bread!

———

Set a fine sieve over a bowl, add the ricotta, and let drain in the fridge for an hour, or until it's dry and firm.

Preheat the oven to 350°F (180°C). Grease an 8-inch (20 cm) springform pan with butter, then sprinkle it with the bread crumbs.

In a large bowl, mix the ricotta, sugar, and cinnamon together with a wooden spoon. Add the eggs one at a time, mixing until the batter is smooth and homogeneous. Fold in the raisins until evenly incorporated.

Pour the batter into the prepared pan and bake for about 50 minutes, until the top is golden and firm to the touch. Let the cake cool completely in the pan.

Remove the side of the springform pan, transfer the cake to a serving plate, and cut into slices. Serve plain, or with a spoonful of whipped cream, if desired.

Cassola is best served on the day it's made, but it can be kept, covered with aluminum foil, in the fridge for a couple of days. Bring to room temperature before serving.

CROSTATA DI RICOTTA E VISCIOLE
Ricotta and Sour Cherry Crostata

MAKES ONE 10-INCH (25 CM) TART; SERVES 6 TO 8

—

FOR THE PASTRY CRUST

2 cups (250 g) all-purpose flour

½ cup (100 g) sugar

9 tablespoons (125 g) cold unsalted butter, diced

Finely grated zest of ½ lemon

1 large (50 g) egg plus 1 large (19 g) egg yolk

FOR THE FILLING

1⅛ pound (500 g) sheep's-milk ricotta, drained in a sieve if very wet

¾ cup (100 g) confectioners' sugar

Scant ¼ cup (40 g) granulated sugar

2 large (100 g) eggs

1 cup (250 g) sour cherry jam

Boccione, the famous bakery of the Roman Ghetto, is known for its two ricotta crostatas, one with chocolate chips and one with sour cherry jam, but the latter is by far the more iconic and successful. If you ever visit the Ghetto, you should absolutely try the original, but until then, the homemade version will surely keep you satisfied.

If you can't find sour cherry jam, you can make the crostata with regular cherry jam; it will still be delicious.

———

To make the crust, in a food processor, pulse together the flour, sugar, butter, and lemon zest to obtain a crumbly mix. Turn the mixture out into a bowl, add the egg and yolk, and mix with your hands until the dough comes together in a smooth ball. Wrap in plastic wrap and let rest in the fridge for an hour.

To make the filling, in the bowl of a stand mixer fitted with the whisk attachment, or in a large bowl, using a handheld mixer, beat the ricotta, confectioners' sugar, granulated sugar, and eggs until smooth and creamy, about 3 minutes. Cover and set aside in the fridge.

Preheat the oven to 350°F (180°C).

When the dough has rested, divide it into 2 pieces, one twice as large as the other. Transfer the larger piece to a well-floured work surface and use a rolling pin to roll it out to a round about ⅛ inch (3 mm) thick. Fit it into a 10-inch (25 cm) pie dish. Trim the edges, and knead the scraps into the remaining piece of dough.

Spread the jam over the dough, then cover it with the ricotta filling.

For the lattice top, roll the second piece of dough out on a well-floured surface to a ⅛-inch (3 mm) thickness. Cut the dough into strips about ½ inch (1 cm) wide. Arrange the strips over the top of the filling to form a simple but tight lattice top. Crimp the edges with a fork to seal.

Bake the crostata for 30 minutes, or until golden. Let cool completely.

Serve the crostata at room temperature or briefly chilled, as you prefer.

The crostata keeps well in the fridge, wrapped in aluminum foil, for up to a week.

HIDDEN CHEESE • This ricotta and cherry crostata was invented to overcome yet another cruel papal decree, which forbade Jews from selling or trading any dairy products. So the ricotta was hidden under a pastry crust, either with a full top crust or a very tightly braided lattice.

SPONGATA
Jam and Nut Cake

MAKES ONE 9-INCH
(23 CM) CAKE;
SERVES 8

—

FOR THE DOUGH

⅓ cup (75 g) packed
brown sugar

7 tablespoons
(100 g) unsalted
butter, at room
temperature

1 large (19 g) egg
yolk

Grated zest of
1 lemon

2 cups (250 g)
all-purpose flour,
plus more for
dusting

3 tablespoons warm
white wine

1 tablespoon
unsalted butter,
softened, for
greasing the pan

Spongata is a traditional cake of Jewish origin that hails from Emilia-Romagna and northern Tuscany. The cake was brought to Italy by Sephardic Jews fleeing the Spanish Inquisition, and it became famous thanks to the entrepreneurial spirit of a Jewish pastry chef by the surname of Muggia in the second half of the nineteenth century. The cake has a shell of pastry dough and is filled with a paste of dried and candied fruit similar to charoset (page 240). While it began as a Jewish dish, today this cake is much more common among Christians, who eat it at Christmas and gift it to friends and family.

———

To make the dough, in a large bowl, combine the brown sugar, butter, egg yolk, and lemon zest and beat with a wooden spoon until creamy. Add the flour and wine and knead the mixture with your hands until a smooth dough forms.

Turn the dough out, divide it into 2 portions, and form each one into a disk. Wrap in plastic wrap and set aside.

To make the cake, preheat the oven to 400°F (200°C). Grease a 9-inch (23 cm) round cake pan with the 1 tablespoon butter.

On a floured surface, roll out one piece of the dough into a 10-inch (25 cm) round. Fit it into the prepared pan.

3 tablespoons fig
jam

3 tablespoons apple
jam

1 tablespoon pear
jam

5 tablespoons (35 g)
chopped candied
orange and citron
peel

2 tablespoons
raisins, soaked
in hot water until
plumped and
drained

10 almonds, roughly
chopped

2 tablespoons pine
nuts

Pinch of ground
cinnamon

Pinch of ground
cloves

Confectioners'
sugar for dusting

To make the filling, in a small bowl, mix the jams together. Spread over the dough in the pan, leaving a ½ inch (1 cm) band of dough uncovered around the edges, then sprinkle the candied fruit, raisins, nuts, cinnamon, and cloves evenly over the top.

Roll out the second piece of dough into a 10-inch (25 cm) round and cover the filling with the pastry. Trim away and discard any excess dough, and crimp the edges of the dough with a fork or press them with your fingers to seal. Pierce the top layer of dough in several spots to make steam vents.

Bake for 20 minutes, or until the top of the cake is golden. Cool completely on a wire rack.

Dust the top of the cake with confectioners' sugar before serving.

NOTE

As an alternative to confectioners' sugar, you can top the cake with a sugar glaze: Combine 3 tablespoons sugar and 1 tablespoon water in a small bowl, stirring until the sugar is dissolved. Brush it over the top of the cake before baking.

Sweet Half-Moon Pie

SERVES 8

FOR THE DOUGH

⅔ cup (130 g) sugar

3 large (150 g) eggs

6 tablespoons
(90 ml) sunflower
or peanut oil

3⅔ cups minus
1 tablespoon
(450 g) all-purpose
flour

1 teaspoon (4 g)
baking powder

FOR THE FILLING

1¾ cups (200 g)
almond flour or
finely ground
almonds

¾ cup (150 g) sugar

1 large (30 g) egg
white

1 cup (380 g)
chopped candied
fruit

FOR DECORATION

2 cups (240 g)
confectioners'
sugar

¼ cup (60 ml) water

Colored sprinkles

Another very festive recipe from the Roman Ghetto is the mezzaluna prepared for Rosh Hashanah. It is a large half-moon–shaped sweet pastry filled with almond paste. The shape is to celebrate the fact that on Rosh Hashanah, there is a new moon rising in the sky.

To make the dough, in the bowl of a stand mixer fitted with the whisk attachment, or in a large bowl, using a handheld mixer, whip the sugar and eggs until pale and thick, about 5 minutes. Add the oil and beat until fully incorporated. Remove the bowl from the mixer stand, if using, add the flour and baking powder, and knead in the bowl with your hands until the dough comes together. Turn the dough out, wrap in plastic wrap, and refrigerate while you prepare the filling.

Preheat the oven to 350°F (180°C). Line a baking sheet with parchment paper.

To make the filling, in a medium bowl, combine the almond flour, sugar, and egg white and mix together with your hands into a thick paste. Mix in the candied fruit.

Take the dough out of the refrigerator and place it on the prepared baking sheet. Using a rolling pin or your fingers, roll or press it into a circle approximately 10 inches (25 cm) in diameter.

Place the filling over one half of the dough. Fold the other end of the dough over to cover the filling. Press down on the edges with your fingers to seal. With your hands, gently bend the corners and round the center of the pie to give it the shape of a half-moon.

Bake the pie for 25 minutes, until golden. Let cool to room temperature on a wire rack.

To decorate the pie, in a small bowl, whisk the confectioners' sugar and water together to make a runny icing. Spread the icing generously over the pie and decorate with sprinkles.

The pie keeps well in the fridge, wrapped in aluminum foil, for a few days.

Almond Custard

SERVES 6

5 large (95 g) egg yolks, at room temperature

¾ cup (150 g) sugar

¾ cup (180 ml) water

2 tablespoons orange blossom water

¾ cup (65 g) almond flour or finely ground almonds

1 teaspoon almond extract

Ground cinnamon for dusting

Ramekins of this rich almond custard are often served on Passover, to end the holiday meal on a sweet note. The recipe is said to come from Livorno, Tuscany, but it is likely of Portuguese origin, as many Portuguese Jews moved to Italy during the Spanish Inquisition, bringing with them their traditional recipes. In the region of Veneto, a similar sweet dish, known as *rosada con le mandorle*, is served on Purim.

———

In a medium bowl, using a handheld mixer, beat the egg yolks until light and thick, about 5 minutes. Set the mixer aside.

In a medium saucepan, combine the sugar, water, and 1 tablespoon of the orange blossom water and heat over low heat, stirring, until the sugar dissolves. Attach a candy thermometer to the side of the pan and bring the mixture to a simmer and cook, stirring occasionally, until it reaches 234 to 239°F (112 to 115°C), the soft-ball stage, about 15 minutes.

With the mixer on low speed, gradually pour the syrup in a slow, steady stream into the egg yolks, then beat for about 2 minutes, until fully incorporated.

Transfer the mixture to a large heavy saucepan and cook over very low heat (or use a double boiler), stirring constantly, until the custard begins to thicken, about 2 minutes. Do not allow the custard to simmer; it should stay below 167°F (75°C), or the eggs will scramble.

Add the almond flour, almond extract, and the remaining tablespoon of orange blossom water, stir well to incorporate, and remove from the heat. Allow to cool slightly.

When the custard is lukewarm, pour it into six 4- or 5-ounce (120 or 150 ml) ramekins or serving cups of your choice.

Dust the tops of the custard with cinnamon and refrigerate for at least an hour before serving.

The custard doesn't keep well, so it should be served the day it is made.

Marzipan Snake

SERVES 10 TO 12

—

Matzo flour or all-purpose flour for sprinkling

4⅓ cups (500 g) blanched almonds (or almond flour)

2½ cups (500 g) granulated sugar

¾ cup plus 1½ tablespoons (200 ml) water

2 tablespoons sunflower or peanut oil

1 large (30 g) egg white

1 tablespoon confectioners' sugar

¼ cup (50 g) candied lemon or orange peel

The marzipan snake is a traditional almond-paste treat prepared for Passover by the Jews of the city of Urbino in the Marche region. The snake is a reminder of the story of Moses and Aaron, whose cane turned into a snake, scaring the Pharaoh and his magicians. This recipe is from my friend Ester Moscati, whose mother, Maria Luisa, was born in Urbino.

———

Preheat the oven to 350°F (180°C). Sprinkle a baking sheet with matzo flour (or all-purpose flour if it's not Passover).

If using whole almonds, finely grind them in a food processor.

Pour the granulated sugar and water into a large shallow pot and cook over medium heat, stirring constantly, until the sugar dissolves. Attach a candy thermometer to the side of the pot and cook until the sugar reaches around 223°F (106°C), the thread stage, about 10 minutes. The syrup will be thick.

Drop the almond flour into the pot and mix it in quickly. Remove from the heat.

Slick your hands with the oil. Spoon the almond paste out onto the prepared pan and shape it into a snake with a long curved body and a large flat head.

In a large bowl, using a handheld mixer, whip the egg white and confectioners' sugar to soft peaks, about 2 minutes. Brush the whipped egg white over the snake.

Decorate the snake with the candied fruit, making a mouth, eyes, and scales.

Bake the snake for 15 minutes, or until golden and almost browned. Remove from the oven and let cool.

Slice and serve as an after-dinner treat.

The snake can be stored in the fridge, in an airtight container or wrapped in aluminum foil, for up to 5 days.

Purim

According to the Book of Esther, about twenty-five hundred years ago, an evil man by the name of Haman, who was the prime minister of the king of Persia, Ahasuerus, became upset because a pious Jew, Mordechai, refused to bow down in front of him. Haman took revenge on the entire Jewish population for Mordechai's offense by asking the king to kill all the Jews in his kingdom. Little did Haman know that one of the wives of the king, Queen Esther, was Mordechai's niece and herself a Jew. At the risk of her own life, Esther spoke to King Ahasuerus and convinced him to stop Haman's evil plan. Thus Haman was defeated, ending up on the very same gallows that he had built to kill the Jews.

At Purim, Jews rejoice at the escaped danger. We celebrate by eating a festive meal, offering donations to the poor, and exchanging gifts of food and drink (known in Hebrew as *mishloach manot*) with friends and family. It's a common custom for kids to wear masks and costumes, much as non-Jews in Italy do for Carnival; many children dress up as the characters of the Book of Esther.

Since Purim falls at around the same time as the Italian Catholic Carnival, and the two celebrations have many common traits, it's no surprise that some dishes have also crossed the border between the two faiths, to the point that today it's difficult to tell if they are Jewish or Italian, and which they were first. One such example is the Jewish Italian orecchie di Aman (page 314) and strufoli (see page 315), thin, crispy sheets of fried pasta dough prepared for Purim that are almost indistinguishable from the Italian Carnival specialty called *chiacchiere*.

Purim is also the holiday for which we prepare one of the oldest documented Jewish Italian dishes, tortolicchio (page 296), a treat that is mentioned in writings dating as far back as 1318. Tortolicchio is a crunchy cookie loaf that is served cut into slices, much like the Ashkenazi mandelbrodt. What is funny about tortolicchio is that it is inextricably paired with beef salami—a rather strange combination—because in Rome, Purim has always been celebrated with these two foods on the table. The best explanation I could find for this odd pairing is that salami, like tortolicchio, was traditionally served on Purim, mostly because soon after Purim it would be too hot to preserve it safely for much longer. However, there is no certainty about this, and the true story of the tradition of serving "salame e tortolicchio" remains, as far as I know, a mystery.

Almond Cake with Sweet Egg Threads

MAKES ONE CAKE;
SERVES 8 TO 10
—

FOR THE CAKE

½ cup (100 g) sugar

¼ cup (60 ml) water

2 tablespoons orange blossom water

1 cup (115 g) almond flour or finely ground almonds

3 to 4 tablespoons finely chopped candied lemon or citron peel

1 large (50 g) egg

FOR THE EGG THREADS

2¾ cups (550 g) sugar

1 cup (240 ml) water

2 tablespoons orange blossom water

1 tablespoon fresh lemon juice

8 large (152 g) egg yolks

SPECIAL EQUIPMENT

Baking syringe (available at baking supply stores and online) or a piping bag fitted with a very small tip

Monte Sinai is an almond cake with a cookie-like texture that is decorated with beautiful, fragile sugarcoated egg threads. This Purim treat dates back to the eighteenth century, possibly even earlier. While the recipe is dutifully recorded in many Jewish Italian cookbooks, it has fallen out of fashion, and few remember what the original version actually looks like, as it is very difficult to make. The preparation of the dish is a bit challenging, because crafting the egg threads is a delicate work of art, but it's also quite rewarding. I've modernized the recipe to make a worthwhile tribute to the original dish in all its splendor.

———

Preheat the oven to 325°F (160°C). Line a baking sheet with parchment paper.

To make the cake, in a large saucepan, combine the sugar, water, and orange blossom water and bring to a simmer over medium heat, stirring to dissolve the sugar, then cook until the mixture is reduced to a thick syrup that coats the back of a spoon, about 10 minutes.

Add the almond flour and candied peel to the sugar syrup, stir vigorously, and remove from the heat. Let cool.

In a small bowl, whisk the egg with a fork. With a whisk or the fork, mix the egg into the almond mixture. You should have a somewhat sticky, but workable, thick paste.

Transfer the paste to the prepared baking sheet and shape it to your liking; see the Variations.

Bake for approximately 30 minutes, or until golden; the baking time will vary, depending on the size and shape of the cake. Let cool.

To make the egg threads, in a large skillet or sauté pan, combine the sugar, water, orange blossom water, and lemon juice and bring to a boil over medium-high heat, then reduce the heat to medium-low and cook for approximately 3 minutes, until the sugar has completely dissolved.

Meanwhile, in a small bowl, whisk the egg yolks to break them up, then pour them through a fine-mesh sieve set over another small bowl (or through sterile gauze) so they are perfectly runny and smooth. Press on the yolks gently with the back of a spoon so most of the liquid goes through.

Set a large sieve over a bowl. Fill a baking syringe or a piping bag fitted with a very small tip with the strained egg yolks and then slowly drizzle them into the sugar syrup, from a height of about 2 inches (5 cm), in circles, dropping only a few strands at a time, to create threads that are about 5 inches (13 cm) long. Let the egg threads cook for a minute or so, using a slotted spoon or a slotted spatula to make sure they are completely submerged in the syrup at least briefly, until they turn a bright yellow-gold, then lift them from the syrup with the slotted spoon or spatula and place in the sieve. Using your fingers, sprinkle ice-cold water over the threads to stop the cooking and then let them drain. Transfer the threads to a plate as you finish each batch.

Untangle the threads from one another using toothpicks and gently drop them over the almond cake to decorate it.

VARIATIONS

- This dessert can have many shapes. Some old recipes describe Monte Sinai as made of two disks of almond cake sandwiched with the egg threads. However, in my humble opinion, there is no point in making the beautiful egg threads and then crushing them between disks of cake. Other recipes call for a large doughnut shape, a single flat disk, or small individual mounds. Pick whichever you prefer; they will all taste great.

- You can cover the cake with a confectioners' sugar icing before decorating it with the egg threads. The icing is optional, but it does make the cake look beautiful and the egg threads shine. To make a simple icing, stir together 1 cup (120 g) confectioners' sugar and 1 tablespoon water until smooth.

Honey Matzo Fritters

MAKES 30 FRITTERS

---

6 matzo sheets

3 large (150 g) eggs

6 tablespoons (75 g) sugar

⅔ cup (100 g) raisins, soaked in hot water until plumped and drained

½ cup (50 g) pine nuts

1 tablespoon grated orange or lemon zest

Up to 3 tablespoons matzo meal

Sunflower or peanut oil for deep-frying

⅓ cup (100 g) honey (see Note)

One of the best culinary inventions from the women of the Roman Ghetto are pizzarelle, small, sweet matzo fritters soaked in honey. These treats can be found in bakeries year-round. I know it might be difficult to believe that anybody would want to eat matzo when it's not Passover, but give pizzarelle a try, and you'll instantly be converted into a matzo lover.

Break the matzo sheets in half, place them in a bowl filled with water, and weigh them down with a plate to keep them submerged. Soak for 2 hours, then drain the matzo and squeeze them to remove all the water.

Transfer the matzo to a large bowl and mash with a potato masher to make a thick and somewhat chunky paste or batter. Mix in the eggs, sugar, raisins, pine nuts, and orange or lemon zest. Stir in some or all of the matzo meal: you are looking to obtain a thick batter that will keep its shape when dropped by the spoonful into the hot oil for frying. It should not look too wet and runny.

Pour 1½ to 2 inches (4 to 5 cm) of oil into a large saucepan and heat over medium heat until a deep-fry thermometer reads 350°F (180°C). You can test the oil by dropping a small piece of food, such as a slice of apple, into it: if it sizzles nicely but doesn't bubble up too wildly, the oil is ready. (An apple is said to help minimize the smell of the frying oil, so I generally go for that, but any bit of food will do.)

Working in batches to avoid crowding, using two spoons, drop small mounds of the matzo mixture into the hot oil and fry the fritters for 5 minutes, or until golden brown, turning them once to ensure even cooking. Drain the cooked fritters on paper towels for a few minutes, then transfer to a plate and drizzle with the honey before serving.

Pizzarelle have to be eaten as soon as they are ready: they are scrumptious hot from the pan, but they get soggy quickly.

NOTE

If the honey is very thick, heat it up in a small saucepan with 3 tablespoons water and a squeeze of fresh lemon juice to liquefy it before drizzling it over the pizzarelle.

VARIATION

For a chocolate version of pizzarelle, omit the matzo meal and add 2 tablespoons unsweetened cocoa powder. Keep in mind, though, that while pizzarelle made with cocoa are delicious, the color is unappealing.

BOMBOLONI ALLA CREMA
Vanilla Custard Doughnuts

MAKES
10 DOUGHNUTS

—

FOR THE DOUGH

½ cup (120 ml) whole
milk

1 tablespoon active
dry yeast

4 cups (500 g)
all-purpose flour,
plus more for
rolling

¼ cup (50 g) sugar

1 large (50 g) egg
plus 2 large (38 g)
egg yolks, at room
temperature

2 tablespoons
unsalted butter, at
room temperature

Sunflower or peanut
oil for deep-frying

Sugar for coating
the doughnuts

FOR THE FILLING

1½ cups (355 ml)
whole milk or
heavy cream, or
a combination

1 teaspoon pure
vanilla extract

½ cup (100 g) sugar

4 large (76 g) egg
yolks

¼ cup (35 g)
all-purpose flour,
sifted

Hanukkah celebrations worldwide feature sufganiyot, deep-fried doughnuts filled with jelly or pastry cream. In Italy, we call them *bomboloni*. While they're sold in pastry shops year-round, as a rich but fairly common breakfast option, Jews eat bomboloni specifically for Hanukkah.

It's best to use a stand mixer for this dough. You could mix the dough with a wooden spoon and then knead it by hand, but it's a lot of effort.

———

To make the dough, in the bowl of a stand mixer fitted with the dough hook, stir together the milk and yeast. Let stand for 5 minutes.

Add most of the flour (reserving a few tablespoons to adjust the texture later), the sugar, egg, and yolks to the mixer bowl and mix on low speed until well combined, about 2 minutes. Turn the speed up to medium and add the butter, 1 tablespoon at a time. Then continue to knead the dough until it pulls away from the sides of the bowl. After about 5 minutes, add the last bit of flour if needed: the dough should be shiny and feel soft, but not sticky. If it feels sticky, add more flour.

Transfer the dough to a lightly floured work surface and stretch and fold it over itself a couple of times with your hands, until it looks springy and smooth.

Place the dough in a lightly oiled bowl, turn to coat, cover with plastic wrap, and let rest and rise in the refrigerator for at least 10 hours, and up to overnight.

Place the dough back on the counter, sprinkle it with flour, and let it sit for 10 minutes.

Roll the dough out into a large rectangle, with a short side toward you. Fold the bottom of the dough up to the center, then fold the top over the dough, much as a letter is folded to fit into an envelope. Rotate it 90 degrees, roll it out again, and repeat the folding.

Line a baking sheet with parchment paper. Roll the dough out to a ½-inch (1 cm) thickness. With a 2½-inch (6 cm) round cookie cutter or a drinking glass, cut out rounds of dough and place them on the baking sheet.

Press the scraps of your dough together and let them rest, covered, for 15 minutes, then roll them out to cut more rounds.

Cover all the dough rounds with a kitchen towel or plastic wrap and let them rise for 1½ hours in a warm spot, or until they have doubled in size.

Pour 2½ inches (6 cm) of oil into a large saucepan and heat over medium heat until a deep-fry thermometer reads 350°F (180°C). You can test the oil by dropping a small piece of food, such as a slice of apple, into it: if it sizzles nicely but doesn't bubble up too wildly, the oil is ready. (An apple is said to help minimize the smell of the frying oil, so I generally go for that, but any bit of food will do.)

Working in batches to avoid crowding the pan, fry the rounds of dough until golden on the first side, about 1 minute, then flip them over and fry for another minute, or until golden on the second side. Transfer the fried doughnuts to a paper towel–lined plate.

When the doughnuts have cooled to room temperature, roll them in sugar.

To make the filling, combine the milk and vanilla in a saucepan and bring to a gentle simmer over medium-low heat.

Meanwhile, in a medium bowl, whisk together the sugar and egg yolks until pale and fluffy.

Gradually pour the warm milk in a slow stream into the egg yolks, whisking constantly. Pour the mixture back into the saucepan and add the sifted flour, whisking until smooth.

Set the saucepan back over medium heat and cook the custard slowly, whisking constantly. until it thickens to the consistency of pudding, a few minutes. Remove from the heat.

Cover the custard with a piece of plastic wrap pressed against its surface and refrigerate until completely chilled.

Fit a pastry bag with a large plain tip and fill it with the custard. Press the nozzle into the side of each doughnut and fill with the custard.

Bomboloni are best freshly made, but they can be stored in the fridge for a day or two, well covered.

Florence and Tuscany

Tuscany occupies Italy's central region, north of Rome, and it includes its capital city, Florence, as well as seaside Livorno to the west.

The earliest record of Jews living in this region dates back to the mid–1100s, but it was not until 1437 that the Jewish community was truly established.

The Jews had a lengthy alliance with the Medici merchant family. Lorenzo il Magnifico defended the Jewish community against expulsions pushed by Friar Bernardino da Feltre until 1490, when a Catholic theocracy installed by Girolamo Savonarola circumvented that protection of the Jews by the family by ordering the expulsion of the Medici along with the Jews. But the Jewish community lent money to the Republic of Florence to delay their expulsion, literally buying themselves time. Then the theocracy fell and the Medici returned in 1512. A second expulsion followed in 1527. Alessandro de' Medici regained influence in 1531, but the protections he offered Jews were short-lived.

Currying favor with Pope Paul IV, Cosimo de' Medici, who succeeded Alessandro, received the title of grand duke of Tuscany, and he began enacting restrictions on Jews, including mandatory badges worn to identify them and segregation into ghettos. The Tuscan border was closed to Jewish refugees in 1569, and a ghetto was opened in 1571.

In 1799, the local Jews—a population by then of only about a thousand—were briefly emancipated when Napoléon's army marched through the region. But the restoration of the grand dukes in 1814 forced them back into ghettos, where they remained until 1848, when their equality was granted in the constitution under Grand Duke Leopold II.

Florence became part of the Kingdom of Italy in 1861. Following unification, the ghetto was completely destroyed, and in 1872, plans to build a temple were approved. By the 1930s, the population of Jews in Florence was about three thousand, but their number was half that following World War II.

With Florence's incredible history, it is easy to overlook other areas of Tuscany. However, Tuscany once bloomed with Jewish culture.

Livorno was a free port city that by the late 1600s had a population of three thousand Jews, which grew to five thousand by 1800. The boom was a direct result of offers from Fernando I de' Medici, who invited Jews to settle there with the promise that he could protect them from the Inquisition and would not establish a ghetto. His motivation was to gain control of Livorno and Pisa as trading hubs, and his offer was successful, as Spanish Jews flocked to Livorno, which served as an oasis between 1600 and 1800. But the Livornese Jewish community dwindled in the post-Napoleonic years, when the city was no longer a free port.

Pitigliano was another Tuscan town Jews turned to in order to avoid ghettoization. For generations, the town's population was one-third Jewish (about five hundred people), which earned it the nickname of "Little Jerusalem."

The exterior and interior of the synagogue in Florence (top); a view of the town of Pitigliano (bottom).

Today there are almost fifteen hundred Jews in Tuscany, most of them in the community of Florence (along with the neighboring towns of Arezzo, Pistoia, and Siena) and in that of Livorno (which also includes Grosseto and Pitigliano).

When visiting Tuscany, you can't miss the Jewish sights of Florence, including the grandiose synagogue, which was said to be inspired by Constantinople's Hagia Sophia, and the Jewish Museum, with its sixteenth-century artifacts.

In Florence, the only kosher restaurant option is Ruth's, where they serve a traditional Jewish caponata (page 225). If kashrut is not an issue, though, try Trattoria da Burdè, Perseus, Buca Lapi, and Da Tito for great regional food.

After Florence and its many attractions, anyone who can afford an extra day trip should visit Pitigliano. It has a beautiful synagogue, which was built in 1598 and remained in operation through 1956, as well as a contemporary Jewish Museum at the foot of the hill the town sits on. In addition, those who travel to Pitigliano get to taste the original sfratti, a walnut and honey treat (page 301).

Biscotti e dolcetti

COOKIES AND SWEETS

PIZZA DE BERIDDE
Nut and Fruit Cookies

**MAKES 10
BIG COOKIES**

———

⅔ cup (100 g) raisins

⅔ cup (160 ml) dry
  white wine

2½ cups minus
  1 tablespoon
  (300 g) all-purpose
  flour (see Note)

1¾ cups (200 g)
  almond flour or
  finely ground
  almonds

¾ cup (150 g) sugar

½ cup (120 ml)
  sunflower or
  peanut oil

⅔ cup (100 g)
  candied citron
  cut into small
  cubes

½ cup (75 g) candied
  cherries, half green,
  half red, cut into
  small cubes

¾ cup (125 g)
  unblanched
  whole almonds

½ cup (70 g) pine
  nuts

Don't let the Italian name of this dish fool you—it's not a pizza but a nut-and-fruit-filled cookie. These cookies are usually offered to celebrate circumcisions. In fact, *beridde* is Roman dialect for the Hebrew word *brit*, as in *brit milah*, the circumcision. More generally, these cookies are also served on the evening before a big event such as a bar or bat mitzvah or a wedding, when friends and family gather for a whole night of studying, praying, and (of course!) eating.

———

Preheat the oven to 475°F (250°C). Line a baking sheet with parchment paper.

In a small bowl, soak the raisins in the wine for 15 to 20 minutes to plump them; drain, reserving the wine.

In the bowl of a stand mixer fitted with the paddle attachment, combine the all-purpose flour, almond flour, and sugar and mix to blend, then add the oil and mix to obtain a crumbly mixture, about 1 minute.

Slowly add about three-quarters of the reserved wine, mixing until you have a moist dough that holds together. Add more of the wine if necessary, but you may not need all it; you just want a fairly firm dough that is not too sticky and can be easily shaped.

Remove the bowl from the mixer stand. Add the raisins, candied fruit, almonds, and pine nuts, and knead them in with your hands.

Shape the dough into a big ½-inch-thick (1 cm) rectangle. Cut it into large bars, approximately 1½ by 5 inches (4 by 13 cm).

Transfer the bars to the prepared pan and bake for 15 to 20 minutes, until golden brown. The cookies should be crunchy and even slightly charred on the outside but still very moist and tender inside. Remove from the oven and let cool.

NOTE

Some people think this recipe should not include any almond flour, just all-purpose flour. But since the recipe for the pizza di beridde prepared by Boccione, the bakery of the Roman Ghetto, is absolutely top secret, we will never know. This is the closest I've been able to get to Ghetto-quality results.

CLOCKWISE FROM TOP LEFT: *Cinnamon and Cocoa Biscotti with Almonds (page 286), Sweet Ring Cookies (page 287), Nut and Fruit Cookies (opposite)*

Cinnamon and Cocoa Biscotti with Almonds

MAKES 50 COOKIES

——

1½ cups (300 g) sugar

3 large (150 g) eggs

½ cup (120 ml) sunflower or peanut oil

3¼ cups (400 g) all-purpose flour, plus more if needed

4 teaspoons ground cinnamon

1 tablespoon unsweetened cocoa powder

1⅓ cups (200 g) blanched whole almonds

Tuscany is the birthplace of biscotti, which are actually called *cantucci* in Italian; *biscotti* is the term we use for *all* cookies. Tozzetti are the Roman version of Tuscan cantucci, and they are one of the classic sweets found in the Roman Ghetto. They differ from traditional biscotti in that they call for cinnamon and cocoa, two special ingredients that make these biscotti very flavorful.

PICTURED ON PAGE 285

————

Preheat the oven to 350°F (180°C). Line two baking sheets with parchment paper.

In the bowl of a stand mixer fitted with the whisk attachment, or in a large bowl, using a handheld mixer, beat the sugar and eggs until light, about 1 minute. Pour in the oil and mix for 2 more minutes, or until creamy. Add the flour, cinnamon, and cocoa and mix well to obtain a soft dough, 1 minute.

Divide the almonds in half and coarsely chop half of them. Add the whole and chopped almonds to the dough and knead in with your hands. Should the dough be too wet and sticky, add another spoonful or so of flour.

Turn the dough out onto a floured work surface and use a bench scraper or a knife to cut it into 6 equal portions. Pat each portion of dough out with your hands to make a 1-inch-thick (3 cm) log. Place the logs on the prepared baking sheets, allowing plenty of room for spreading.

Bake the logs for 20 minutes, or until they are golden and dry to the touch. Let cool for 15 minutes (leave the oven on).

With a sharp knife, cut the logs into ½-inch-thick (1 cm) slices. Return the slices to the baking sheet, standing them up, and bake for about 5 minutes, until completely dry and golden on all sides. Remove from the oven and let cool.

The biscotti can be stored for weeks in an airtight container or cookie tin.

CIAMBELLETTE
Sweet Ring Cookies

MAKES 20 TO 25 COOKIES

—

3 large (150 g) eggs

½ cup plus 2 tablespoons (150 ml) sunflower or peanut oil

¾ cup (150 g) sugar

4 cups (500 g) all-purpose flour (see Note)

Ciambellette are very simple, plain cookies shaped into chubby rings. Until a few years ago, the women of the Roman Ghetto used to prepare ciambellette for Passover, using a special certified kosher-for-Passover flour; however, since these days it is difficult to find that flour outside of Israel, now we eat them at other times of the year rather than at Passover.

The original recipe used a peculiar unit of measurement: half an eggshell. For example, a dough made with 6 eggs called for 12 half eggshells of oil and 12 half eggshells of sugar. And traditionally, if the cookies were being prepared for Passover, they would be set aside in cotton pillowcases, to prevent them from being contaminated by foods that were not kosher for the holiday. PICTURED ON PAGE 285

———

Preheat the oven to 350°F (180°C). Line a baking sheet with parchment paper.

In a large bowl, combine the eggs, oil, and sugar and stir together with a fork. Add half of the flour and mix it in with the fork, then add the remaining flour and start working the dough with your hands. When the bowl gets in the way of your kneading, transfer the dough to a lightly floured work surface and continue to knead for about a minute, until it is smooth.

Divide the dough into 20 to 25 pieces and form into balls. Shape the balls into rings, either by making a hole in the center of each one with your finger or by rolling the balls into ropes and bringing the ends of the ropes together.

Transfer the rings to the prepared pan and bake for 8 to 10 minutes, then flip them with a spatula and let bake for another 2 minutes, or until the cookies are golden and lightly toasted on both sides. Remove from the oven and let cool.

NOTE

This recipe is obviously not kosher for Passover unless you can get your hands on that precious flour; see headnote. You can, however, substitute a mix of potato starch and matzo cake meal for the all-purpose flour to make similar ciambellette that are approved for Passover.

Crunchy Nut Bars

SERVES 4 TO 6

—

2½ cups (250 g) mixed almonds, walnuts, and hazelnuts

1 tablespoon sunflower or peanut oil

¾ cup (150 g) sugar

2½ tablespoons honey

This confection of nuts cooked in sugar and honey is a fourteenth-century recipe traditionally prepared for Purim and Shavuot. Over the centuries, some Jews have abandoned this specialty, but the recipe lives on as a Christmas treat in various regions of Italy.

———

Preheat the oven to 350°F (180°C). Line a baking sheet with parchment paper.

Spread the nuts on the prepared pan and roast for 5 minutes, or until slightly toasted and fragrant. Remove from the oven.

Line a second baking sheet with parchment paper and brush the paper with the oil. In a medium nonstick saucepan, combine the sugar and honey and cook, without stirring, over medium heat for 5 minutes.

Add the toasted nuts to the sugar and honey mixture and stir with a wooden or heatproof spoon to coat the nuts well. Be careful; the honey syrup is hot! Transfer the nuts to the oiled parchment paper and press down on the mixture with a well-oiled spatula so it's no thicker than 1 inch (3 cm).

Before the nuts cool completely, oil the blade of a chef's knife and cut the nuts into smaller bars for serving. Let cool.

Nociata keeps well wrapped in parchment paper for a week or longer.

VARIATION

Use pine nuts and about ¼ cup (30 g) chopped candied citron instead of the mixed nuts to make a version called *pignoccata*.

GINETTI
Chunky Breakfast Cookies

MAKES 6 BIG COOKIES

———

2 large (100 g) eggs plus 2 large (38 g) egg yolks

6 tablespoons (90 ml) sunflower or peanut oil

½ cup (100 g) sugar

A few drops of pure vanilla extract (optional)

Heaping ¾ cup (85 g) almond flour or finely ground almonds

2¾ cups (340 g) all-purpose flour, plus more for dusting

All the recipes for the delicious treats Boccione Bakery, in the Roman Ghetto, prepares are top secret, so this recipe is my close approximation of their ginetti. These are simple, plain cookies that make the best sweet breakfast or afternoon snack, dipped in milk or coffee. The cookies are quite large—one cookie is filling enough to get you going in the morning or to pick you up in the afternoon.

———

Preheat the oven to 350°F (180°C). Line a baking sheet with parchment paper.

In a large bowl, combine the eggs, yolks, oil, sugar, and vanilla, if using, and stir together with a fork. Add the almond flour and half of the all-purpose flour and mix it in with the fork, then add the remaining flour and start working the dough with your hands. When the bowl gets in the way of your kneading, transfer the dough to a generously floured work surface and knead for about 2 minutes, until the dough is smooth and soft.

You can shape the dough directly or let it rest for 30 minutes in the fridge for easier handling.

Shape the dough into a big 1-inch-thick (3 cm) rectangle. Cut it into 6 large bars, approximately 1½ by 5 inches (4 by 13 cm).

Transfer the bars to the prepared pan and bake for 15 to 20 minutes, until golden. The cookies should be crunchy on the outside but still very moist and tender on the inside. Remove from the oven and let cool.

The cookies will keep for a week or longer in an airtight container or cookie tin.

ZUCCHERINI
Sugar Cookies

MAKES 20 COOKIES

—

2½ cups minus
1 tablespoon
(300 g) all-purpose
flour (see Note)

2 large (100 g) eggs

¼ cup (60 ml) light
extra-virgin olive
oil or sunflower oil

¾ cup (150 g) sugar,
plus 1 cup (200 g)
for shaping

Pinch of grated
lemon zest

Zuccherini—the name translates literally to "little sugars"—are crunchy sugar-rolled cookies that are part of the Venetian Passover tradition. With their sugar coating, these cookies are a kids' favorite. They keep well and are great to make ahead and store in a cookie tin for when the craving for something sweet strikes unexpectedly. PICTURED ON PAGE 292

———

Preheat the oven to 350°F (180°C). Line two baking sheets with parchment paper.

Pour the flour onto a clean counter and make a well in the center.

In a small bowl, beat the eggs lightly with a fork, then pour them into the well. Pour in the oil and sugar and add the lemon zest. Mix the flour into the wet ingredients and knead with your hands for a minute or two, until they all come together into a smooth dough.

Clean the counter and pour the sugar for shaping onto it. Pull off a generous tablespoon of the dough and roll it between your palms to form a ball. Then place the ball on the sugarcoated counter and press into a thin disk about ¼ inch (6 mm) thick and 3 inches (8 cm) in diameter. (Only one side of the disk will be covered in sugar.) Make a hole in the center of the disk with your finger, like you would to form a bagel. Place the cookie on one of the prepared baking sheets, sugarcoated side up, and repeat with the remaining dough.

Bake the cookies one sheet at a time for 8 to 10 minutes, or until golden. Remove from the oven and let cool.

Stored in an airtight container or cookie tin, the cookies will keep well for a few weeks.

NOTE

The Jewish community of Venice bakes these cookies with a special kosher-for-Passover-certified flour, so the cookies can be eaten for the holiday even though they contain flour. This would not be the case when you make them at home.

APERE

Sponge Cookies

MAKES 12 LARGE COOKIES

—

5 large (250 g) eggs

1½ cups (300 g) granulated sugar

2¾ cups plus 2 tablespoons (360 g) all-purpose flour (see Note, opposite)

Grated zest of 1 lemon

Confectioners' sugar for dusting

Apere are soft cookies made with an egg-based batter that bakes into a sponge cake–like treat with a texture similar to that of ladyfingers. Along with bisse (page 294), zuccherini (opposite), and azzime dolci (page 295), apere are one of the traditional sweets that are prepared for Passover in Venice in the great all-volunteer baking marathon before the holiday. While delicious on their own, these cookies also make a great base for tiramisu. PICTURED ON THE FOLLOWING PAGE

———

Preheat the oven to 400°F (200°C). Line three large baking sheets with parchment paper.

In the bowl of a stand mixer fitted with the whisk attachment, or in a large bowl, using a handheld mixer, whip the eggs until light and airy, about 5 minutes. Add the granulated sugar and whip for another 5 minutes, or until pale and very fluffy. With a rubber spatula, gently fold in the flour and lemon zest.

Spoon the batter in large dollops—about ¼ cup (70 g) each—onto the prepared baking sheets, leaving plenty of room between them, and then spread into 3- to 3½-inch (8 to 9 cm) circles. (The cookies will spread further while baking.)

Bake the cookies one sheet at a time for 12 minutes, or until they are golden and peel off the parchment paper easily. Remove from the oven and let cool.

The plain cookies can be stored in an airtight container or cookie tin for a few days. Sprinkle with confectioners' sugar just before serving.

CLOCKWISE FROM TOP LEFT: *Sponge Cookies (page 291), Sugar Cookies (page 290), S Cookies (page 294), Aniseed Cookies (page 295)*

S Cookies

MAKES 30 COOKIES

—

4 cups (500 g)
all-purpose
flour (see Note,
page 290)

3 large (150 g) eggs

1¼ cups (250 g)
sugar

Grated zest of
1 lemon

½ cup (120 ml)
extra-virgin olive
oil or sunflower oil,
plus a little extra
for greasing your
hands and work
space

Bisse, unleavened oil-based cookies shaped into the letter S, are one of the most iconic foods of the Jewish Ghetto in Venice. Their Italian name is the plural of the word *bissa*, which is Venetian dialect for *biscia*, a grass snake. Similarly shaped cookies called *essi buranei* can be found outside the ghetto, but essi are crumblier because they contain leavening, and they are usually served with sweet wine. Bisse are eaten on their own or with creamy zabaione (page 242).

In Venice, these cookies are traditionally prepared for Passover using a special Passover-certified flour, but you can also find them year-round in the kosher bakery. I learned how to make them from my friend Sandra Levis, who is a prominent member of the Venetian Jewish community. Every year, she and a team of volunteers spend two weeks baking bisse and many other treats for the community to enjoy on Passover. PICTURED ON PAGE 293

—

Place the flour in a large bowl and make a well in the center of it. Break the eggs into the well and add the sugar and lemon zest. Using a fork, start mixing the eggs, sugar, and flour together as you gradually add the oil. Then continue mixing to form a soft, elastic dough.

Turn the dough out onto a lightly floured counter and knead it by stretching it and tearing it apart multiple times, using a motion we call *stracciare*, which is considered essential to the success of the recipe, as it helps to develop the gluten and absorb all the oil. Wrap the dough in plastic wrap and let rest in the fridge for 30 minutes.

Preheat the oven to 325°F (160°C). Line two baking sheets with parchment paper.

Grease your hands and your work surface with oil. Cut the dough into 30 pieces approximately 1¾ ounces (50 g) each and the size of a golf ball, and roll them into little snakes about 4 inches (10 cm) in length. Gently place the snakes on the prepared baking sheets as you go, shaping them like the letter S.

Bake the cookies for 20 minutes, or until golden. Remove from the oven and let cool.

Stored in an airtight container or cookie tin, these will keep well for a few weeks.

Aniseed Cookies

MAKES 20 LARGE COOKIES

—

8 cups (1 kg) all-purpose flour (see Note, page 290)

2½ cups (500 g) sugar

1 cup plus 2 teaspoons (250 ml) light extra-virgin olive oil or sunflower oil

5 large (250 g) eggs

4 tablespoon (25 g) anise, fennel, or caraway seeds

Grated zest of 1 lemon

Azzime dolci are homey cookies spiced with anise (or fennel) seeds, so they taste a bit like licorice. They are slightly crunchier than the rest of the Venetian repertoire of cookies, but they make up in flavor for what they lack in texture. They are also a beautiful sight to behold, thanks to their elaborate decoration, so they are great for gifting.

PICTURED ON PAGE 292

————

Preheat the oven to 400°F (200°C). Line two baking sheets with parchment paper.

In a very large bowl, combine the flour, sugar, oil, eggs, seeds, and lemon zest. Mix with your hands until the dough comes together, then transfer to a lightly floured counter and knead the dough for a minute or so, until smooth.

Lay a sheet of parchment paper on the counter. Divide the dough into 20 balls. One at a time, working on the parchment, flatten each ball to a ¼-inch-thick (6 mm) disk, using a rolling pin or your fingers. Pinch the edges of the disk with your fingers to flute them. Make multiple indentations all over the surface of the disk, using a thimble or your fingers. Use the edge of a spoon to make a decorative motif all around the edges of the disk. Arrange the cookies on the prepared baking sheets as you shape them.

Bake the cookies one sheet at a time for 10 to 12 minutes, until pale gold. Remove from the oven and let cool.

Stored in an airtight container or cookie tin, the cookies will keep well for a few weeks.

TORTOLICCHIO
Biscotti for Purim

MAKES 8 COOKIES

—

4 cups (500 g)
all-purpose flour,
plus more as
needed

1½ cups (500 g)
honey

1 cup (200 g)
unblanched
whole almonds,
or a mix of
almonds and
Italian "confetti"
(sugarcoated
almonds)

Pinch of ground
cinnamon

Grated zest of
½ orange

1 egg for brushing

Tortolicchio is a very ancient Jewish recipe prepared to celebrate Purim. The name derives from the word *tortore*, which in Roman dialect means "stick"; tortolicchio are, in fact, little sticks.

They are very crunchy cookies, similar in texture to the biscotti we see in the United States. Serve with a sweet wine for dunking.

———————

Preheat the oven to 350°F (180°C). Line a baking sheet with parchment paper.

In a big bowl, mix together the flour, honey, almonds, cinnamon, and zest with your hands, working quickly. (If the honey is too thick or has solidified, heat it for a couple of minutes in a saucepan on the stovetop, or in a microwave oven, until it is liquefied and runny before adding it to the other ingredients. If the dough is too dry or too wet, adjust the consistency by adding either a bit more honey or a bit more flour.) You should have a heavy but workable dough.

Shape the dough into bars that are 4 inches (10 cm) long, 2½ inches (6 cm) wide, and ½ inch (1 cm) thick. As you shape them, transfer the bars to the prepared pan.

Gently whisk the egg and brush it over the top of the bars.

Bake for approximately 20 minutes, until the tortolicchio are golden brown. Be careful not to overbake. Remove from the oven.

While they're still warm, slice the logs into finger-sized sticks; once it's cooled completely, tortolicchio are tough to cut without shattering.

Tortolicchio will keep for a very long time in an airtight container.

VARIATION

If you can find sugarcoated aniseeds, which are sometimes sold in Indian and Pakistani markets, add a tablespoon to the recipe when you add the almonds. The oldest tortolicchio recipes often featured the seeds, as they add a unique flavor to the cookies.

A COOKIE AS A TOKEN OF LOVE · The first mention of this cookie is in a document from 1318, when Kalonimos ben Kalonimos, a writer from Provence, visited Rome and had a taste of tortolicchio. He liked it so much that he included it in his treatise on the holiday of Purim. This is not, however, the only evidence of the long history of tortolicchio. A couple of hundred years later, in a document from 1543, a rabbi from Rome named Isacco Lattes recounted the story of a married woman who became enamored with a younger man and exchanged with him, as a token of love . . . you guessed it: a tortolicchio.

Almond Shortbread Turnovers

MAKES 24
TURNOVERS

—

FOR THE FILLING

2⅔ cups (300 g)
    almond flour or
    finely ground
    almonds

1½ cups (300 g)
    sugar

Grated zest of
    ½ lemon

2 large (60 g) egg
    whites

FOR THE DOUGH

½ cup plus
    1 tablespoon
    (135 ml) sunflower
    or peanut oil

3 large (150 g) eggs

4¾ cups (600 g)
    all-purpose flour

1½ cups (300 g)
    sugar

Grated zest of
    ½ lemon

Confectioners'
    sugar for dusting

The recipe for these almond cookies dates back to the time in the Middle Ages when Spanish Jews fled the Inquisition and settled in Venice. The Italian name *impade* is believed to come from the same Spanish root as the word *empanadas*, and these cookies are small turnovers made of short-crust pastry. They are filled with almond paste, and they look somewhat similar to empanadas, though with a curvier shape.

————

Preheat the oven to 325°F (160°C). Line a baking sheet with parchment paper.

To prepare the filling, place the almond flour, sugar, and lemon zest in a large bowl. Add one of the egg whites, mixing it in with your fingers. You might need some or all of the second egg white, but the result should be the consistency of a soft, pliable dough. Knead the almond dough in the bowl with your hands until smooth. Cover the bowl with a kitchen towel and let rest at room temperature while you prepare the short-crust dough.

In a small bowl, whisk together the oil and eggs with a fork for a couple of minutes.

In a large bowl, combine the flour, sugar, and lemon zest. Make a well in the center and pour in the egg and oil mixture. Stir and knead with your hands to form a soft dough.

Pinch off a golf ball–sized portion (1¾ ounces/50 g) of dough. Working on a lightly floured surface, flatten the dough ball into an oval 3 inches (8 cm) long. Place a little ball of the almond filling, about a tablespoon, in the center of the dough. Pull the two long sides of the dough over to meet in the center and pinch them together into a ridge, sealing the filling inside.

Curve the cookie into a C shape and transfer it to the prepared pan. Repeat with the remaining dough and filling.

Bake for 18 to 20 minutes, until the bottoms of the cookies are golden brown; flip them over with a spatula to check for doneness. Remove from the oven and let cool.

Sprinkle the cookies with confectioners' sugar before serving.

These keep well in an airtight container or cookie tin for a couple of days. They can also be frozen, well wrapped, and refreshed in a warm oven if needed.

Cutout Cookies

**MAKES
APPROXIMATELY
40 COOKIES**

—

2 large (100 g) eggs

½ cup minus
1 tablespoon
(100 ml) sunflower
or peanut oil

3 cups (370 g)
all-purpose flour,
plus more for
dusting

1½ teaspoons (7 g)
baking powder

¾ cup plus
2 tablespoons
(170 g) sugar

Simple short-crust cutout cookies (biscotti di pasta frolla, or frollini) and jam tarts (crostate) are classic Italian breakfast and snack options. There is no better way to start the day or have a little break in the afternoon than with a cup of tea and a short-crust cookie or a slice of jam tart.

All over Italy, cookies and crostatas are generally made with butter, but you can use oil instead.

This is the simplest and healthiest short-crust dough recipe you'll ever try. It's a real keeper. You can use it to make a jam crostata as well (see Variation).

———

In a medium bowl, combine the eggs and oil and mix with a fork until well blended.

Sift the flour and baking powder together into a large bowl. Make a well in the center of the flour and add the sugar and the egg mixture. Mix the ingredients with your hands until they come together, then turn out onto a lightly floured counter and knead to form a soft dough.

Shape the dough into a ball, wrap in plastic wrap, and refrigerate until firm, about 30 minutes.

Preheat the oven to 350°F (180°C). Line two baking sheets with parchment paper.

Place the dough on a piece of parchment paper and, with a rolling pin, roll out ¼ inch (6 mm) thick. Cut out cookies with your favorite cutters and arrange them on the baking sheets.

Bake the cookies for 15 minutes or so, depending on size, until golden. Remove from the oven and let cool.

The cookies will keep for at least a week in an airtight container or cookie tin.

VARIATION
Crostata with Jam

Preheat the oven to 350°F (180°C). Line the bottom of a 10-inch (25 cm) cake pan with parchment paper. Divide the dough in half and roll one piece out to a round about ¼ inch (6 mm) thick. Trim the dough to the size of the cake pan and fit it into the pan. Spread ½ cup (125 g) jam of your choice over the dough, leaving a small border all around the edges.

Roll out the second piece of dough ¼ inch (6 mm) thick. Using a pastry cutter, cut the dough into ¼-inch-wide (6 mm) strips. Arrange the strips on top of the jam, forming a diamond lattice pattern. Bake for 25 minutes, or until golden. Remove from the oven and let cool. Serves 6 to 8.

EVICTION COOKIES • This recipe hails from Pitigliano, a medieval village in the Tuscan region of Maremma. Jews and gentiles lived side by side in Pitigliano for generations, earning the town the nickname "Little Jerusalem." In the 1600s, Jews were evicted from their homes by landlords armed with sticks. Generations later, the town's Jewish bakers created stick-shaped cookies called *sfratti*, which means "evictions," to commemorate their persecution. The history of the Jews of Pitigliano is preserved in the cookbook *The Classic Cuisine of the Italian Jews* by Edda Servi Machlin. The book is now out of print and difficult to find, but this recipe is adapted from it.

Walnut and Honey Cookies

MAKES ABOUT
9 DOZEN COOKIES
—

FOR THE DOUGH

3¼ cups (400 g)
all-purpose flour,
plus more for
dusting

1 cup (200 g) sugar

2 tablespoons plus
2 teaspoons
(40 ml) sunflower
or peanut oil

⅔ to 1 cup (150 to
240 ml) dry white
wine

FOR THE FILLING

4½ cups (15 ounces/
425 g) walnuts

1 cup (340 g) honey

½ teaspoon ground
cinnamon

Generous
¼ teaspoon
ground cloves

Pinch of grated
nutmeg

Grated zest of
1 orange

2 tablespoons
confectioners'
sugar for dusting

These cookies, filled with chopped walnuts, honey, spices, and orange zest, are a typical Rosh Hashanah treat, generally served with a glass of dessert wine. The dough is rolled out thin, filled, and shaped into logs to bake, then sliced into cookies immediately after baking.

———

To make the dough, pour the flour and sugar into a bowl and add the oil and ⅔ cup wine. Knead with your hands until a smooth dough forms, about 2 minutes. If the dough is dry, add the remaining wine.

Turn the dough out, divide it into 6 portions, and wrap them individually in plastic wrap. Set aside in the fridge to chill.

Preheat the oven to 350°F (180°C). Line a baking sheet with parchment paper.

To prepare the filling, coarsely chop the walnuts, by hand with a knife or in a food processor.

In a nonstick saucepan, bring the honey to a boil over medium heat. Let boil for a couple of minutes, then add the cinnamon, cloves, nutmeg, orange zest, and chopped walnuts and reduce the heat to low. Cook, stirring, for 5 minutes, then remove from the heat and continue to stir until the filling is cool enough to handle.

Sprinkle your work surface with the confectioners' sugar. Divide the filling into 6 portions. Roll each one into a cylinder, using the confectioners' sugar to help you with the shaping.

Take the dough from the refrigerator. One at a time, with a rolling pin, roll each portion out on a lightly floured surface into a long rectangle. Wrap each rectangle of dough around a portion of filling and pinch the seam and ends to seal the roll. The rolls should be approximately 9 inches (23 cm) long and 1½ to 2 inches (4 to 5 cm) thick.

Place the sfratti on the prepared pan, seam side down. Bake for about 20 minutes, until lightly golden. Remove from the oven.

Wrap the logs in foil and let cool completely (the foil keeps the logs from becoming too hard to slice as they cool), then unwrap and cut into ½-inch-thick (1 cm) slices to serve.

Sfratti keep well for many weeks in an airtight container.

Almond Cookies

**MAKES 15 TO
20 AMARETTI**

2⅔ cups (300 g)
almond flour or
finely ground
almonds

1 cup (200 g) sugar

2 large (60 g) egg
whites, beaten

15 to 20 almonds for
decoration

My grandmother Malu used to make the best amaretti, delicious yet extremely simple almond cookies. We eat them for Passover, and year-round as well, as everybody enjoys them for an afternoon snack along with a cup of coffee. In Italy, you can find two types of amaretti: crunchy ones and soft ones. This recipe is for the soft type, which are common among Sephardic Jews.

Preheat the oven to 300°F (150°C). Line a baking sheet with parchment paper.

In a medium bowl, whisk together the almond flour and sugar.

In the bowl of a stand mixer fitted with the whisk attachment, or in a large bowl, using a handheld mixer, whisk the egg whites until they hold firm peaks, about 5 minutes.

Add the beaten egg whites to the flour and sugar mixture and stir until a soft, sticky dough forms.

Use a small cookie scoop or your fingers to portion the dough into mounds about the size of a walnut (¾ ounce/20 g if you have a scale). Roll each one into a ball and place on the prepared pan, leaving 1 inch (3 cm) of space between the cookies. Press gently on each ball to flatten the top and insert an almond into the center of the cookie for decoration.

Bake for 20 to 25 minutes, until the cookies are slightly cracked and golden on top. Keep an eye on the amaretti while they are baking, because they tend to burn quickly on the bottom. If the bottoms of the amaretti start to color too fast, move the pan to a rack closer to the top of the oven, and reduce the baking time if necessary. When they are done, transfer the amaretti to a wire rack to cool.

Stored in an airtight container or cookie tin, amaretti will keep for up to 5 days.

Almond and Chocolate Cookies

MAKES 15 TO 20 COOKIES

—

2 cups (300 g) blanched whole almonds

3½ ounces (100 g) dark chocolate, broken into pieces

2 large (100 g) eggs

1½ cups (300 g) sugar

½ cup (50 g) pine nuts

Pinch of ground cloves

Pinch of ground cinnamon

Grated zest of 1 orange

Juice of ½ lemon

All-purpose flour for dusting

These Venetian Purim cookies are made with almonds, chocolate, pine nuts, cinnamon, and cloves. They are very easy to prepare and work well as *mishloach manot*, that is, a holiday gift for family or friends. This is another recipe I learned from my friend Anna Campos, who also taught me all the secrets of goose prosciutto (page 49).

———

Finely grind three-quarters of the almonds in a food processor; transfer to a small bowl and set aside. Coarsely grind the remaining almonds; set aside in another small bowl.

Finely grind the chocolate in the food processor, very briefly so it doesn't begin to melt; or grate it with a cheese grater.

In the bowl of a stand mixer fitted with the whisk attachment, or in a large bowl, using a handheld mixer, beat the eggs until light and fluffy, about 2 minutes. Add the almonds, sugar, ground chocolate, pine nuts, cloves, cinnamon, orange zest, and lemon juice and mix well.

Turn the dough out, wrap in plastic wrap, and chill in the refrigerator for 15 minutes.

Preheat the oven to 350°F (180°C). Line a baking sheet with parchment paper.

Dust your hands with flour. Pull off pieces of dough the size of a walnut, shape into balls, and place them on the prepared pan, leaving at least 1½ inches (4 cm) between them. Flatten the balls with your fingers to a ½-inch (1 cm) thickness.

Bake for 10 to 15 minutes, until the mustazzoni are firm on top but still soft inside; they will harden while cooling. Remove from the oven and let cool.

Stored in an airtight container or cookie tin, the cookies will keep well for a week or so.

Passover

Pesach—Passover in English—is the great holiday of freedom.
It commemorates the emancipation of the Jews from their long years
of slavery in Egypt and the exodus from that land.

During Passover, eating any leavened food, and food that contains wheat, barley, rye, oats, or spelt, is prohibited. Jews cannot even keep such foods at home, so we give our homes a thorough cleaning before the holiday.

On Passover, in the ceremony called a seder, we eat foods with a strong symbolic value: matzo, unleavened bread, in memory of the Jews' hasty escape from Egypt; a roasted leg of lamb, reminiscent of the Passover sacrifice prescribed in the Torah; hard-boiled eggs, representing the eternity of life; bitter herbs, which remind us of the bitterness of slavery in Egypt; and charoset (page 240), a kind of fruit jam, said to resemble the mortar that our ancestors used to make brick walls for the pharaoh's constructions.

For those who love to cook and eat, Passover is both the most interesting and the most challenging of holidays. While it is fine to simply go gluten-free and avoid eating bread, pasta, and desserts for the seven days of the holiday, Jewish people take special pride in producing delicious meals and sweets that overcome the Passover culinary prohibitions. With creative recipes and clever substitutions for proscribed ingredients, adapting common foods to make them appropriate for Passover is not very difficult. And Italian Jews are no exception here.

We make Passover lasagna with matzo instead of pasta (see page 122) and scacchi, a matzo casserole (page 132).

Dayenu (page 78), a soup with eggs and matzo pieces gently scrambled in it, is prepared in most households, especially for the first evening of Passover. On the sweet side, pizzarelle (page 274), matzo fritters dipped in honey, are everyone's favorite in Rome.

Those who prefer to limit their matzo intake have a number of other delicious Passover specialties to choose from. For savory dishes, the most traditional ones are classic Roman agnello di Pesach (page 206)—lamb cooked especially for Passover with artichokes and fava beans into a very seasonal, bright green main dish—and the elaborate Venetian turkey meatloaf (page 155).

For dessert, do not miss my famous chocolate mousse cake (page 246); my grandmother's soft amaretti (page 302); the fluffy bocca di dama almond cake (page 257); and the traditional creamy scodelline, or almond custard (page 269).

In Venice, every Passover, a small group of volunteers prepares cookies for the entire community, using a special certified-kosher-for-Passover all-purpose flour whose use has essentially been banned in most places other than Israel. The special cookies—bisse (page 294), apere (page 291), zuccherini (page 290), impade (page 297), and azzime dolci (page 295)—are not kosher for Passover if they are made without that special flour. But they are certainly well worth baking at other times of the year.

Passover desserts include (clockwise from top left) Passover Almond Cake (page 257), Almond Cookies (page 302), Passover Chocolate Mousse Cake (page 246), Almond Custard (page 269), Honey Matzo Fritters (page 274)

MONTINI
Almond Paste Mounds

MAKES 50 COOKIES

—

5¼ cups (600 g) almond flour or finely ground almonds

2 cups (400 g) sugar

2 large (100 g) eggs

2 tablespoons plus 2 teaspoons (40 ml) liqueur, such as cognac or other brandy

Chopped candied or dried fruit for decoration (optional)

Food coloring (optional; see Variations)

The shape of these little almond cookies is supposed to remind you of Mount Sinai. They are generally given to family and friends in the Purim gift basket, because they travel well and last a long time.

The traditional recipe for montini is quite hard to prepare, as it requires sugar cooked to the thread stage, not something everyone can master, so I've settled on a much easier version made with eggs that was taught to me by Anna Levi Cogoi many years ago. I promise you, no one will be able to tell the difference between the difficult classic recipe—which you'll find in the sidebar—and this modernized one.

————

Preheat the oven to 350°F (180°C). Line two baking sheets with parchment paper.

Pour the almond flour into a large bowl. Add the sugar, eggs, and liqueur. Mix and knead the ingredients with your hands in the bowl until they come together into a soft dough.

Pull off walnut-sized portions of dough and shape them into small mountain-shaped mounds, or into slightly flattened balls, if you prefer. Place the little mounds on the prepared pans and decorate them with candied or dried fruit, if desired.

Bake the cookies one sheet at a time for 7 to 10 minutes, just until they are golden on the bottom and dry on the outside. Remove from the oven and let cool.

Montini keep well in an airtight container or cookie tin for a week.

VARIATIONS

• Montini can be white or colored. For brown montini, add a teaspoon of unsweetened cocoa powder to the dough. For a pink version, add 1 teaspoon maraschino liqueur plus some red food coloring. If you want to make a multicolored cookie, divide the dough into two or three portions, color each one, and then sandwich the portions of dough together.

• You can use this recipe to make walnut paste. Substitute walnut flour for the almond flour and brewed coffee for the liqueur.

• The almond dough, which is essentially almond paste, can also be used for stuffed dried fruits. Dates, dried apricots, and dried plums (prunes) filled with almond paste are served, especially in Venice, at Passover and Tu B'Shvat; walnuts can also be sandwiched with almond paste and served as well.

- continued -

TRADITIONAL MONTINI MADE WITH COOKED SUGAR

MAKES 20 COOKIES

——

1¾ cups (200 g) almond flour or finely ground almonds

½ cup minus 1 tablespoon (100 ml) water

1 cup (200 g) granulated sugar, plus more for rolling

1 tablespoon confectioners' sugar

Candied or dried fruit for decoration (optional)

Food coloring (optional; see Variations)

Pour the almond flour into a bowl.

In a small nonstick saucepan, combine the water and sugar and bring to a boil, stirring to dissolve the sugar, then attach a candy thermometer to the side of the pan and cook until the sugar syrup reaches 230°F (110°C), the thread stage. Pour the sugar syrup over the almond flour and mix with a heatproof spoon, then knead with your hands until a smooth dough forms.

Sprinkle the confectioners' sugar on the counter, turn the almond dough out onto the counter, and shape into a flat disk. Wrap it with plastic wrap and let rest for 12 hours in the fridge before using it, following the instructions on page 308.

DICTINOBIS (FICHI NOBIS)
Fried Doughnuts

**MAKES 8 TO
10 DOUGHNUTS**

—

FOR THE DOUGH

1 cup (200 g)
granulated sugar

⅓ cup (80 ml) sweet
dessert wine or
milk

3 tablespoons
sunflower or
peanut oil

2 large (100 g) eggs

Approximately
4 cups (520 g)
all-purpose flour
(you may need a
little more or less),
plus more
for dusting

¼ cup (40 g) potato
starch

Scant 2 teaspoons
(8 g) baking
powder

1 teaspoon
unsweetened
cocoa powder

Pinch of salt

⅔ cup (100 g)
chocolate chips
or chopped mixed
candied fruit
(optional)

Sunflower or peanut
oil for deep-frying

Confectioners'
sugar for sprinkling

These cakey doughnuts can be eaten to celebrate the end of Yom Kippur, as well as the holidays of Purim and Sukkot (although not everyone agrees about the latter). After Yom Kippur, some people prefer to break the fast with something light and easily digestible, but others really want to make up for the calories they missed out on, and fried doughnuts, which are often served with zabaione (page 242), fit the bill!

No one seems to remember the origin of the Latin name of this dish. In Italy, it goes by a simplified misspelling of the original name, fichi nobis, which makes no sense: *fichi* means "figs," and there are no figs in the recipe!

———

In a large bowl, combine the granulated sugar, wine or milk, oil, and eggs and stir with a spoon to mix. Add about half of the flour, the potato starch, baking powder, cocoa, and salt and stir until you have a very sticky dough. Gradually add enough of the remaining flour, stirring, to make a soft, pliable dough with a texture similar to that of short-crust pastry. The amount of flour will vary based on many factors, including humidity, so trust your intuition to decide how much flour to use.

At this point, you can add the chocolate chips or candied fruit, or leave the dough plain.

Pour 1½ inches (4 cm) of oil into a medium saucepan and heat over medium heat until a deep-fry thermometer reads 350°F (180°C). You can test the oil by dropping a small piece of food, such as a slice of apple, into it: if it sizzles nicely but doesn't bubble up too wildly, the oil is ready. (An apple is said to help minimize the smell of the frying oil, so I generally go for that, but any food will do.)

With lightly floured hands, roll a small piece of dough into a rope about ¾ inch (2 cm) thick and shape it into a 2½-inch (6 cm) ring, pinching the ends to seal, then drop it gently into the oil. Fry the doughnut for 2 minutes per side, until golden on both sides. Remove the doughnut from the pot with a slotted spatula and drain it on a paper towel–lined plate.

Proceed to shape and fry the doughnuts until you run out of dough.

Let the doughnuts cool down, then sprinkle with confectioners' sugar. Serve immediately, ideally with a side of zabaione (page 242).

CASTAGNOLE
Fried Cocoa Cookies

MAKES ABOUT
50 BITE-SIZE
COOKIES

—

FOR THE DOUGH

3 tablespoons
sunflower or
peanut oil

3 tablespoons
dessert wine or
milk

½ cup (100 g) sugar

1 large (50 g) egg

2 to 2½ cups
(250 to 300 g)
all-purpose flour,
plus more for
dusting

3 tablespoons
unsweetened
cocoa powder

Pinch of salt

Sunflower or peanut
oil for deep-frying

Castagnole are a traditional Roman Sukkot treat. They look like mini crunchy chocolate cookies, but the dough is fried, so they are surprisingly soft on the inside. In the old days, especially in the Roman Ghetto, no one would ever show up for dinner in the sukkah without a tray of freshly fried castagnole. Some families prepare these for Purim too, as they fit the holiday tradition of eating fried foods.

Italian Catholics have fried treats they prepare for Carnival, which are also called castagnole, but those are fluffy and spongy like doughnuts, while the Jewish cookies are more dense and cakey.

———

To make the dough, in a large bowl, combine the oil, wine or milk, sugar, and egg and stir with a spoon to blend. Add about 1 cup (125 g) of the flour, the cocoa, and salt and stir until you have a very sticky dough. Gradually add enough of the remaining flour, stirring, until you have a soft, pliable dough with a texture similar to that of short-crust pastry or Play-Doh. The amount of flour will vary based on many factors, including humidity, so trust your intuition about how much flour to use.

Pour 1½ inches (4 cm) of oil into a medium saucepan and heat over medium heat until a deep-fry thermometer reads 350°F (180°C). You can test the oil by dropping a small piece of food, such as a slice of apple, into it: if it sizzles nicely but doesn't bubble up too wildly, the oil is ready. (An apple is said to help minimize the smell of the frying oil, so I generally go for that, but any bit of food will do.)

While the oil heats, with lightly floured hands, roll the dough into long ropes about ¾ inch (2 cm) thick and place them on a lightly floured cutting board. With a knife, cut the ropes into small bites approximately the size of gnocchi, ¾ inch (2 cm) long.

Working in batches to avoid crowding, drop the pieces of dough into the oil and fry for about 3 minutes, stirring once, until cooked through. Remove the castagnole from the pan with a slotted spoon or a slotted spatula and drain them on a paper towel–lined plate.

Serve the castagnole slightly warm or at room temperature.

Castagnole can be stored in an airtight container or cookie tin for up to a week.

Crispy Fried Haman's Ears

MAKES 15 PASTRIES

—

2¼ cups (275 g) all-purpose flour, or as needed

Pinch of salt

¼ cup (50 g) granulated sugar

3 tablespoons sunflower or peanut oil

2 large (100 g) eggs

¼ cup (60 ml) grappa, rum, or Marsala

Up to 3 tablespoons milk (or rice milk) or orange juice if necessary

Sunflower or peanut oil for deep-frying

Confectioners' sugar for dusting

The festive season of Carnival occurs immediately before Lent, usually in the month of February. At this time of the year, all over Italy and especially in Venice, you can see colorful parade, with both adults and children dressed up in masks and costumes throwing confetti and streamers at each other.

For Italian Jews, Carnival is associated with Purim, because the two holidays take place at around the same time and have the same joyful spirit. Both are celebrated with an abundance of food and drink, public displays of jubilance, and, most important, masquerades, a custom that probably originated among Italian Jews at the end of the fifteenth century and spread across Europe to gentiles.

Considering the similarities between the holidays, it's not surprising that Italian Jews have adopted one of the most traditional Carnival recipes, chiacchiere, although they have been reshaped and renamed orecchie di Aman, or Haman's ears. Haman's ears, not to be confused with Ashkenazi hamantaschen, are thin, crispy sheets of fried pasta dough covered in sugar; they're the same as chiacchiere, just made in a different shape. Italian chiacchiere are simply cut into strips, while orecchie di Aman are usually triangular or pointy on top.

———

In a large bowl, combine the flour and salt. Make a well in the center of the flour, add the granulated sugar, oil, eggs, and alcohol of your choice, and mix well. Knead the dough with your hands until smooth and elastic. If the dough is too firm, add a little milk or juice; if it is too soft, add a little more flour. The dough should be pliable but not sticky. Allow the dough to rest, covered, for 15 minutes.

Turn the dough out onto a lightly floured work surface. With a rolling pin, roll it out into very thin sheets, about ⅛ inch (3 mm) thick (you could also use a pasta machine to roll out the dough).

With a sharp knife, cut the sheets into rectangles, aiming for about 3 by 2½ inches (8 by 6 cm). Fold, press, and pinch the two top corners of each rectangle together to give it the shape of a pointy animal ear. You can also simply cut the dough into tall triangles with slightly curved sides, or cut it into thinner strips and twist them slightly.

Pour 1½ to 2 inches (4 to 5 cm) of oil into a large saucepan and heat over medium heat until a deep-fry thermometer reads 350°F (180°C). You can test the oil by dropping a small piece of food, such as a slice of apple, into it: if it sizzles nicely but doesn't bubble up too wildly, the oil

is ready. (An apple is said to help minimize the smell of the frying oil, so I generally go for that, but any bit of food will do.)

Gently lower each "ear" of dough into the hot oil using metal tongs, which will help you hold the folded corners in place when the dough starts cooking. Fry the treats in batches, flipping them gently once or twice, until golden, 1 to 2 minutes. Remove with a slotted spoon and drain well on a plate lined with paper towels.

Sprinkle the orecchie with confectioners' sugar and serve warm.

VARIATION

Strufoli is a Purim specialty that is a variation of this recipe. It is short ribbons made out of the same dough. The ribbons are tied in a knot, fried, and drizzled with honey.

MANICOTTI
Sweet Fried Pasta Swirls

MAKES ABOUT
12 LARGE MANICOTTI
(OR 24 SMALL ONES)

—

FOR THE RIBBONS

A triple recipe
  Fresh Egg Pasta
  (page 103)

About 1 tablespoon
  cornmeal

Sunflower or peanut
  oil for deep-frying

FOR THE SUGAR
SYRUP

2 cups (400 g) sugar

1 cup (240 ml) water

1 teaspoon fresh
  lemon juice

Sesame seeds
  for sprinkling
  (optional)

Jewish Italian manicotti, which we prepare to celebrate Purim, bear no relationship to the pasta dish called manicotti in the States, other than the fact that both recipes are made with egg pasta. Our manicotti are ribbons of fresh pasta rolled into swirls as they fry, and then glazed with sugar syrup. It may take a few tries to get the hang of the technique, as the rolling and frying takes a bit of practice, but they make an impressive dessert and a wonderful gift as well.

———

Divide the dough into 12 portions. Using a rolling pin or a pasta machine, roll each one into a rectangular sheet about 3 by 12 inches (8 by 30 cm). If you are not confident in your frying skills, you can cut the larger sheets in half to make 24 smaller sheets, 1½ by 6 inches (4 by 15 cm).

Lay the sheets out on a wet dish towel dusted with cornmeal, making sure to use enough cornmeal to keep the sheets from sticking. Line a large tray with paper towels.

Pour 1½ to 2 inches (4 to 5 cm) of oil into a medium saucepan and heat over medium heat until a deep-fry thermometer reads 350°F (180°C). You can test the oil by dropping a small piece of food, such as a slice of apple, into it: if it sizzles nicely but doesn't bubble up too wildly, the oil is ready. (An apple is said to help minimize the smell of the frying oil, so I generally go for that, but any bit of food will do.)

Pick up a fork and roll the end of one of the pasta ribbons around the tines. Dip the fork into the hot oil, holding the other end of the pasta ribbon with your other hand, then gradually roll the pasta ribbon up on the fork into a swirl. The pasta will bubble and puff up as it fries, so you need to be gentle and fast at the same time. Fry the pasta ribbon, turning it over once, until golden.

Carefully lift out the swirl and drop it onto the paper towels to drain and cool. Repeat with the remaining pasta, adding more oil if needed and letting it heat up before frying another swirl.

While the fried pasta cools, prepare the sugar syrup: In a medium saucepan, combine the sugar, water, and lemon juice and bring to a simmer over medium-low heat, stirring until the sugar is fully dissolved, then continue to simmer until reduced to a thick syrup that coats the back of a spoon, 10 to 15 minutes. Remove from the heat.

Dip the pasta rolls into the syrup to coat, or drizzle the syrup over the pasta rolls if you prefer. Sprinkle with sesame seeds, if desired, then serve.

Bologna, Ferrara, and Emilia-Romagna

Emilia-Romagna, the region due south of Lombardy and Veneto,
has a rich Jewish history. Its capital, Bologna; the city of Ferrara; and a number
of smaller towns, including Modena, Reggio Emilia, Parma, Soragna, and many
others (thirty in total), have or have had at some point in time a Jewish community.

The first Jews of Emilia-Romagna settled in the area adjacent to the Adriatic coast back in the eleventh century, because of its favorable position close to the trade routes between Venice and the Levant.

During the fourteenth and fifteenth centuries, thanks to the generous policies of the dukes of Este, the community in Emilia-Romagna grew, welcoming Jews who were expelled from Spain (in 1492), Portugal (in 1498), and Germany (in 1530).

One of the most prosperous Jewish communities, whose members were not only moneylenders but also rich merchants, was the one in Bologna. Throughout its history, Bologna has been a major cultural center (it is home to the first university ever founded, as early as 1088!), and the Jewish culture there bloomed along with the mainstream one. In 1488, the University of Bologna even established a course in Judaism.

However, the good relationship between Jews and Christians was not meant to last, as a wave of Christian preachers orchestrated a polemical campaign against the Jews and the Marranos, Jews from Spain and Portugal who had converted during the Inquisition but were suspected of maintaining Jewish customs in their homes.

Under the influence of the papacy, the Jews experienced a worsening of their social conditions, especially following the violently anti-Jewish bull *Cum nimis absurdum*, published in 1555. In various urban centers, Jewish freedom was suddenly limited, and Jews were either expelled, as happened in Parma in 1488 and in Piacenza in 1570, or locked into ghettos. Ghettos were established in Bologna in 1566 (then shut down in 1593 with the definitive expulsion), in Ferrara in 1627, in Modena in 1630, and in other cities later on.

Throughout the nineteenth century, the ghettos of Emilia-Romagna were abolished, restored, or partially opened several times until they disappeared completely with the unification of the country.

With greater social integration came a dilution of the Italian Jewish culture in the region. Many smaller Jewish communities shrank to almost nothing or merged with larger ones.

Unfortunately, with the racial laws established in 1938, Italian Jews were once again a legally separate and actively discriminated-against body of citizens within the state. Approximately two hundred Jews were deported from Bologna and Ferrara. In Emilia-Romagna, or, more precisely, in Fossoli di Carpi, a concentration camp functioned from 1942: a total of five thousand prisoners,

The synagogue in Modena

Jews, and political opponents destined for extermination camps were imprisoned there.

The Jewish communities of Emilia-Romagna—Bologna, Ferrara, and the nearby towns—have fewer than four hundred residents today. However, Emilia-Romagna is still home to some great Jewish sights, cherished by the small but active congregations living in the region.

In Ferrara, you can visit the old ghetto, with its original structure and appearance preserved; three fascinating synagogues that have been housed under a single roof on Via Mazzini since 1485; the famous cemetery along Via delle Vigne, a very evocative and emotional place; and the impressive recently opened MEIS, Museum of Italian Judaism and the Shoah.

In Bologna, you can go for a stroll through the old ghetto in the heart of the historic city center, visit the Art Nouveau synagogue, spend some time in the Jewish Museum, and walk by the dramatic Shoah memorial.

There aren't any kosher restaurants in Ferrara or Bologna, but the local Jewish institutions can arrange kosher meals on request. For those who don't mind eating nonkosher, in Ferrara, try Osteria del Ghetto and Trattoria da Noemi, where you can taste local specialties such as pasta filled with pumpkin (page 129) and torta tenerina (page 259). In Bologna, dining at Trattoria Bertozzi and at Ristorante da Bertino are a must, and make sure to have a taste of the legendary lasagna Bolognese (page 121), as well as other pasta dishes.

Great day trips in the region include the towns of Modena, Parma, and Soragna, where you can visit beautiful old synagogues and, of course, also enjoy excellent food.

Pane

BREAD

HALLÀH
Challah

MAKES 2 LARGE LOAVES

—

1⅓ cups (315 ml) water

½ cup (100 g) sugar

1 packet (¼ ounce/ 7 g) active dry yeast

⅓ cup (80 ml) sunflower or peanut oil, plus more for greasing the bowl

3 large (150 g) eggs

1 teaspoon salt

4 to 5 cups (550 to 680 g) bread flour (all-purpose flour will also work), plus more for dusting

Sesame or poppy seeds for sprinkling (optional)

Challah belongs on every Jewish table on Shabbat, including those in Italy. The soft, fluffy loaf of egg bread is the same all over the world. Most old Jewish-Italian books, as well as family recipe books, include a recipe for challah.

This is my best recipe for challah, but I consider it a never-ending work in progress. I have tried more challah recipes than I can recall, and I still experiment whenever I come across a recipe that intrigues me. I hope you will use this challah to bless your table on Shabbat.

———

In the bowl of a stand mixer, or in a large bowl, if you are working by hand, combine the water and sugar. Sprinkle the yeast over the top and let stand for 5 minutes.

Add the oil and 2 (100 g) of the eggs to the bowl and stir everything together.

If using a stand mixer, attach the bowl to the mixer stand and fit it with the dough hook. Add the salt and 1½ cups (200 g) of the flour to the liquid mixture and mix well. Add 2½ cups (350 g) more flour and knead on low speed for 5 minutes. The amount of flour you will need depends on many variables, so proceed gradually, adding up to 1 cup (130 g) more flour if necessary, kneading until the dough comes together and no longer sticks to the sides of the bowl or to your fingers. If you are working by hand, add the salt and then add the flour as above, mixing the dough with your hands in the bowl until it's no longer possible, then turn it out onto a floured counter and knead for about 10 minutes.

If using a stand mixer, turn the dough out onto a floured counter and knead by hand for 2 minutes or so, to get a feel for it: it should be soft, smooth, and elastic. If in doubt about the texture, err on the side of a wetter, stickier dough, as you can add more flour after the dough has risen if necessary; a dough that's too dry can't really be saved and will yield a doughy, dense bread with a tight crumb.

Place the dough in an oiled bowl, cover with plastic wrap, set in a warm place, and let rise until doubled in bulk, 1½ to 2 hours. I find that beyond the 3-hour mark, the dough will deflate, so keep an eye on the clock. (However, the dough can be given a slower, longer rise, up to 24 hours, in the refrigerator to accommodate your schedule if needed; see Note.)

- continued -

When the dough has risen, turn it out on a counter dusted with flour and divide it into 6 equal pieces. Roll each piece into a rope about 12 inches (30 cm) long. If the ropes shrink back as you try to roll them out, let them rest for 5 minutes to relax the gluten and then try again.

For each loaf, arrange 3 of the ropes side by side and, starting in the middle, braid them together as you would braid hair. Squeeze the ends together when you get to the first end of the braid and fold the end under itself. Turn the challah around and repeat the braiding on the other half of the dough. (I start braiding in the middle because it makes the resulting challah more evenly shaped, but if you find it confusing, you can just braid the ropes from top to bottom, like a regular braid, and you'll be just fine.)

Line a baking sheet with parchment paper and place the braided challahs on top. Cover with a clean kitchen towel and let rise in a warm place for about 1 hour, until well puffed up.

At least 15 minutes before baking, preheat the oven to 400°F (200°C).

When you are ready to bake, whisk the remaining egg with 1 tablespoon water and brush it all over the challah. Sprinkle with sesame or poppy seeds, if desired.

Bake the challah for 15 minutes, then lower the temperature to 350°F (180°C) and continue baking until the challah is golden brown, 15 to 20 more minutes. Remove from the oven and let cool before serving.

NOTE

I like to make the challah and bake it right before dinner, so it's the freshest it can be, but that's not always possible in terms of schedule. If this is an issue, make the dough with slightly less than half the amount of yeast called for in the recipe one full day ahead of when you need to bake it (for example, on Thursday night for Friday night) and let it sit in the fridge for 24 hours, covered with plastic wrap. After 24 hours, take the dough out of the fridge, divide it and shape into ropes while it's still cold, braid it, and let rise until puffed and pillowy, approximately 1½ hours. Bake it as directed.

Crunchy Buns

**MAKES ABOUT
16 BUNS**

—

3 cups (720 ml)
  water

1 packet (¼ ounce/
  7 g) active dry
  yeast

½ teaspoon sugar

7½ cups (1 kg) bread
  flour (or a mix of
  bread flour and
  durum wheat
  flour), plus more
  for dusting

1 tablespoon salt

Sunflower or peanut
  oil for greasing the
  bowl

Ossi—the name translates as "bones"—are small, super-crunchy buns. They make a great base for sandwiches and are a perfect vehicle for scooping up the last drops of any pasta sauce. They are quite easy and quick to make, which is a great advantage on a day when you forget to buy bread. Because they are made with yeast instead of a sourdough starter, they keep for only a day, so plan accordingly, and consider preparing less than a whole recipe if you think you won't eat them all in that time.

———

In the bowl of a stand mixer fitted with the dough hook, or in a large bowl, if you are making the dough by hand, stir together the water, yeast, and sugar. Let stand for 5 minutes.

Add half of the flour to the yeast mixture, then add the salt and start kneading on low speed or by hand. When the flour has been absorbed, gradually add the remaining flour (you may not need the full amount, or you may need slightly more flour, so proceed slowly), mixing until the dough comes together, pulls away from the sides of the bowl, and wraps around the dough hook, if using. The dough should feel smooth, soft, and elastic and still be somewhat damp and soggy.

Lightly oil a large bowl, transfer the dough to the bowl, cover with plastic wrap, and let rest and rise for an hour at room temperature.

Line two baking sheets with parchment paper.

Turn the dough out onto a well-floured counter. Divide the dough in half, handling it as little as possible so as not to deflate it. It should still feel wet and sticky. With your fingers coated in flour, gently form each piece of dough into a roll, then cut each one into small buns, 3 inches (8 cm) square. Dust the buns generously with flour and gently place them on the prepared baking sheets. (The shape of the buns will not be perfect, as the dough is soft and wobbly, and that's fine.)

Let the buns rise for 20 more minutes. In the meantime, preheat the oven to 400°F (200°C).

Bake the buns for 20 to 25 minutes, until golden and firm to the touch. Remove from the oven and serve warm or at room temperature.

Ossi are best eaten fresh out of the oven, or at least on the same day they are baked.

White Pizza

SERVES 6

—

1 teaspoon diastatic malt powder (optional; see Note)

½ teaspoon (2 g) active dry yeast

1¾ cups (425 ml) water

3¾ cups (500 g) bread flour

2½ teaspoons kosher salt, plus more for sprinkling

1½ tablespoons extra-virgin olive oil, plus more for coating the pan and for drizzling

½ cup (70 g) semolina

Practically every bakery in Rome offers pizza bianca, as well as pizza rossa (pizza bianca is plain and dressed with olive oil and salt, like focaccia, while pizza rossa has tomato sauce), because Italians really love it!

Roman Jews serve pizza bianca to accompany charcuterie specialties like coppiette (page 69) or goose prosciutto (page 49). This recipe requires a bit of patience, as the dough contains very little yeast and therefore is given a long, slow rise in the fridge, but the result is well worth the wait.

———

In the bowl of a stand mixer fitted with the dough hook, or in a large bowl if you are making the dough by hand, stir together the malt, if using, yeast, and a little more than ¼ cup (60 ml) of the water. Add 1 cup (135 g) of the flour and mix for a minute to combine. Remove the bowl from the mixer stand, if using, cover with plastic wrap, and set aside to rest in a warm place (I put it in the oven, with just the oven light on) for 1½ hours.

Add the remaining water, the remaining flour, and the salt to the bowl (return it to the mixer stand if necessary) and knead until you have a dough that pulls away from the sides of the bowl and wraps around the hook, if using. Add the olive oil and knead a few more minutes, until the oil is absorbed and the dough pulls away from the sides of the bowl again.

Remove the bowl from the stand again, if necessary, cover the dough with plastic wrap, and let rest at room temperature for 30 minutes, then transfer to the fridge. Let the dough rest in the fridge for 6 to 7 hours.

Take the dough out of the fridge and place the bowl back in the oven, with just the light on, for an hour. Remove from the oven.

Preheat the oven to 500°F (260°C). Grease a half sheet pan (or a large rimmed baking sheet) generously with olive oil.

Sprinkle a clean work surface with the semolina and turn the dough out onto it, then pat it down into a rough rectangle, with a short side toward you. Fold the dough as follows: Lift up one of the long sides of the dough and fold it to the center of the dough. Brush off any excess flour. Lift up the opposite side of the dough and fold and stretch it over the first fold, as you would fold a letter. Brush off the excess flour.

Let the dough rest for a minute, then turn it 90 degrees, pat it out into a large rectangle again, and repeat the folding process. Slice the dough open with a knife so it opens like a butterfly or a book and repeat the folding one last time.

Place the dough back in the bowl, cover it with plastic wrap, and let rest for 5 more minutes, then transfer it to the prepared pan.

Lightly flour your hands. Very gently, grab the dough from underneath, starting at the center, and pull it slowly in all directions to stretch it, trying not to tear it. When it gets too difficult to stretch this way (because your fingers won't reach the center of the dough anymore), gently press the dough down with your fingertips, still moving from the center outward, to spread the dough all the way into the corners of the pan. Should the dough spring back and resist spreading, let it rest for 5 minutes and then resume pressing. Don't overwork the dough by pressing it down too much: it's OK for the dough to look uneven and a bit messy. Let the dough rest one last time for 5 minutes.

Drizzle olive oil over the top of the dough, and sprinkle with a few generous pinches of salt.

Bake the pizza bianca for 10 to 12 minutes, until golden and crispy. Or, for a pizza bianca with charred spots on top, which some people enjoy, reduce the baking time by 5 minutes, turn on the broiler, and broil until you reach the desired darkness (but keep an eye on it so the whole pizza hasn't burned before you notice!). Remove from the oven and let cool on a wire rack until just warm or room temperature.

Pizza bianca is best the day it's made, but it can be kept for a day or two and reheated briefly in the oven or toasted before serving.

NOTE

Diastatic malt powder is a special baking ingredient that promotes a strong rise and a better crust. It can be easily found online, but if you don't have it, you can skip it.

VARIATION

You can use this dough to make small buns similar to ossi (page 327). When the dough is ready for shaping, follow the instructions on page 327 to make small buns and bake accordingly.

ROSCHETTE ALL'HEBREA
Breadstick Rings

MAKES 140 VERY
SMALL ROSCHETTE

—

1 teaspoon (4 g)
    active dry yeast

1 cup (240 ml) water

½ cup minus
    1 teaspoon (115 ml)
    oil: equal parts
    extra-virgin olive
    oil and sunflower
    or peanut oil

3⅔ cups minus
    1 tablespoon
    (450 g) all-purpose
    flour

2 tablespoons
    durum wheat
    semolina flour
    or additional
    all-purpose flour
    (see Note)

Scant 1 teaspoon
    salt

Roschette all'hebrea, the Italian version of Spanish rosquillas, are little ring-shaped breadsticks that are traditionally served on the night before a brit milah, the circumcision ceremony, when people gather to pray and study together in preparation for the big event.

For years, I thought of this recipe as Libyan, because I learned it from my Libyan grandmother, Malu, but I was wrong: roschette have been a Jewish specialty in the city of Livorno since the seventeenth century. Apparently, the addictive roschette traveled all the way from Livorno to the Italian colonies, including Libya, where they became widely appreciated: there they were always offered as a welcoming treat for guests, along with a cup of coffee, and that's the way I serve them in my house.

This recipe makes almost 12 dozen roschette, but don't worry: even if that sounds like a lot, they are very small and will disappear in seconds.

———

In a large bowl, mix the yeast with the water and oil. Let stand for 5 minutes.

Add the flour, semolina (or additional all-purpose flour), and salt to the bowl, stir, and knead vigorously until you get a dough that is no longer sticky. It should feel a little softer and more elastic than bread dough and should form easily into a ball.

Put the dough in a large bowl, cover with plastic wrap, and let rise in a warm place for 1 hour, or until roughly doubled in size.

Preheat the oven to 350°F (180°C). Line two baking sheets with parchment paper.

To shape the roschette, pull off a very small portion of dough, the size of a hazelnut (⅛ ounce/5 g is ideal), and roll into a very thin rope approximately 4 inches (10 cm) in length, then form it into a ring approximately 1½ inches (4 cm) across, pinch the ends to seal, and place it on one of the prepared pans. The rings should be really thin, because the roschette will puff up a bit as they bake. You can shape enough roschette to fill the second baking sheet now, and then continue filling the baking sheets as you go, but the roschette are best baked one sheet at a time.

Bake the roschette one sheet at a time for 15 to 20 minutes, until they are starting to turn golden but are still a bit pale. Remove the roschette from the oven and let cool on a wire rack.

Roschette will keep very well in tins or a paper bag (do not store in plastic bags or containers, and do not freeze) for 7 to 10 days.

NOTE

The semolina makes the roschette crunchier, but you can simply use more flour if you don't have it.

VARIATIONS

Roschette can also be made with sesame seeds sprinkled on top before baking (brush them with water first, so the sesame sticks!), or with about 2 tablespoons fennel seeds mixed into the dough.

Raisin Rolls

MAKES 10 ROLLS

—

2 packets (½ ounce/ 14 g) active dry yeast

1 cup (240 ml) water

1½ cups (300 g) sugar

1 cup (240 ml) sunflower or peanut oil

3 large (150 g) eggs, plus 1 large (19 g) egg yolk

8 cups (1 kg) all-purpose flour, plus more for dusting

1 cup raisins (150 g), soaked in water until plumped and drained

Sesame seeds for sprinkling

Sweet raisin bread was likely brought to Italy by the Spanish Jews in the fifteenth century. It was served to conclude festive meals, and it was also distributed to the poor under the sukkah for the holiday of Sukkot, together with quince jelly (page 239). Today this sweet raisin bread is still eaten on Sukkot, but also on Yom Kippur. Some Jewish women have been known to smuggle their bulo rolls into the synagogue and hand some out right after the sound of the shofar that announces the end of the fast, so family members can snack on something even before they get home.

———

In the bowl of a stand mixer fitted with the dough hook, or in a large bowl, if you are making the dough by hand, combine the yeast and water. Let stand for 5 minutes.

Add the sugar, oil, and whole eggs to the yeast mixture and mix well. Add the flour a couple of cups (about 250 g) at a time, kneading vigorously until the dough comes together. This dough will feel tougher and denser than most bread doughs, and that's the way it should be.

Put the dough in a large bowl, cover with plastic wrap, set in a warm spot, and let rise for 1½ hours, until almost doubled in volume.

Line two baking sheets with parchment paper. Turn the dough out onto a floured counter, press it down gently, and knead in the raisins.

Divide the dough into 10 portions and form into 5-inch-long (13 cm) rolls. Place them on the prepared baking sheets and let rise for another hour, or until nicely puffed.

Preheat the oven to 350°F (180°C).

Lightly beat the egg yolk in a small cup and brush the rolls with the egg. Sprinkle them with sesame seeds and bake for 10 to 12 minutes. Reduce the heat to 325°F (160°C) and bake for another 5 to 10 minutes, until golden brown. Keep an eye on the rolls, and don't let them get too dark. Remove from the oven and let cool.

The rolls can be wrapped in aluminum foil and kept for up to a day. For longer storage, wrap them in foil, place them in a plastic bag, and freeze for up to a few months.

VARIATIONS

• The oldest recipes for this bread include anise seeds, lemon peel, and candied fruit (most often citron), along with the raisins, but these days most people make them with raisins only.

• You can swap chocolate chips for the raisins; your kids will love it!

Shavuot, Lag Ba'omer, Tu B'Shvat, and Tu B'Av

The life of a Jew has its own special rhythm, marked by the many holidays in our calendar that reconnect us with God, our family, and our community. Here are some other holidays worth mentioning, and the traditional foods we eat to celebrate them.

Shavuot

Shavuot commemorates the revelation of God on Mount Sinai and the gift of the Torah, the Jewish law. On this holiday, we eat dairy products, because it is said (among many other symbolical interpretations) that the Torah nourishes our souls the way milk nourishes babies.

Italian Jews typically celebrate with the cheesy semolina dumplings called *gnocchi alla romana* (page 138); crostata di ricotta e visciole (page 263), which is a short-crust tart filled with ricotta and jam; and cassola, a baked ricotta cheesecake (page 260).

Lag Ba'omer

Lag Ba'omer is a minor holiday that occurs on the thirty-third day of the Omer, the forty-nine-day period between Passover (see page 305) and Shavuot. The Omer is a time of semi-mourning, because according to the Talmud, during this season a plague killed thousands of students of Rabbi Akiva. The plague is believed to have ended on Lag Ba'omer, the thirty-third day of the Omer, so as a result, Lag Ba'omer is celebrated as a joyful twenty-four hour break from the sadness of the Omer period. On this holiday, Jews all over the world traditionally go for picnics and light bonfires. Torta di erbette (page 32), tibuia (page 37), tortiglioni (page 40), and buricche (page 43) are a great fit for a picnic as they travel very well.

Tu B'Shvat

Tu B'Shvat is the New Year of the Trees. On this holiday, we plant new trees and eat the seven types of grains and fruit for which Israel was historically renowned: wheat, barley, olives, dates, grapes, figs, and pomegranate. Traditional dishes of this holiday include carrots with raisins (page 222), rice dressed in tomato and chicken giblet sauce (page 136), and a dense cake with dried fruit and nuts (page 264).

Tu B'Av

Tu B'Av is a Jewish holiday that celebrates love and is similar to Valentine's Day. While many Jews don't do anything special on this day, it is considered an auspicious day for weddings. On Tu B'Av, we generally prepare the same recipes we would for a romantic Valentine's Day treat, and that might include chocolate, such as the decadent, flourless chocolate cake called *torta tenerina* (page 259).

PUTIZZA DI NOCI
Sweet Nut Loaf

MAKES ONE 10-INCH
(25 CM) ROUND LOAF;
SERVES 8 TO 10

—

FOR THE FILLING

1½ cups (150 g)
walnuts

⅔ cup (100 g)
almonds

⅓ cup (50 g)
hazelnuts

2 tablespoons
pine nuts

½ cup (100 g) sugar

1½ ounces (40 g)
dark chocolate

1⅓ cups (200 g)
raisins, soaked
in warm water to
plump and drained

3 tablespoons rum

1½ teaspoons honey

1½ teaspoons
apricot jam
(or additional
honey)

Grated zest of
¼ orange

Grated zest of
¼ lemon

1 large (50 g) egg,
separated, plus
2 large (60 g) egg
whites

- ingredients continued -

While the home country of this rich, festive bread is Slovenia, in the area of Trieste and Gorizia, Italian Christians have adopted it to celebrate Christmas and Easter and Italian Jews to celebrate Rosh Hashanah.

There are countless versions of this sweet nut bread, which is often confused with a similar local bread called *gubana*, and every family uses different ingredients in the filling. The simplest versions feature only walnuts, raisins, honey, and cinnamon; more elaborate ones include hazelnuts, pine nuts, and almonds. The richest versions also have cookie crumbs and jam thrown into the mix, although some people theorize that these ingredients were added by merchants to make the loaf heavier, and therefore more expensive.

Thanks to the presence of a generous amount of nuts and dried fruit, this bread is also well suited to the holiday of Tu B'Shvat.

————

To prepare the filling, in a food processor, grind the walnuts, almonds, hazelnuts, and pine nuts with the sugar to coarse crumbs. Transfer the nut crumble to a large bowl.

Coarsely chop the chocolate and add it to the bowl with the nut crumble. Add the raisins as well.

In a small bowl, stir together the rum, honey, jam, and orange and lemon zest. Add to the nut crumble, mix well to combine, and set aside.

To prepare the dough, in a medium bowl, combine the water, yeast, 1 tablespoon of the sugar, and 1 cup (125 g) of the flour to make a quick starter. Cover with plastic wrap and let rest for 30 minutes at room temperature.

In the meantime, mound the remaining 3 cups (375 g) flour on a clean work surface and make a well in the center. Add the remaining sugar, the egg and egg yolks, rum, orange and lemon zest, salt, and melted butter to the center of the well and mix them together with a spoon, trying to avoid mixing in the flour yet. Add the prepared starter to the mixture in the center of the well, then start to mix in the flour, continuing until you have a smooth dough.

Knead the dough into a ball, transfer it to a bowl, cover, set in a warm place, and let rise for an hour, or until doubled in size.

- continued -

⅓ cup (80 ml) water

1 packet (¼ ounce/
   7 g) active dry
   yeast

¾ cup (150 g) sugar

4 cups (500 g)
   all-purpose flour,
   plus more for
   dusting

1 large (50 g) egg
   plus 2 large (38 g)
   egg yolks

2 tablespoons rum

Grated zest of
   ¼ orange

Grated zest of
   ¼ lemon

Pinch of salt

4 tablespoons
   (½ stick/57 g)
   butter or
   margarine,
   melted

1 egg, beaten with
   a few drops of
   water, for glaze

Line the bottom of a 10-inch (25 cm) cake pan with parchment paper.

When the dough has doubled, turn it out onto a generously floured work surface, flatten it with a rolling pin, and roll out into a large rectangle about ⅛ inch (3 mm) thick.

Add the egg yolk to the reserved filling and stir well.

In a large bowl, whip the egg whites in a bowl with a handheld mixer for about 5 minutes, until stiff peaks form. Gently fold the egg whites into the filling.

With a spatula, spread the filling evenly over the rolled-out dough. Roll the dough up from a long side to form a rope and then coil the rope on itself to form a snail. Fit it into the prepared pan and let the roll rest for 30 minutes at room temperature, covered with a kitchen towel.

Preheat the oven to 425°F (220°C).

Brush the egg glaze over the top of the dough. Bake for 10 minutes, then reduce the temperature to 350°F (180°C) and bake for 35 minutes.

In the meantime, crumple up a piece of parchment paper and soak it in water briefly, then squeeze out the excess water.

After the loaf has baked for a total of 45 minutes and has started to get a nice golden-brown crust, cover it with the wet parchment paper, which will keep the loaf moist and prevent it from burning, and bake for 5 to 10 more minutes (total baking time is 50 to 55 minutes), until fully baked through. Remove from the oven.

Let the loaf cool in the cake pan for at least 30 minutes, then run a knife around the edges of the loaf to release it and turn it out onto a wire rack, then invert onto the rack and let cool to room temperature.

Serve cut into wedges, with a nice cup of tea or coffee.

The loaf keeps well wrapped in aluminum foil for a couple of days.

Smaller Italian Jewish Communities

With its long and multifaceted Jewish history, Italy has many cities, towns, and villages where Jews have established themselves over the two thousand years since they originally came to the country. The regions discussed below have smaller populations of Jewish citizens today, but they are important to note for historical and cultural context, as they did have lively Jewish communities in the past.

Friuli–Venezia Giulia

On a short day trip from Venice, less than two hours by car, you can visit Trieste and Gorizia, in the region of Friuli–Venezia Giulia.

Trieste is one of the oldest holdings of the Habsburg monarchy, home to Jewish settlements as early as the thirteenth century. In the nineteenth century, a community of six thousand Jews lived in Trieste, and among them were many famous artists and intellectuals, such as the poet Umberto Saba and the writer Italo Svevo.

After World War II, the Jewish population had shrunk to only six hundred, but the beautiful local synagogue, built in 1912, still stands. In addition to the synagogue, the Carlo and Vera Wagner Museum is worth a visit.

Gorizia, also ruled by the Habsburgs, had its first Jewish settlements in the sixteenth century. Despite being locked in the ghetto there for a hundred years, Jews enjoyed relative freedom in Gorizia, and the community had grown to more than three hundred members by 1850, when the population started to dwindle. The community was eventually wiped out in concentration camps from 1943 to 1944, but in town you can still visit the baroque synagogue and the Jewish Museum.

When it comes to Jewish Italian food, both in Trieste and Gorizia, you can easily find in most bakeries the delicious putizza di noci (page 335), a sweet bread filled with nuts, honey, and chocolate, as well as simple almond pastries that closely resemble Jewish montini (page 308).

Marche

There were few Jews living in the Marche region before the year 1000, but the Jewish population grew substantially in subsequent years thanks to Sephardic immigrants from the Kingdom of Naples, Ashkenazis from Germany, and Levantini from the Levant. These immigrants were hardworking people, as evidenced by their surnames, including Orefice (jeweler), Tessitori (weavers), and Tintori (dyers), among others.

Because of the attitude of the popes toward them, Jews in the Marche region experienced both privileges and restrictions over time. Many small Jewish settlements in the Marche region disappeared when Jews were forced into ghettos in Ancona, Urbino, Pesaro, and Senigallia. However, these four cities still offer testimonies of their past with their beautiful synagogues, three of which remain in use.

It is difficult to find local Jewish Italian foods in the Marche region today, but the Jews there proudly prepare the legendary marzipan snake (page 270).

- continued -

ABOVE: *The facade of the Synagogue of Trieste (top) and a view of Urbino (bottom)*
OPPOSITE: *The Scolanova Synagogue in Trani, Apulia*

Naples and Southern Italy

The Jewish community of Naples, in Campania, is the southernmost one of Italy, and it is responsible for all the other smaller Jewish settlements that exist in the regions of Molise, Apulia, Basilicata, Calabria, and Sicily.

A Jewish presence was recorded in Campania as early as the first century BCE, but it was only in the nineteenth century that this community was fully brought back to life, after centuries of dramatic changes. The Jews in this region lived through very positive phases of freedom (under the Aragonese domain) and very dark times (under the Anjovin domain), but they eventually had to leave Southern Italy after the 1541 expulsion—only to return to Naples in 1831, thanks to the financial support of a German family of bankers, the Rothschilds.

At the beginning of the twentieth century, the Jewish community of Naples counted one thousand people, but by the end of World War II, only a few more than five hundred remained, and today they number approximately two hundred, including the Jews in the rest of Southern Italy.

Among the Jews of the Neapolitan community we count the people of Trani, in Apulia, a Jewish community whose history began in ancient Roman times and, again, lasted until the 1541 expulsion. The Jews of Trani lived in their own quarter, called Giudecca, for centuries, and they had as many as four synagogues, although these were later converted into churches. In 2007, the ancient Scolanova Synagogue, built in 1243 and later used as a church, was returned to the community, which now celebrates the holidays there.

Sicily once boasted one of the largest Jewish populations in the Diaspora, with a fascinating history that started in 59 BCE and lasted fifteen centuries. Sicily has had more than fifty Jewish

settlements, and in particularly favorable times, Jews accounted for 20 to 30 percent of the population, until the expulsion in 1493, when the community—about thirty-five thousand people—scattered and disappeared or converted to Christianity.

Among the remnants of Sicilian Jewish life, the most impressive is the Jewish quarter of Ortigia, in Syracuse, which has preserved its fifteenth-century layout as well as an original mikveh (ritual bath).

Luckily, though, Jewish life has seen a rebirth in Sicily. After more than five centuries, a small Jewish community was established in Syracuse in 2010.

Resources

BEANS

Camellia
camelliabrand.com

CHEESE

Murray's Cheese
murrayscheese.com

Saxelby Cheese
saxelbycheese.com

COOKWARE

Falcon
falconenamelware.com

Food52
food52.com/shop

IKEA
ikea.com/us/en

Le Creuset
lecreuset.com

Lodge
lodgecastiron.com

Sur La Table
surlatable.com

Webstaurant Store
webstaurantstore.com

FLOUR

Bakers Authority
bakersauthority.com

Bob's Red Mill
bobsredmill.com

King Arthur Baking
kingarthurbaking.com

FRUITS AND NUTS

Bella Viva Orchards
bellaviva.com

Nuts.com
nuts.com

Paradise Brands
paradisefruitco.com

ITALIAN IMPORTED GOODS

Eataly
eataly.com/us_en/

Guidi Marcello
guidimarcello.com

Gustiamo
gustiamo.com

Italian Harvest
italianharvest.com

Sogno Toscano
sognotoscano.com

Yümmy Bazaar
yummybazaar.co
/collections/italy

MEAT, FISH, CHARCUTERIE

Aqua Best
aquabestnyc.com

Bella Bella Gourmet
bellabellagourmet.com

Browne Trading Company
brownetrading.com

D'Artagnan
www.dartagnan.com

DeBragga
debragga.com

Grow & Behold
growandbehold.com

Heritage Foods
heritagefoods.com

Joe Jurgielewicz & Son
tastyduck.com

Porter Road
porterroad.com

Sea to Table
sea2table.com

Snake River Farms
snakeriverfarms.com

ONLINE SPECIALTY FOODS

Goldbelly
goldbelly.com

Mercato
mercato.com

OTHER GOURMET OR SPECIAL INTEREST PRODUCTS

Di Bruno Bros.
dibruno.com

Glatt Kosher Store
glattkosherstore.com

Gourmet Food World
gourmetfoodworld.com

SPICES AND HERBS

Diaspora Co.
diasporaco.com

Mountain Rose Herbs
mountainroseherbs.com

Penzey's
penzeys.com

Rumi Spice
rumispice.com

Bibliography

ENGLISH

Cooper, John. *Eat and Be Satisfied: A Social History of Jewish Food.* Northvale, NJ: Jason Aronson, 1993.

Gitlitz, David M., and Linda Kay Davidson. *A Drizzle of Honey: The Life and Recipes of Spain's Secret Jews.* New York: St. Martin's Press, 1999.

Goldstein, Joyce. *Cucina Ebraica: Flavors of the Italian Jewish Kitchen.* San Francisco: Chronicle, 1998.

Machlin, Edda Servi. *The Classic Cuisine of the Italian Jews: Traditional Recipes and Menus and a Memoir of a Vanished Way of Life.* New York: Giro Press, 1993.

Parla, Katie, and Kristina Gill. *Tasting Rome: Fresh Flavors and Forgotten Recipes from an Ancient City.* New York: Clarkson Potter, 2016.

Roden, Claudia. *The Book of Jewish Food: An Odyssey from Samarkand to New York.* London: Penguin Books, 1996.

———. "The Dishes of the Jews of Italy: A Historical Survey." *Notes from Zamir,* Spring 2003.

Roth, Cecil. *The History of the Jews of Italy.* Philadelphia: Jewish Publication Society of America, 1946.

Sacerdoti, Annie. *The Guide to Jewish Italy.* Venice: Marsilio, 2013.

Zanini De Vita, Oretta. *Popes, Peasants and Shepherds: Recipes and Lore from Rome and Lazio.* Berkeley: University of California Press, 2013.

ITALIAN AND OTHER LANGUAGES

Agostini, Maria. *Dolci ebraici della tradizione veneziana.* Venice: Filippi Editore, 1995.

Anau, Roberta, and Elena Loewenthal. *Cucina ebraica.* Milan: Fabbri, 2003.

Artusi, Pellegrino. *La scienza in cucina e l'arte di mangiar bene.* Florence: A. Salani, 1908.

Ascoli Vitali-Norsa, Giuliana. *La cucina nella tradizione ebraica: Ricette di cucina ebraica, italiana, askenazita e sefardita.* Florence: Giuntina, 1987.

Belgrado Passigli, Milka. *Le ricette di casa mia: La cucina casher in una famiglia ebraica italiana.* Florence: Giuntina, 1993.

———. *Nuove ricette di casa mia: La cucina casher in una famiglia ebraica italiana.* Florence: Giuntina, 2005.

Benbassa, Esther. *Cuisine judéo-espagnole: Recettes et traditions.* Paris: Éditions du Scribe, 1984.

Brandes, Francesca. *Veneto: Itinerari ebraici.* Venice: Marsilio, 1995.

Cia, Eramo. *La cucina mantovana.* Padua: Franco Muzzio Editore.

Comunità Ebraica di Casale Monferrato. *La cucina della memoria: Ricette giudaico monferrine raccolte dai ricettari di famiglia.* Casale Monferrato: Fondazione arte, storia e cultura ebraica, 2001.

De Benedetti, Ines. *Poesia nascosta: Le ricette della cucina tradizionale ebraica italiana.* Milan: ADEI, 1949.

Di Segni, Riccardo. *Beteavon–Buon appetito! Incontro di culture e ricette della tradizione ebraico-romana.* Rome: GP, 2010.

Di Segni, Sandra. *L'ebraismo vien mangiando.* Florence: Giuntina, 1999.

Freda, Secondino. "Cucina romanesca ebraica." *La Strenna dei Romanisti* 36. Rome: Staderini Editore, 1975.

Gandolfi, F. "La tradizione dei dolci ebrei." *Veneto ieri, oggi, domani* 1, no. 7 (August 1990).

Loewenthal, Elena. *Buon Appetito, Elia!* Milan: Baldini & Castoldi, 2001.

Malizia, Giuliano. *La cucina romana ed ebraico-romanesca.* Rome: Newton Compton Editori, 1995.

Marconi, Enzo. *La cucina tradizionale degli ebrei di Venezia.* Catania: F. Guaitolini, 1929.

Milano, Attilio. *Storia degli ebrei in Italia.* Torino: Einaudi, 1963.

Montanari, Massimo. *Il mondo in cucina: Storia, identità, scambi.* Rome: Laterza, 2006.

Pavoncello Limentani, Donatella. *Dal 1880 ad oggi: La cucina ebraica della mia famiglia.* Rome: Carucci Editore, 1982.

———. *Gastronomia e folklore.* N.p.: Rome, 1984.

Pesaro Norsa, Valeria. *La cucina ebraica di casa nostra.* Milan: Proedi, 2000.

Pontoni, Germani. *L'oca: La storia, il folklore, le ricette antiche.* Lodi: Bibliotheca culinarian, 1997.

Rundo, Joan. *La cucina ebraica in Italia.* Casale Monferrato: Sonda, 2001.

Sabban, Françoise, and Silvano Serventi. *A tavola nel Rinascimento.* Rome: Laterza, 2005.

Sacerdoti, Annie, Annamarcella Tedeschi Falco, and Vincenza Maugeri. *Emilia-Romagna. Itinerari ebraici.* Venice: Marsilio, 1992.

Sacerdoti, Mira. *Cucina ebraica in italia.* Casale Monferrato: Piemme, 1994.

Sada, Luigi. *La cucina pugliese.* Rome: Newton Compton Editori, 2012.

Tedeschi, Bruna. *La mia cucina ebraica romanesca.* Rome: Logart Press, 2008.

Toaff, Ariel. *Mangiare alla giudia: La cucina ebraica in Italia del Rinascimento all'età moderna.* Bologna: Il Mulino, 2000.

Viccei, Angelo Antonio. *Il pasto degli ebrei.* Lucca: Salvatore e Giandomenico Marescandoli, 1731.

Acknowledgments

Writing this book has been a wonderful adventure I've shared with family, friends, and many generous people who love Jewish Italian cuisine as much as I do and who felt the need to share their knowledge. I am grateful and obliged to many, so here are some thank-you notes.

- Ima, for teaching me all I know in life (especially how to cook!), and for expressing your love to me through the food you make; you are my greatest inspiration.

- Aba, for believing in me through the highs and lows of my path; your unconditional support means a lot to me.

- Shlomi, for seeing the potential in me and for giving me the courage to realize it; you are the source of all my happiness, as well as my inspiration for writing this book.

- Ellen Scordato, my agent, for believing in this book when it only existed in my head.

- Judy Pray, my editor, for taking a very rough manuscript and turning it into a book I'm proud of.

- Manuel, for starting Labna with me back in 2009; it's been a privilege to share a blog with you for more than ten years—and counting!

- Anna Campos, Sandra Levis, Marta Morello, Alessandro Marzo Magno, Dana Raccah, Giordana Sermoneta, and Lorella Ascoli, for patiently answering my endless questions.

- Jonah Lehrer, for crafting a great book proposal with me, and for reviewing the final manuscript.

- Julianne "Tony" McGinn, for helping me with writing and researching when I thought this book would never see the light of day.

- Ray Kachatorian, Carrie Purcell, and Jen Barguiarena, for bearing with me on set and making this book so beautiful.

- All the staff at the CDEC in Milan, and in particular director Gadi Luzzatto Voghera, for allowing me to use your library for research and for overseeing my content; your dedication to preserving Jewish history is invaluable.

- All the readers of my blog, and particularly the hundreds of them who tested the recipes for this book, for your enthusiastic support; your appreciation for my work makes me feel I have so many distant but wonderful friends out there.

Kashrut Index

General Index

BENEDETTA JASMINE GUETTA is an Italian food writer and photographer. She was born in Milan, and now lives in Santa Monica, California. In 2009, she cofounded a website called Labna, the only Jewish/kosher cooking blog in Italy, specializing in Italian and Jewish cuisine. Since then, she has been spreading the word about the marvels of Italian Jewish food in Italy and abroad, teaching the recipes of the cuisine to a growing number of people in cooking schools, synagogues, and community centers, among others. Her work has been featured by numerous news outlets in Italy and abroad, including the *Washington Post*, *Cosmopolitan*, *Elle à Table*, *Saveur*, and *Tablet*. Guetta has previously coauthored and illustrated two cookbooks in Italian; this is her first English-language cookbook.